ResultsPlusRevision

Edexcel GCSE
360Science

With diagnostic tests on CD-ROM

A PEARSON COMPANY

How to use the book and CD-ROM

Welcome to the ResultsPlus Revision guide for Edexcel's GCSE 360Science.

This book will help you prepare for your exams with more confidence. It contains the key information you need to know, along with plenty of practice questions and tips from the people that write and mark your exams.

But before you start revising, why not take a diagnostic test? This will help you to identify what you already know and where you need to improve.

Insert the CD-ROM and follow the easy installation instructions. Then choose a test from the Tests menu. You can take each diagnostic test as many times as you want! Your latest results will be saved on your computer.

After taking a test, click on the Results tab. The Analysis screen shows your scores, question-by-question. Test review lets you look back at your answers and compare them with the correct answers. And your personalised skills map shows you how you performed in each area of your course. By copying across the red, amber and green symbols to the revision tracker at the front of your book, you can see where to spend more time revising...

Which tier are you taking?

Higher – you need to cover all the material in this book.

Foundation – you can leave out the sections marked with the 'Higher' tabs.

The book is divided into the 12 topics from your specification.

At the start of each section you'll find a list of skills. A complete list of the skills is given in your revision tracker at the start of the book.

Each section explains what you need to know about that topic. We've also included some helpful ResultsPlus features.

CD tests

There are 12 tests on the CD-ROM. Tests 1-6 cover the Foundation Tier: Test 1 covers B1a; Test 2 covers B1b; Test 3 covers C1a; Test 4 covers C1b; Test 5 covers P1a; Test 6 covers P1b. Tests 7-12 cover the same topics at Higher Tier.

Need more help? details of where to look in the main student book for more information. (ISBN 978-1-903133-68-2)

4.5: Tuberculosis and new drugs

- B1.b.4.13 Explain what causes tuberculosis (TB)
- B1.b.4.13 Explain how tuberculosis (TB) is spread
- B1.b.4.14 Describe the prevention and control of TB
- B1.b.4.14 Explain why the emergence of drug-resistan
- B1.b.4.15 Interpret data on the number of cases of TB of time
- B1.b.4.16 Use secondary data to explore the costs of

Need more help? For more on this topic, see pages 82–84.

edexcel key terms
tuberculosis A disease caused by a bacterium that causes severe damage to the lungs and can lead to death.

ResultsPlus Watch out!
Some questions ask you to read values from a graph and then do a calculation based on these values. Many students get these answers wrong because they don't read the values off the graph correctly.

Higher tier For more on this topic, see pages 83–85.

Tuberculosis

Tuberculosis (TB) is a disease caused by a bacterium. It is s in droplets produced when an infected person coughs or sne bacteria quite quickly, so most people who become infected because they have spent time indoors with an infected pers as a 'disease of poverty', which means that it spreads easily overcrowded conditions.

TB mainly affects the lungs, but can also affect bones, joints treated with antibiotics. It can be fatal if it is not treated. The is not very effective in adults or against all forms of TB.

Preventing and controlling TB

The best way of preventing TB is to try to cure those people to stop them passing it on. The TB bacterium can survive for without causing symptoms, so it is not easy to eradicate.

TB can be treated with antibiotics, which are drugs that kill b bacteria can develop resistance to antibiotics. This happens

- people stop taking antibiotics as soon as they feel better
- there will be a few bacteria with mutations that make ther and these will be the ones most likely to survive
- these resistant bacteria reproduce and may infect anothe

The development of drug-resistant bacteria can be reduced course of antibiotics that their doctor gives them.

The development of drug-resistant bacteria (of any kind) is may lead to the development of bacteria that we can't kill at

Some strains of TB have developed resistance to various an antibiotics' (several different antibiotics used at the same t them. Treatments are given for six months. A system called Treatment, Short Course (DOTS) is used, where a nurse watc antibiotics each day, to make sure that they complete their

Watch out! common mistakes that students make in the exams. Make sure that you don't fall into the same traps!

Higher tier indicates material which only Higher tier students need to revise. Higher Tier skills and questions are indicated by blue tick-circles and question numbers.

Revision tracker

Topic 1: Environment

Explain what a food chain is	10
Explain that many food chains link together to make a food web	10
Explain what pyramids of numbers and pyramids of biomass show	10
Explain why pyramids of biomass are a more accurate representation of the energy in a food chain than pyramids of numbers	10
Describe food chains quantitatively using pyramids of biomass	10
Describe how organisms in an ecosystem compete with each other for things they need	12
Give examples of how and why predators compete with each other for prey	12
Explain how animal populations are affected by numbers of predators	12
Explain how animal populations are affected by competition for resources	12
State why it is more cost-effective, in terms of energy, to produce a field of wheat rather than a field of beef cows	10
Interpret population data in terms of predator-prey interdependence	12
Interpret population data in terms of intra-species competition	12
Use secondary data to explain how human activity can affect the environment (Higher tier)	14
Use secondary data to explain how changes in human population size can affect the environment (Higher tier)	14
Use secondary data to explain how changes in human activity can affect the environment, particularly changes in economic and industrial conditions (Higher tier)	14
Describe how computer models can be used to study populations	14
Suggest some advantages of using computer models compared with real data	14
Suggest some disadvantages of using computer models compared with real data	14
Explain natural selection	18
Explain that individuals can have characteristics that mean they are more successful at breeding	18
Describe how natural selection can lead to the formation of new species	18
Explain how natural selection results in new species from variants that are better adapted to their environment	18
Explain why less well adapted species may become extinct	18
Explain how fossils provide evidence for evolution	20
Explain selective breeding	18
Describe genetic engineering; show how crops can be genetically modified	22
Compare natural selection, selective breeding and genetic engineering in terms of changing the characteristics of a species	22
Describe Charles Darwin's theory of evolution (Higher tier)	20
Discuss why Charles Darwin had difficulty in getting his theory of evolution accepted by the scientific community in the 19th century (Higher tier)	20
Explain why classification of organisms is necessary, and how this is done, including the five kingdoms, the different levels of classification and the five vertebrate groups	16
State some of the difficulties of classifying organisms	16
Discuss the principles and ethics of organic farming; explain why organic products are more expensive than non-organic products	22
Describe how crop plants can be genetically modified; give examples of how and why crop plants might be genetically modified (Higher tier)	22
Describe some of the ethical concerns raised by the genetic modification of plants (Higher tier)	22

Topic 2: Genes

Describe genes as parts of chromosomes which are found within the nucleus	24
Describe genes as parts of chromosomes which control the cell's activity	24
State that the unit of inheritance is the gene	24
State that a gene is a section of a long-chain (DNA) molecule	24
Suggest how DNA evidence can be used to solve crimes	24
Describe some of the implications of the outcome of the Human Genome Project, including the use of DNA evidence in medicine	24
Describe how gene therapy works (Higher tier)	30
Discuss how the life of a person suffering from cystic fibrosis or breast cancer would change if this disease could be treated genetically (Higher tier)	30
Describe how plants reproduce by asexual reproduction; explain how this produces genetically identical organisms called clones	26
Outline what sexual reproduction is; discuss how this leads to a mixing up of genes and variation in the new generation	26, 28
State how some characteristics can be changed by changes in environmental conditions, including the food we eat (Higher tier)	26
Explain that plant growth is influenced by mineral resources in the soil (Higher tier)	26
Explain the difference between dominant and recessive alleles	28
Explain how alternative forms of a gene cause variation in a characteristic	28
Explain how some alleles cause diseases which can be inherited, including sickle-cell anaemia, Huntington's disease and haemophilia	30
Explain how mammals can be cloned (Higher tier)	32
Describe how transgenic animals can be used for the production of 'designer milk' (Higher tier)	32
Investigate ways in which we might use transgenic animals (Higher tier)	32
Discuss the social and ethical concerns of cloning mammals	32
Discuss the possibility of cloning human body parts for transplant surgery	32
Describe what is meant by 'designer babies' (Higher tier)	32
Discuss the contemporary scientific theory of 'designer babies' (Higher tier)	32
Explain why the idea of 'designer babies' is so controversial (Higher tier)	32

Topic 3: Electrical and Chemical Signals

Explain what reaction time is	34
Suggest why reaction time is important	34
State how reaction time can be measured	34
Describe the structure of the central nervous system	34
Describe the structure of the brain	38
Describe the functions of the brain	38
Describe how the central nervous system carries electrical impulses from sense organs to muscles	34
Describe how strokes disrupt the functioning of the brain (Higher tier)	38
Describe how brain tumours disrupt the functioning of the brain (Higher tier)	38
Describe how Parkinson's disease disrupts the functioning of the brain (Higher tier)	38
Describe how grand mal epilepsy disrupts the functioning of the brain (Higher tier)	38
Explain that receptors in sense organs detect internal and external changes	34
Explain how the body responds to the stimuli of internal and external changes	34
Explain how the eye focuses light on the retina	36
Explain why the iris reflex is useful in helping to protect the body	36
Suggest some advantages of the accommodation reflex in helping to safeguard the body	36
Give examples of the 'ducking' reaction to objects travelling close to the head in helping to safeguard the body	36
Describe the difference between voluntary and reflex responses	36
Describe the composition of the blood	40
Describe the transport function of the blood	40
Explain how hormones act as chemical messengers	40
Explain how hormones act as chemical messages affecting target organs	40
Explain how hormones act as chemical messages affecting cells	40
Interpret data to explain how oestrogen causes the lining of the uterus to thicken during the early part of the menstrual cycle (Higher tier)	42
Interpret data to explain how progesterone maintains the lining of the uterus during the middle part of the menstrual cycle and during pregnancy (Higher tier)	42
Explain how manufactured sex hormones can be used for contraception	42
Explain how manufactured sex hormones can be used to treat infertility in women	42
Discuss the social and ethical implications of IVF treatment	42
Discuss the social and ethical implications of IVF treatment in mature clients	42
Explain how insulin produced by the pancreas regulates glucose concentrations in the blood	40
Describe the advantages for people with diabetes of the use of human insulin produced by genetically modified bacteria	40

Topic 4: Use, Misuse and Abuse

Describe the main mental and physical effects of solvents (including effects on lungs and neurones)	46
Describe the main mental and physical effects of alcohol (including effects on reaction times, the liver and the brain)	46
Describe the main mental and physical effects of tobacco (including effects on the gaseous exchange and circulatory systems)	46
Describe how the use of drugs may affect activities such as driving, produce abnormal behaviour and create the risk of viral infections	46
Explain the effects on nerve transmission and reaction times of stimulants, including caffeine	44
Explain the effects on nerve transmission and reaction times of sedatives, including barbiturates	44
Explain the effects on nerve transmission of painkillers, including paracetamol	44
Explain the effects on reaction times of depressants, including alcohol and solvents	44
Discuss the use of opiates and cannabinoids in pain-relief for terminally ill patients, including the dangers of addiction	44
Describe the uses of paracetamol and the dangers of overdose	44
Discuss why medical opinion on the use of cannabis for pain-relief has fluctuated over the years	44
Describe a pathogen as a disease-causing organism	48
Explore secondary sources of data about the main physical and mental effects of the misuse of drugs	46
Use data on drug misuse to present information to different audiences	46
Explain that microbes can be transmitted by direct contact	48
Explain that microbes can be transmitted by vertical direct contact from mother to fetus	48
Explain that microbes can be transmitted by horizontal direct contact	48
Explain that microbes can be transmitted by indirect contact	48
Explain how microbes can be transmitted by vehicle-borne mechanisms	48
Explain how microbes can be transmitted by vector-borne mechanisms	48
Describe the body's physical barriers as the first line of defence against microorganisms, including skin, nasal hairs and cilia	48
Describe the body's chemical barriers as the first line of defence against microorganisms (lysozyme in tears)	48
Describe how infection can lead to inflammation	50
Describe how white blood cells defend against microorganisms	50
Describe the second line of defence against infection as non-specific	50
Describe how the immune system works	50
Describe the difference between antibodies and antigens	50
Describe the third line of defence as the specific immune system	50
Explain what causes tuberculosis (TB)	52
Explain how tuberculosis (TB) is spread	52
Describe the prevention and control of TB (Higher tier)	52
Explain why the emergence of drug-resistant TB is a problem (Higher tier)	52
Interpret data on the number of cases of TB in the UK over a period of time (Higher tier)	52
Use secondary data to explore the costs of developing new drugs	52

Revision tracker

Topic 5: Patterns in Properties

	Description	Page
	Explain how flame tests are used to identify the presence of a particular metal	66
	Use the result of a flame test to identify the presence of a particular metal	66
	Use results of analysis to identify substances found at a crime scene	66
	Interpret data describing the properties of chlorine and iodine	64
	Give examples of the uses of chlorine and iodine	64
	Interpret data describing the properties of helium, neon and argon	60
	Give examples of the uses of helium, neon and argon	60
	Interpret data describing the properties of iron, copper, silver and gold	60
	Give examples of the uses of iron, copper, silver and gold	60
	Describe how to identify iron, copper and zinc using sodium hydroxide solution	66
	Use the periodic table to find the symbol of an element	54
	Identify and recall the position of metals and non-metals in the periodic table	54
	Identify and recall the positions of the alkali metals, halogens, noble gases and transition metals in the periodic table	54
	Recall that elements in the same group have similar properties	54
	Recall that a row in the periodic table is called a period and that a column is called a group	54
	Use secondary data to explore the arrangement of elements in the periodic table	54
	Describe how an atom consists of neutrons and positively charged protons in a nucleus surrounded by negatively charged electrons	56
	Explain how the periodic table was used to predict the discovery of new elements	56
	Use secondary data to explore the use of atomic number in the periodic table (Higher tier)	56
	Recall that all atoms of the same element have the same number of protons and that this is the atomic number	56
	Recall that the alkali metals' reactivity with water increases with increase in atomic number	62
	Describe the reactions of alkali metals with water	62
	Recall that chemical reactions happen at different rates	62
	Recall that chemical reactions that give out heat are exothermic	62
	Recall that chemical reactions that take in heat are endothermic	62
	Recognise the gradual change in the properties of elements from the top to the bottom of each group	60
	Describe the variation in colour of the halogens	64
	List the physical states at room temperature of the halogens	64
	Recall the trends in boiling points of the halogens	64
	Describe how the reactivity of the halogens decreases as the group descends	64
	Describe the displacement reactions of halogens with solutions of other halides	64
	Describe the noble gases as chemically inert compared with other elements	60
	Recall that elements in the same group of the periodic table have similar chemical properties	62
	Explain the use of the endings -ide and -ate in chemical names (Higher tier)	58
	Represent chemical reactions in topic 5 by word equations	58
	Represent a range of chemical reactions by balanced equations, including state symbols (Higher tier)	58, 62
	Recall the symbols of elements in topic 5 and identify their positions in the periodic table	54
	Identify and recall the formulae of simple compounds topic 5	56

Topic 6: Making Changes

	Description	Page
	Describe how neutralisation can be used to make salts	68
	Recall that some salts are used in fertilisers and that some salts can be used to produce colours in fireworks	68
	Recall the reactions of metal oxides, hydroxides and carbonates with dilute sulphuric and hydrochloric acids	68
	Describe the preparation of pure, dry samples of insoluble salts from solutions of soluble salts	68
	Explain that most metals have to be extracted from their ores	72
	Recall that metal ores are found in the Earth's crust	72
	Recall that some metals occur as their oxides	72
	Recall how metals can be extracted from oxides by reaction with carbon	72
	Explain that the addition of oxygen to a substance is oxidation	70
	Explain that the loss of oxygen from a substance is reduction	70
	Recall that the least reactive metals are found uncombined in the Earth's crust	72
	Recall that the more reactive metals have more stable ores	72
	Describe how the method of extraction of a metal depends on the stability of its ore	72
	Discuss the differences between 'natural' and 'artificial' substances	76
	Discuss the impacts on health of artificial food additives	76
	Describe the use of sodium hydrogen carbonate in baking powder	70
	Recall that heating carbonates and hydrogen carbonates produces carbon dioxide gas and that this is an example of thermal decomposition	70
	Describe hydration and dehydration	70
	Recall that cooking involves chemical changes leading to new products	70
	Interpret data linking a chemical in food with a health impact, and recognise that a correlation does not imply a cause (Higher tier)	76
	Describe how to test for hydrogen, oxygen, carbon dioxide, ammonia and chlorine	74
	Describe how to collect gases by upward delivery	74
	Describe how to collect gases by downward delivery	74
	Describe how to collect gases over water	74
	Describe how to collect gases using a gas syringe	74
	Relate the method used to collect a gas to the solubility and density of the gas	74
	Describe the uses of hazard labels in the chemistry laboratory	70
	Give some examples of the uses of ammonia, carbohydrates, carbon dioxide, caustic soda, sodium chloride and water	76

Give some examples of the uses of citric acid, ethanoic acid, hydrochloric acid and phosphoric acid	76	
Represent chemical reactions in topic 6 by word equations	68	
Represent chemical reactions in topic 6 by balanced simple formulae equations (Higher tier)	68	

Topic 7: There's One Earth

Recall what is meant by global warming	84
Recall that the idea of global warming started as a single scientist's idea	84
Explain how the idea of global warming became a widely accepted theory	84
Recall that energy is released when fuels burn	78
Recall that the products of the complete combustion of hydrocarbons are carbon dioxide and water	78
Explain how burning fossil fuels may lead to global warming	84
Describe how the composition of the Earth's atmosphere and the Earth's temperature has varied over time	84
Recall that predictions about global warming use computer models, which carry uncertainties	84
Suggest what could be done to combat global warming (Higher tier)	84
Explain the importance of recycling waste products such as glass, metal and papers	92
Evaluate economic and environmental reasons for recycling	92
Evaluate economic and environmental reasons for the desalination of sea water	92
Explain what we mean by sustainable development	92
Describe how the Internet can be used to obtain information about environmental change	92
Recognise the need to check the reliability of information from the Internet	92
Describe the properties of a useful fuel	86
Explain why bio-fuels are sometimes an attractive alternative to fossil fuels	86
Discuss the benefits and drawbacks of hydrogen as a fuel	86
Recall that alcohol obtained from crops is a useful bio-fuel	86
Recall that large areas of fertile land are needed to produce bio-fuels	86
Describe the fractional distillation of crude oil	81
Give examples of the uses for the main fractions of crude oil	81
Explain where the main fractions are produced on the fractionating column (Higher tier)	81
Outline the relationship between boiling point, the size of molecule, viscosity, ease of ignition and uses of the main fractions of crude oil (Higher tier)	81
Explain why incomplete combustion can occur in faulty appliances	78
Describe how incomplete combustion can produce carbon and carbon monoxide	78
Explain why carbon monoxide is a toxic gas	78
Interpret data relating respiratory diseases to atmospheric pollutants (Higher tier)	78
Describe how nitrogen and oxygen can be obtained from liquid air	89
Give examples of useful substances obtained from sea water and rock salt	89
Represent chemical reactions in topic 7 by word equations	78
Represent chemical reactions in topic 7 by balanced simple formulae equations (Higher tier)	78

Topic 8: Designer Products

Relate properties to uses of materials in clothing and sports equipment, including carbon fibres, Thinsulate® and Lycra®	94
Explain that smart materials change their properties in response to changing conditions	94
Describe how scientists create new materials with special properties; suggest why some new materials have unexpected novel properties	94
Suggest why uses for some new materials are only discovered after they have been made	94
Explain the breathability of fabrics like Gore-Tex® in terms of their structure	94
Suggest how the properties of a material such as Kevlar® might be used in everyday life	94
Compare sizes of nanoparticles with conventionally produced materials	97
Describe the special properties nanoparticles have because of their size	97
Relate the size of nanoparticles to their uses	97
Discuss the risks and uncertainties of nanotechnologies (Higher tier)	97
Discuss how nanotechnology is presented in the media (Higher tier)	97
Describe how beer and wine can be made by fermentation	99
Describe how fermentation uses yeast to convert sugars to alcohol	99
Describe the effects of ethanol in alcoholic drinks on the human body	99
Discuss the social issues of drinking alcohol	99
Explain what intelligent packaging is	102
Explain how intelligent packaging can show whether food is fresh	102
Describe how emulsifiers work	102
Give examples of the use of emulsifiers in foods like mayonnaise	102
Design a list of properties for a product, based on its end use (Higher tier)	94

Topic 9: Producing and Measuring Electricity

Describe the difference between alternating current and direct current	112
Recall that batteries and solar cells are both sources of direct current	112
Describe how to produce an electric current by rotating a magnet in a coil of wire, as in a dynamo	112
List the factors that affect the size of an induced voltage	112
List the factors that affect the direction of an induced voltage	112
Explain how a change in the resistance in a series circuit changes the current	104

Revision tracker

☐ ☐ ☐	Explain how a change in the resistance in a parallel circuit changes the current (Higher tier)	104
☐ ☐ ☐	Describe how the resistance of a light-dependent resistor (LDR) changes with light intensity	107
☐ ☐ ☐	Describe how the resistance of a thermistor changes with a change of temperature	107
☐ ☐ ☐	Describe applications depending on resistance change, such as controlling the exposure time in a digital camera	107
☐ ☐ ☐	Recall that current is a rate of flow of negatively charged electrons, which can be measured by an ammeter placed in series in a circuit	104
☐ ☐ ☐	Recall that a battery's stated capacity is given in terms of amp-hours	110
☐ ☐ ☐	Use the capacity in amp-hours to predict the number of hours a battery should last when supplying a given current	110
☐ ☐ ☐	Use data to explain how current varies with voltage for fixed value resistors and filament lamps	104, 107
☐ ☐ ☐	Describe how to investigate how the current varies with the voltage for fixed value resistors or filament lamps	104, 107
☐ ☐ ☐	Use the relationship between the voltage, current and resistance: $V = I \times R$	104
☐ ☐ ☐	Identify different battery types	110
☐ ☐ ☐	Investigate the voltage and current output from dry or rechargeable cells	110
☐ ☐ ☐	Discuss the advantages/disadvantages of battery technology including considerations of their cost, performance and impact on the environment	110
☐ ☐ ☐	Discuss the impact that electricity has had on making the modern world	114
☐ ☐ ☐	Discuss the impact that the electric telephone has had on making the modern world	114
☐ ☐ ☐	Explain what is meant by superconductivity (Higher tier)	114
☐ ☐ ☐	Explain how a new technology, such as Maglev trains, develops as a result of scientific advances, such as the discovery of superconductivity (Higher tier)	114
☐ ☐ ☐	Use data relating the size of electric circuits to the processing speed of computers	114
☐ ☐ ☐	Suggest future applications of computers	114
☐ ☐ ☐	Explain how to use ICT to collect and display data from electric circuits for analysis	114
☐ ☐ ☐	Compare the use of ICT to collect and display data with traditional methods in terms of reliability and validity of data	114

Topic 10: You're in Charge

☐ ☐ ☐	Describe some different forms of renewable energy	116
☐ ☐ ☐	Evaluate whether solar power can meet the UK's future electricity needs	116
☐ ☐ ☐	Evaluate whether wind power can meet the UK's future electricity needs	116
☐ ☐ ☐	Evaluate the economic impact of different forms of renewable energy	118
☐ ☐ ☐	Evaluate the environmental impact of different forms of renewable energy	118
☐ ☐ ☐	Evaluate the social impact of different forms of renewable energy	118
☐ ☐ ☐	Evaluate the possible benefits and drawbacks of implementing technology such as a new national grid for distribution of electricity (Higher tier)	118
☐ ☐ ☐	Describe how scientific ideas change over time, such as the medical uses of electricity (Higher tier)	118
☐ ☐ ☐	Label a diagram of a simple electric motor	124
☐ ☐ ☐	Describe how a simple electric motor works	124
☐ ☐ ☐	Recall that electrical power is the rate of transfer of electrical energy	120
☐ ☐ ☐	Use power = current × voltage to calculate electrical power	120
☐ ☐ ☐	Explain what 'efficiency' means	122
☐ ☐ ☐	Use the equation efficiency = useful output/total input × 100%	122
☐ ☐ ☐	Interpret data about the efficiency of solar cells	116
☐ ☐ ☐	Suggest why solar cells are not yet in widespread use	116
☐ ☐ ☐	Use the equation cost = power × time × cost of 1 kWh, where power is measured in kilowatts and time is measured in hours	120
☐ ☐ ☐	Discuss whether an energy efficiency measure, such as insulating a home, is cost-effective	122
☐ ☐ ☐	Use data to compare energy efficiency measures	122
☐ ☐ ☐	Explain how the earth wire, together with a fuse, provides protection for the user	124
☐ ☐ ☐	Recall the advantages of a residual current circuit breaker (RCCB) and explain how it works (Higher tier)	124

Topic 11: Now You See it, Now You Don't

☐ ☐ ☐	Evaluate evidence suggesting that microwave radiation from mobile phones or masts poses health risks	136
☐ ☐ ☐	Discuss how evidence about possible health risks from microwave radiation has been reported in the media	136
☐ ☐ ☐	Describe the characteristics of ultraviolet light in terms of amplitude, frequency and wavelength	128
☐ ☐ ☐	Relate the characteristics of ultraviolet light in terms of frequency, wavelength and energy to the dangers of over-exposure	128
☐ ☐ ☐	Describe the detrimental effects of excessive exposure to microwaves (internal heating of body tissue), to infrared (skin burns) and to X-rays and gamma-rays (mutation or destruction of cells in the body)	128
☐ ☐ ☐	Explain the detrimental effects of excessive exposure to microwaves, infrared, X-rays and gamma-rays in terms of increasing frequency (Higher tier)	128
☐ ☐ ☐	Describe how reflection occurs in materials of different densities	130
☐ ☐ ☐	Describe how refraction occurs in materials of different densities	130
☐ ☐ ☐	Explain how scanning by reflection can be used for ultrasound scanning of a fetus during pregnancy	132
☐ ☐ ☐	Explain how reflection of visible light can be used in iris recognition	132
☐ ☐ ☐	Discuss the advantages/disadvantages of scanning by reflection	132
☐ ☐ ☐	Explain how scanning by absorption enables bone fractures to be 'seen' using X-rays	132
☐ ☐ ☐	Explain how scanning by absorption enables rain to be monitored using microwaves	132
☐ ☐ ☐	Explain how scanning by absorption enables forged bank notes to be detected by fluorescence using ultraviolet light	132

Explain how scanning by emission enables the use of infrared sensors to monitor temperature	132
Discuss the benefits and drawbacks to society of a technology that is based on the properties of waves (Higher tier)	136
Describe the advantages of sending information in the form of a digital signal	134
Describe how the production of digital signals has created a range of music technologies	134
Describe how digital signals have altered the way we listen to music	134
Describe how digital signals have altered the way we distribute music	134
Describe the total internal reflection of light waves	130
Explain how total internal reflection allows optical fibres to transfer large amounts of information over long distances	130
Describe the similarities and differences between longitudinal and transverse waves	126
Give examples of longitudinal waves including sound waves, ultrasound and seismic waves	126
Give examples of transverse waves including seismic waves and electromagnetic waves	126
Suggest reasons why scientists find it difficult to predict earthquakes even with suitable data (Higher tier)	136
Suggest reasons why scientists find it difficult to predict tsunami waves even with suitable data (Higher tier)	136
Explain the terms amplitude, frequency and wavelength	126
Describe the speed of a wave	126
Use speed = frequency × wavelength	126
Use speed = distance/time to calculate the distance to a reflecting surface	126
Use data about seismic waves passing through the Earth to draw conclusions about the types of materials that are found in the planet's interior (Higher tier)	130
Describe the similarities and differences of the waves in the electromagnetic spectrum	128
Recall that all electromagnetic waves travel at the same speed in a vacuum	128

Topic 12: Space and its Mysteries

Recall that there is no air in interplanetary space and that the temperature in interplanetary space can vary widely	138
Describe why astronauts feel weightlessness in orbit or in interplanetary space	138
Recall how lack of air, temperature variations, lack of activity and weightlessness in interplanetary space can be partly allowed for in spacecraft (Higher tier)	138
Explain the difference between mass and weight	138
Use weight = mass × acceleration of free-fall W = mg	138
Explain how a spacecraft might be powered in terms of action and reaction	140
Describe the energy changes that take place when a spacecraft is launched	140
Describe how force = mass × acceleration can be used to predict how an object behaves	140
List and discuss the social and economic benefits of knowledge about the Universe (Higher tier)	146
List and discuss the technological advances which might arise from exploration of the Universe (Higher tier)	146
Describe ways of discovering information about the Universe that don't involve human travel, such as soil experiments on landers and the Hubble Space Telescope	146
Describe the Search for Extraterrestrial Intelligence (SETI) mission	146
Recall how scientists are overcoming the dangers of radiation and the deterioration of bones and heart on long space flights	138
Describe the role of gravity on Earth	140
Describe the role of gravity in astronomy	140, 144
Describe the idea of black holes (Higher tier)	144
Use the unit of gravitational field strength, newton per kilogram (N/kg)	138
Describe stellar evolution from the nebula stage for small stars like our Sun	144
Describe stellar evolution from the nebula stage for more massive stars than the Sun	144
Discuss the chance and the possible consequences of a comet or asteroid hitting the Earth and any uncertainties in there	142
Describe how the orbit of a comet differs from that of a planet or an asteroid	142
Use data sources to compare the relative sizes of and distances between Earth, our Moon, the planets, the Sun, galaxies and the Universe	142
List objects in the Solar System and Universe in order of size	142
Describe the Solar System as part of the Milky Way galaxy	144
Describe how the Milky Way is related to other galaxies, and the Universe	144
Use scientific evidence to develop an argument in favour of the idea that intelligent life exists elsewhere in the galaxy (Higher tier)	146
Use scientific evidence to develop an argument against the idea that intelligent life exists elsewhere in the galaxy (Higher tier)	146
Suggest ways of finding intelligent life elsewhere in the galaxy (Higher tier)	146
Recall that there are unanswered scientific questions about the existence of extraterrestrial life	146
Recall that there are unanswered scientific questions about the nature of 'dark matter' that makes up much of the Universe's mass (Higher tier)	148
Describe the origin, current state and fate of the Universe using the main theories (Big Bang, oscillating and steady state)	148
Describe the supporting evidence for the main theories including the microwave background radiation (Higher tier)	148
Describe the supporting evidence for the main theories including red shift (Higher tier)	148
Describe how the existence of life on a planet is determined by the nature of the planet and its position in its solar system (Higher tier)	142
Describe how the position of a star in its lifecycle determines the existence of life on a planet (Higher tier)	144

1.1: Chains and pyramids

- B1.a.1.1 Explain what a food chain is
- B1.a.1.1 Explain that many food chains link together to make a food web
- B1.a.1.1 Explain what pyramids of numbers and pyramids of biomass show
- B1.a.1.1 Explain why pyramids of biomass are a more accurate representation of the energy in a food chain than pyramids of numbers
- B1.a.1.1 Describe food chains quantitatively using pyramids of biomass
- B1.a.1.3 State why it is more cost-effective, in terms of energy, to produce a field of wheat rather than a field of beef cows

Need more help?
For more on this topic, see pages 16–19 of the main student book (ISBN 978-1-903133-68-2).

edexcel key terms

biomass The mass of an organism (or a population) when all the water has been removed.
ecosystem A group of plants and animals that live and interact together, and their environment.
food chain A chain to show how energy moves from plants to different animals.
organism Any living thing.
predator An animal that kills and eats other animals.
prey An animal that is hunted and killed by another animal.
quantitatively Using numbers to describe something.

ResultsPlus Watch out!

Don't confuse predators and scavengers. A predator is an animal that kills other animals to eat them. Some animals, such as maggots, feed on dead animals, but they aren't predators because they didn't kill the animals. Maggots are scavengers.

A food chain shows how energy passes through the different organisms in an ecosystem. Nearly all the food chains on Earth (and all the ones you need to know about) start with a plant.

As well as understanding what predators and prey are (see the key terms box), you need to remember what these words mean:

- **producer** – an organism (usually a plant) that produces its own food using energy from sunlight
- **consumer** – an organism (usually an animal) that eats other organisms
- **herbivore** – an animal that only eats plants
- **carnivore** – an animal that only eats other animals
- **omnivore** – an animal that eats both plants and animals
- **scavenger** – an animal that eats the remains of animals killed by predators.

An animal such as a gazelle can be described using several of these words: it is a consumer because it eats plants; it is a herbivore because it only eats plants; and it is prey because other animals such as lions will hunt and kill it.

Most animals eat more than one kind of food, so food chains are linked together into food webs to show the feeding relationships in an ecosystem.

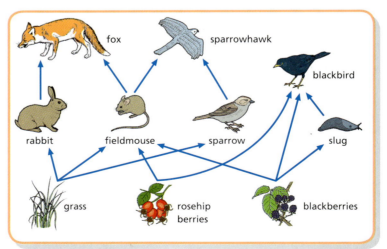

A food web (not to scale).

Pyramids of numbers and biomass

Food chains and webs tell you what kinds of food different organisms eat, but they don't tell you *how much* food. Pyramids of numbers and biomass are quantitative (numerical) ways of showing feeding relationships.

A pyramid of numbers shows the number of organisms at each feeding level. The top pyramid shows that one fox will eat several rabbits, and that the rabbits eat a lot of grass plants. However, pyramids of numbers don't always look like pyramids! The bottom diagram shows that one oak tree can feed many caterpillars. A few blackbirds can feed on these caterpillars, and lots of fleas can live on these blackbirds.

A pyramid of biomass is a more accurate way of showing the energy in a food chain. Biomass is the dry mass of living things (what the mass would be if all the water was removed). The pyramid of numbers with the oak tree looks like this if you use the biomass of all the organisms at each level instead of the number of organisms.

Energy in food chains

When a mouse eats wheat, only about 10 per cent of the energy in the wheat ends up being stored in the body of the mouse. Most of the energy from the wheat is 'wasted', i.e. used in respiration or excreted in droppings. If an owl eats the mouse, only about 10 per cent of the energy in the mouse ends up being stored in the body of the owl.

We could feed the world more efficiently if people ate less meat and more plants, as 90 per cent of the energy in plants is wasted if we feed them to animals and then eat the animals. This doesn't apply to animals that feed on moorland or mountains where crops can't be grown. It is still true that only about 10 per cent of the energy in the grass is stored in the meat of these animals, but we couldn't use the land to produce food any other way.

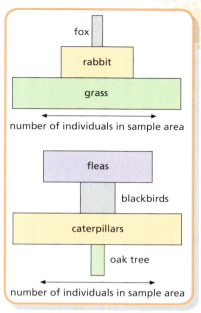

Pyramids of numbers.

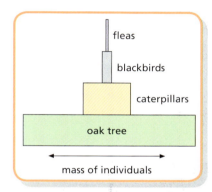

Pyramid of biomass.

Test yourself

1. Phytoplankton are organisms that use sunlight to make food. These organisms are known as:
   A consumers   B decomposers   C herbivores   D producers

2. Explain what the following words mean:
   a herbivore   b omnivore   c producer   d prey

3. Look at the drawing of the food web on page 10. Write down three feeding terms that describe:
   a the blackbird   b the sparrowhawk   c the rabbit

4. a Explain why the pyramid of numbers that starts with the oak tree is not shaped like a pyramid.
   b Why is a pyramid of biomass a better way of showing the energy in a food chain than a pyramid of numbers?

5. Greenfly live on a sycamore tree. Bluetits eat ladybirds that feed on the greenfly.
   a Sketch a food chain for the tree and the organisms that live on it.
   b Sketch a pyramid of numbers and a pyramid of biomass for the food chain.

6. 'Feed the world – give up meat.' Explain this slogan in as much detail as you can.

ResultsPlus Exam tip

An exam question may ask you to identify a pyramid of biomass. Remember that a pyramid of biomass is *always* pyramid-shaped – it is always widest at the bottom and narrowest at the top.

Need more help
For more on this topic, see pages 10–11.

1.2: Competition and populations

- B1.a.1.2 Describe how organisms in an ecosystem compete with each other for things they need
- B1.a.1.2 Give examples of how and why predators compete with each other for prey
- B1.a.1.2 Explain how animal populations are affected by numbers of predators
- B1.a.1.2 Explain how animal populations are affected by competition for resources
- B1.a.1.4 Interpret population data in terms of predator–prey interdependence
- B1.a.1.4 Interpret population data in terms of intra-species and inter-species competition

edexcel key terms

competition Where two organisms both need the same thing, such as food, space or light.
interdependence When a change to one organism brings about a change in another organism.
inter-species Between members of different species.
intra-species Between members of the same species.
population The total number of one species of an organism living in an area.

ResultsPlus Watch out!

With key terms that are very similar, such as interspecific and intraspecific, make sure you can remember which one is which!

Interspecific means the same as **inter**-species (between *different* species).

Intraspecific means the same as **intra**-species (between members of the *same* species).

Animals within an ecosystem compete with each other for food and mates. Plants compete for space, light and water.

Competition can be between animals of different species (such as zebra and wildebeest competing for grass). This is called inter-species (or interspecific) competition. Competition can also be between members of the same species (such as two lions competing to eat a zebra they have killed). This is called intra-species (or intraspecific) competition.

A population is the number of individuals of one species in a particular habitat. The size of a population depends on the resources available, and on the numbers of predators.

The organisms in a food web are interdependent. This means that a change in the population of one species will affect the other species in the area.

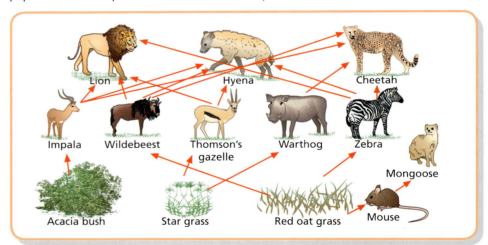

A food web.

In the food web above, if the numbers of hyenas go down (perhaps due to a disease):
- the numbers of impala, wildebeest, gazelle and zebra will go up, because there are fewer predators to eat them
- the numbers of lions and cheetahs will go up, because there is less competition for prey
- eventually the numbers of plants may go down, because now there are more herbivores to eat them.

Intra-species competition happens when resources are in short supply. For example, if there hasn't been much rain and the plants don't grow well, there will be competition between the different wildebeest for food, as well as inter-species competition between wildebeest and other species.

The populations of a predator and its prey also depend on one another. The graph shows how populations change over time.

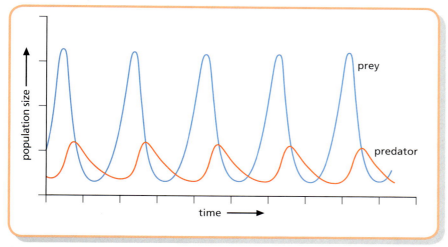

Changes in populations of predators and prey.

If there are plenty of plants, the prey population increases. This means there is more food for the predators, so their numbers increase too. However, more predators kill more prey, so then the prey numbers go down again. Fewer prey animals means less food for the predators, so their numbers go down too. Fewer predators allows the number of prey animals to increase, and so the cycle repeats itself.

Test yourself

1. Which is true?
   A predators compete with prey for food
   B predators compete with each other for food
   C predators are food for prey
   D predators cannot be scavengers

2. Explain what 'inter-species' and 'intra-species' mean.

3. Look at the food web on the opposite page.
   a Which animals does the wildebeest compete with for food?
   b List three animals that won't be in inter-species competition for food. Explain your answer.

4. Look at the food web again. What will happen to the populations of the different organisms if:
   a all the gazelles migrate to a different area
   b a new pride of lions comes into the area
   c a disease kills all the acacia bushes?

Need more help
For more on this topic, see pages 13–15.

1.3: Modelling and human activity

- B1.a.1.6 Describe how computer models can be used to study populations
- B1.a.1.6 Suggest some advantages of using computer models compared with real data
- B1.a.1.6 Suggest some disadvantages of using computer models compared with real data
- B1.a.1.5 Use secondary data to explain how human activity can affect the environment
- B1.a.1.5 Use secondary data to explain how changes in human population size can affect the environment
- B1.a.1.5 Use secondary data to explain how changes in human activity can affect the environment, particularly changes in economic and industrial conditions

Computer modelling

Populations of different organisms change over time. It is difficult and time-consuming to observe an ecosystem over a long period of time, so scientists often use computer models to study population changes.

The scientists need to study some ecosystems first, to find out what can affect the sizes of different populations. They work out rules for how ecosystems work, and program these into a computer. They then put in real data about the ecosystem they are studying, and use the computer to predict how the populations will change in the future. The model should be checked by seeing if its predictions are correct before it is used to study other ecosystems.

The advantages and disadvantages of computer models are given in the table below.

Advantages of computer models
• It can produce results faster than collecting data.
• It can predict a variety of different outcomes (such as population changes for many different organisms).
Disadvantages of computer models
• It can be unreliable, as ecosystems are complicated.
• The model is only as good as the data fed into it.

This scientist is taking samples of water and mud to study the ecosystem in a pond.

Environment

Human activity

Higher tier

Most human activities affect the environment in some way. For example:

- burning fossil fuels puts extra carbon dioxide into the atmosphere
- clearing forests for farming can result in floods and soils washing away
- changing the way land is used can cause desertification (land turning into desert) and loss of species
- building roads and cities reduces the habitats for wildlife.

Carbon dioxide is a 'greenhouse gas' that traps heat in the atmosphere. The extra carbon dioxide that humans are putting into the atmosphere is making the Earth warm up. This is called 'global warming' or 'climate change'. It could lead to rising sea levels, and different climate conditions that could lead to crops failing and species of plants and animals becoming extinct.

The effect of humans on the environment depends on:

- the population size
- the amount of industry and the economy.

The more people there are, the more fuel is burned for energy, and the more land is needed for growing food. The standard of living also makes a difference. A person in a country like the UK, with a rich economy and lots of industry, uses more energy and resources than a person in a developing country with a lower standard of living and little industry.

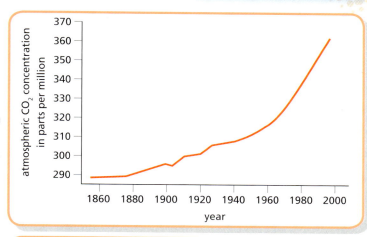

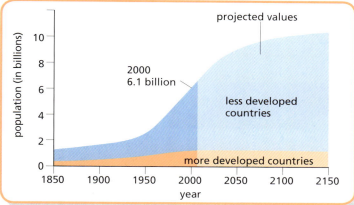

Population size and carbon dioxide emissions.

Test yourself

1. a Write down **two** advantages of using computer models to study ecosystems.
   b Write down **one** disadvantage.
2. Why do scientists need to study real ecosystems before they build computer models to predict what will happen to them in the future?
3. Look at the graph of carbon dioxide levels.
   a How has the concentration of carbon dioxide in the atmosphere changed since 1860?
   b Suggest how this could be linked to the increase in human population over the same period.
   c What other environmental effects are linked to population size?
4. Explain why someone in the UK has more effect on the environment than a person living in a developing country.

ResultsPlus
Exam Question Report

A computer was programmed to model the effects of changing global temperatures on endangered animals. It was found that as the global temperature increased more species became extinct. Why was a computer used to model this rather than experimental evidence?

A computers are more accurate
B computers give results faster
C experimental evidence cannot be proven
D experimental evidence is less reliable

Answer: The correct answer is B.

How students answered
More than half of students got this wrong. Many students find questions about computer modelling difficult.

58% 0 marks

You need to memorise the advantages and disadvantages given in the table to make sure you can answer questions like this correctly.

42% 1 mark

> **Need more help**
> For more on this topic, see pages 28–29.

1.4: Classification

 B1.a.1.11 Explain why classification of organisms is necessary, and how this is done, including the five kingdoms, the different levels of classification and the five vertebrate groups

 B1.a.1.11 State some of the difficulties of classifying organisms

There are millions of different kinds of organism – far too many to study unless they can be organised into groups. This process is called classification.

All biologists use the same classification system, and each type of organism is given a name in Latin. This means that scientists from all countries know they are all talking about the same organism when they discuss their work.

The table below shows the different 'levels' of classification, together with some examples. The top 'level' is kingdom. There are five kingdoms: animals, plants, bacteria, fungi and protoctista (single-celled organisms).

edexcel key terms
characteristic A feature of an organism that can be inherited or modified by the environment.
classification A systematic way of grouping things.
species A population of organisms that can breed together and produce fertile young.

Level	Human example	In English	Bird example	In English
kingdom	Animalia	animals	Animalia	animals
phylum	Chordata	with spinal cords	Chordata	with spinal cords
class	Mammalia	mammals – see below	Aves	birds
order	Primates	ape-like animals	Passeriformes	perching birds
family	Hominidae	human-like animals	Muscicapidae	flycatchers
genus	*Homo*	humans	*Turdus*	thrushes
species	*sapiens*	modern-day humans	*merula*	blackbird

Exam tip

Many students lose marks because they can't remember the order in which things are classified: kingdom, phylum, class, order, family, genus and species. The sentence King Philip Came Over For Gooey Sweets may help you to remember it. (Or you might find it easier to remember a phrase you make up yourself — especially if it is a rude one!) It will also be helpful to memorise the complete classification for humans — there is often a question on it. Don't worry about learning the blackbird example though.

The vertebrates

All vertebrates (animals with a backbone) belong to the phylum Chordata. You need to learn the characteristics of the five different classes of vertebrates.

Class	Characteristics	
Mammals (Mammalia)	• have hair • give birth to live young	• produce milk • warm-blooded
Birds (Aves)	• have feathers • lay hard-shelled eggs	• warm-blooded
Reptiles (Reptilia)	• have dry scales • lay leathery-shelled eggs	• cold-blooded
Amphibians (Amphibia)	• have moist skin • lay jelly-coated eggs in water	• cold-blooded
Fish (Pisces)	• have wet scales • lay eggs in water	• cold-blooded

Exam tip

You *do* need to remember the characteristics of the different vertebrate groups. It is also worth memorising the fact that all vertebrates belong to the phylum Chordata.

Some organisms are not easy to identify. For example, the platypus is covered in fur and feeds its young with milk, but the young are born from leathery-shelled eggs, not born live. The platypus has some characteristics of both mammals and reptiles. It is classified as a mammal.

A platypus.

ResultsPlus
Exam Question Report

A new species has been discovered in the dry forests of Madagascar. The new species has wings and can fly. It gives birth to live young and is covered in body hair.

The new species is a:
A mammal   B bird   C reptile   D amphibian
Answer: The correct answer is A.

How students answered
Many students put B, because it has wings, but wings aren't a feature used to decide whether an animal is a bird or not.

57% 0 marks

Some students realised that having live young and hair meant this animal was a mammal.

43% 1 mark

ResultsPlus
Exam Question Report

The peppered moth, *Biston betularia*, can have light wings or dark wings. The two kinds of peppered moth belong to:
A the same kingdom and species
B a different kingdom but the same species
C a different kingdom and species
D the same kingdom but a different species
Answer: The correct answer is A.

How students answered
Less than half the students got this right.

58% 0 marks

The clue here is the name. Both types of moth have the same Latin name, so they must be the same species. If they are the same species, they *must* belong to the same kingdom.

42% 1 mark

Test yourself

1. Put these classification terms in order, starting with the biggest group: class, genus, phylum, species, family, order

2. Modern horses are called *Equus callabus*. Fossils of earlier horses include *Equus scotti* and *Equus stenonis*. These horses do not belong to the same:
   A class   B order   C species   D genus

3. These animals are all part of the cat family: lions (*Panthera leo*), jaguars (*Panthera onca*), leopards (*Panthera pardus*) and tigers (*Panthera tigris*). These animals are from different:
   A classes   B species   C orders   D kingdoms

4. Which kingdom, phylum and class do the animals in question 3 all belong to?

5. Which class (or classes) of vertebrates:
   a lay eggs   b give birth to live young   c have scales?

6. Leatherback turtles live in the sea. They do not have hard shells. They lay eggs in holes in sandy beaches. What kingdom, phylum and class do these turtles belong to? Explain your answer.

> **Need more help?**
> For more on this topic, see pages 22, 24–25.

1.5: Natural selection

- **B1.a.1.7** Explain natural selection
- **B1.a.1.7** Explain that individuals can have characteristics that mean they are more successful at breeding
- **B1.a.1.7** Describe how natural selection can lead to the formation of new species
- **B1.a.1.7** Explain how natural selection results in new species from variants that are better adapted to their environment
- **B1.a.1.7** Explain why less well adapted species may become extinct
- **B1.a.1.9** Explain selective breeding

edexcel key terms

adaptation How organisms change over generations to become more suited to their environment.
environment The place and conditions where an organism lives.
mutation A change in DNA.
natural selection How environmental factors such as disease or predation alter the characteristics of a species.
reproduction The process of producing the next generation of individuals.
selective breeding Deliberately mating together organisms to produce plants or animals that have useful combinations of characteristics.

Most organisms are adapted to the environment in which they live. For example, polar bears have very good insulation to allow them to live in cold climates.

The genes that pass on characteristics can sometimes mutate (change). Most mutations do not affect an organism, and others are harmful, but sometimes there may be a mutation that gives an organism an advantage. This causes variation within a species.

For example, some herbivores may have longer legs than others in the species, which would allow them to run faster. These longer-legged animals are more likely to escape when they are being hunted, and so they are more likely to survive to reproduce.

Many of an organism's characteristics are inherited. This means that longer-legged herbivores may pass on the characteristic of having long legs. Eventually all the herbivores of that species will have longer legs. This is known as natural selection.

Over long periods of time organisms in an area undergo other changes that make them better adapted to that particular environment. Eventually these changes might make them so different from the original species that the organisms will be classed as a new species.

How natural selection can lead to changes in a species.

If the environment changes, some of the species that live there will be able to cope with the new conditions better than others. These species will be more successful in the competition for food, and the less well adapted species may become extinct (die out).

Natural selection occurs because natural events (such as disease, increase in predators, etc.) kill off the organisms within a species that are not well adapted to their environment. It happens over very long periods of time, and is not controlled by humans.

Environment

Selective breeding

Humans have kept animals such as cows, sheep, horses and dogs for thousands of years. Humans can change the characteristics of their animals by selective breeding. They choose animals with characteristics that make them useful to humans and only breed from those animals. It is similar to natural selection except that humans are making the breeding choices, rather than natural events. Animals may be selectively bred to produce more milk or meat, or to run faster. Plants can also be selectively bred, e.g. to produce more grain or to survive in different conditions. Selective breeding usually produces varieties within a species rather than new species.

ResultsPlus — Watch out!

Make sure you are clear about the difference between natural selection (due to natural events) and selective breeding (controlled by humans). Some students get them mixed up.

ResultsPlus — Exam Question Report

Which is an example of natural selection?
A the cultivation of flowers with a particular colour
B putting DNA into bacteria
C the development of long necks in giraffes
D breeding cows that produce lots of milk

Answer: The correct answer is C.

How students answered
Three quarters of students picked one of the wrong answers.

75% 0 marks

Only a quarter of students worked out that cultivation is a human activity so it is not an example of natural selection. Putting DNA into bacteria is genetic modification (you'll learn more about this on pages 22–23). Breeding cows that produce lots of milk is selective breeding.

25% 1 mark

Test yourself

1. a Giraffes have long necks. What advantage do you think this gives them in the inter-species competition for food?
   b Suggest how giraffes came to have long necks.
2. Explain the difference between natural selection and selective breeding.
3. On the Galapagos Islands Charles Darwin found species of finches that had different shaped beaks on each different island. Darwin suggested that species with different shaped beaks evolved from one common ancestor.

   The evolution of the different beaks was due to the availability of:
   A different types of food   B different nesting sites
   C mates   D water

Two species of finches from the Galapagos Islands.

19

1.6: The theory of evolution

Need more help
For more on this topic, see pages 26–27.

- B1.a.1.8 Explain how fossils provide evidence for evolution
- B1.a.1.10 Describe Charles Darwin's theory of evolution
- B1.a.1.10 Discuss why Charles Darwin had difficulty in getting his theory of evolution accepted by the scientific community in the 19th century

edexcel key terms

evolution A gradual change in the characteristics of a species over many generations.
extinct When a group of organisms dies out because it cannot adapt itself to a new situation.
fossil An imprint in rock left by an organism that lived thousands or even millions of years ago.

Charles Darwin developed a theory to explain why there were so many different species of plants and animals. He said that over vast periods of time, natural selection resulted in some species changing into new ones and some species becoming extinct.

Fossils provide evidence to support the theory of evolution. Fossils are the shapes of dead organisms (or their skeletons or shells) preserved in rocks. This happens when the remains become covered in sediments before they get eaten or rot. Over time, more and more sediments build up above the remains and turn into rock. This means that fossils found in lower layers of rock are *older* than those found nearer the surface.

Higher tier

Darwin's theory of evolution tried to explain all his observations about different species and fossils. He said that all the species in the world today could have evolved from an earlier species through the process of natural selection. However, he couldn't explain *how* characteristics were passed on from parents to offspring, or why characteristics changed (DNA and mutations hadn't been discovered at that time).

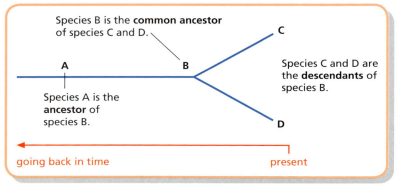

This evolutionary tree shows that fossil organism A evolved into fossil organism B, which then evolved into species C and D.

Most scientists at the time agreed with Darwin's observations, but they *didn't* all agree that his theory of evolution explained them. His theory was weakened because Darwin couldn't explain how characteristics were passed on. Also, many people at the time didn't like Darwin's ideas because he said that humans and apes had evolved from a common ancestor, so humans were related to animals such as chimpanzees.

Darwin's ideas were also unpopular because they disagreed with what the Christian Bible said about how the world and the organisms on it had been created. Many people did not *want* to believe that Darwin's theory was the true explanation for the many different species on the planet.

Today the theory of evolution is accepted by nearly all scientists because there is much more evidence (from DNA, and from the discovery of many more fossils) that supports it.

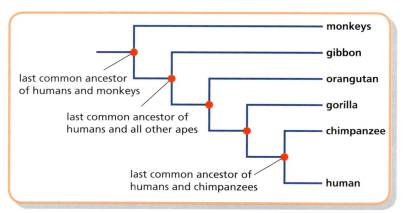

A 'family tree' for monkeys and apes. The species marked with red dots are all extinct.

Environment

Test yourself

1 The diagram shows some fossils in layers of rock.

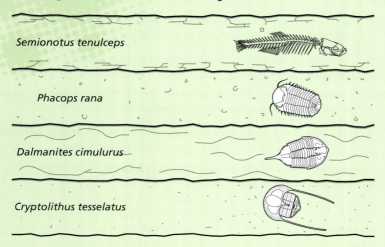

a What is a fossil?
b Which of the fossils shown in the diagram is the oldest?
c None of these fossils are of animals that are alive today. Suggest why we cannot find these animals alive on the Earth.

2 Darwin published his ideas in a book called *On The Origin of Species*, which was published in 1859. At the time, most of the scientific community:
A agreed with Darwin's observations and his interpretations
B agreed with Darwin's observations but not his interpretations
C agreed with Darwin's interpretations but not his observations
D disagreed with Darwin's observations and interpretations

3 Some people were upset with Darwin's ideas because he said that:
A humans evolved from Adam and Eve
B humans evolved from chimpanzees
C humans and apes had common ancestors
D humans and apes evolved from a single cell

4 a What evidence did Darwin use to support his ideas?
b Scientists today have a lot more knowledge that supports the theory of evolution. What do scientists know about today that Darwin did not know about?

ResultsPlus Exam tip

Be careful if you are asked a question about Darwin and human evolution. Humans did *not* evolve from apes (gorillas, orangutans and chimpanzees). Apes and humans *all* evolved from a species that is now extinct (referred to as our common ancestor). The diagram on page 20 shows the different common ancestors of humans and chimps, humans and all apes, and humans and monkeys.

Need more help
For more on this topic, see pages 20–21, 23.

edexcel key terms

genetic engineering Transferring genes from one organism to another, or changing genes in an organism by altering the DNA.
genetically modified An organism that has had its characteristics altered by the use of genetic engineering.
organic (when applied to food) Food produced without artificial fertilisers, pesticides or herbicides.

ResultsPlus
Exam Question Report

The most likely reason for farmers to produce an organic crop is:
A to increase shelf-life
B to increase profit margin
C to decrease crop yield
D to decrease biodiversity

Answer: The correct answer here is B (although some organic farmers just believe that too much use of chemicals is wrong).

How students answered
Some students chose A or D, which are incorrect. Organic produce is more likely to have a shorter shelf-life, and organic farming increases biodiversity. Others chose C, which is correct but isn't a *reason* why farmers produce organic crops. Some students knew that farmers can charge more for organic food, increasing the profit margin.

1.7: Organic farming and genetic modification

- **B1.a.1.12** Discuss the principles and ethics of organic farming; explain why organic products are more expensive than non-organic products
- **B1.a.1.9** Describe genetic engineering; show how crops can be genetically modified
- **B1.a.1.9** Compare natural selection, selective breeding and genetic engineering in terms of changing the characteristics of a species
- **B1.a.1.13** Describe how crop plants can be genetically modified; give examples of how and why crop plants might be genetically modified
- **B1.a.1.13** Describe some of the ethical concerns raised by the genetic modification of plants

Organic farming

Modern farming methods involve the use of many different chemicals, including fertilisers and pesticides. Some people think that these methods are harmful to wildlife and may leave residues in food. Organic farming is a way of farming without using chemical fertilisers and pesticides. Land is fertilised using animal manure or by growing certain crops that can add nitrogen to the soil. Pests are controlled using biological methods (by introducing predators of the pests, for example).

Organic products are often more expensive than non-organic products because yields (the amount of food produced) are lower.

Genetic modification

Scientists have been improving crops and farm animals for hundreds of years, using selective breeding. Today, scientists can change the characteristics of organisms more directly, by changing their DNA. A genetically modified (GM) organism has had its genes changed, or genes from other species added to it. GM bacteria can be used to made drugs and hormones needed for medical treatments. GM crops can be made resistant to pests or weedkillers.

Test yourself

1 Which of the following is **not** a technique used to produce organic crops?
   A use of crop rotation to maintain nitrates in the soil
   B obeying strict rules about the use of pesticides
   C use of chemical fertilisers to maintain nitrates in the soil
   D a ban on the use of genetically modified crops

2 What is likely to be the main reason why consumers are buying more organic produce?

3 Why are organic products generally more costly than non-organic products?

4 Explain the difference between natural selection, selective breeding and genetic modification.

Environment

GM crops can be developed that have various benefits:

- GM tomatoes stay firm for longer so they have a longer shelf-life and are easier to transport.
- GM crops can be developed that are resistant to certain pests.
- Crops that are resistant to a particular weedkiller make controlling weeds easier.
- GM rice ('golden rice') contains more vitamin A than normal rice. Vitamin A is often missing from the diets of people in poor countries where rice is the main food.

Supporters of genetic modification say that GM crops can improve people's diets and allow farmers to grow more food. Opponents say that:

- GM crops are just aimed at making more profits for big companies
- the modified genes may 'escape' and get into wild plants
- eating GM food may have long-term effects that we don't yet know about.

How are crops genetically modified?

The gene needed is identified. This gene can come from another type of plant, or even from bacteria. Enzymes are used to 'cut' the required gene out of the plant chromosomes or out of the plasmid (a ring of DNA) in the bacteria. Enzymes are also used to add the gene to DNA from the crop plant being modified, and this DNA is inserted into the plant. If the new gene is inserted into a plant embryo at an early stage of its development, all the cells in the new plant will have the gene, and the gene will be passed on when the plant reproduces.

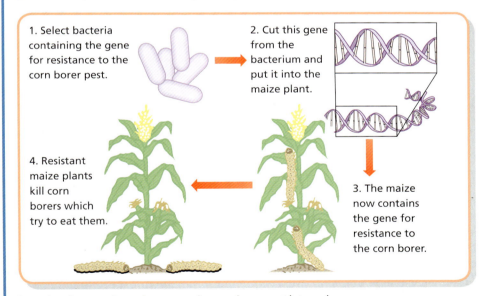

Inserting the gene for resistance to the corn borer pest into maize.

Higher tier

ResultsPlus
Exam tip

You need to understand the differences between natural selection, selective breeding and genetic modification. Natural selection involves animals or plants becoming more adapted to their environment through the generations as they reproduce naturally. Selective breeding is when *humans* choose which animals or plants produce offspring. Genetic modification *does not involve breeding* (so it doesn't involve fertilisation or pollination). Genes are changed directly, and the change is seen in just one generation.

ResultsPlus
Exam Question Report

Corn is genetically modified by inserting foreign genes into its genome. This is carried out using:
A plasmids and enzymes
B plasmids and hormones
C hormones and enzymes
D hormones, plasmids and enzymes
Answer: The correct answer here is A.

How students answered
Most students got this one wrong. Even if you can't remember what plasmids are, the key thing to know is that hormones are *not* involved. Hormones are chemical messengers in animals and plants, and are not used in genetic engineering.

Test yourself

5. Hormones, carbohydrates and enzymes are all types of chemical found in organisms. Which type is used in genetic engineering?

6. Describe **two** reasons why crop plants may be genetically modified.

7. Write down **two** reasons why some people think that crops should *not* be genetically modified.

2.1: DNA, genes and chromosomes

Need more help?
For more on this topic, see pages 36–37, 46–47.

- B1.a.2.1 Describe genes as parts of chromosomes, which are found within the nucleus
- B1.a.2.1 Describe genes as parts of chromosomes, which control the cell's activity
- B1.a.2.2 State that the unit of inheritance is the gene
- B1.a.2.2 State that a gene is a section of a long-chain (DNA) molecule
- B1.a.2.3 Suggest how DNA evidence can be used to solve crimes
- B1.a.2.3 Describe some of the implications of the outcome of the Human Genome Project, including the use of DNA evidence in medicine

edexcel key terms

alleles Alternative forms of the same gene.
cancer A disease resulting from the rapid, uncontrolled growth of cells.
cell The basic 'unit' from which living things are made.
characteristic A feature of an organism.
chromosome Thread-like structures in the nucleus made up of strings of genes.
DNA A chemical containing the code that tells a cell how to develop.
forensic The knowledge used in the investigation of crime.
gene A piece of DNA that contains the instructions needed for a particular characteristic, such as eye colour.
genetics The science concerning the inheritance of characteristics.
Human Genome Project (HGP) A project to map the human genetic code by working out the sequence of genes in human DNA.
nucleus The part of a cell that contains genetic material in the form of chromosomes.

Most of the cells in our bodies (and in all animals and plants) contain a nucleus. Inside the nucleus are chromosomes, which are very long molecules of DNA. Smaller sections of this DNA are called genes. The genes in our bodies control the way we grow and how our bodies work by controlling the activities of the cells. Genes are sometimes referred to as the 'units of inheritance'.

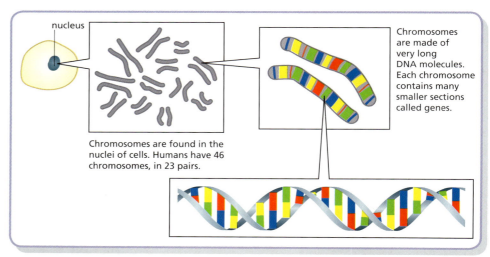

Chromosomes are found in the nuclei of cells. Humans have 46 chromosomes, in 23 pairs.

Chromosomes are made of very long DNA molecules. Each chromosome contains many smaller sections called genes.

Genes in the nucleus.

Chromosomes come in pairs. The genes on each of a pair of chromosomes do the same job, although there might be slight differences between each gene in a pair. These pairs of genes are called alleles.

ResultsPlus Exam tip

Students often lose easy marks because they can't remember the differences between genes, chromosomes, and so on. You need to remember:
- chromosomes are found in the nucleus of a cell
- chromosomes are made from DNA
- a gene is a section of a chromosome (so genes are also made from DNA)
- a gene is a unit of inheritance
- alleles are alternative terms of the *same* gene.

Genes and crime

Each person has a unique set of genes. Criminals often leave small traces of skin or blood at the scene of a crime. Forensic scientists can extract DNA from these traces and make a 'DNA fingerprint' or 'genetic profile' from it. This can be compared to the genetic profiles of suspects, and help to solve a crime. DNA tests can also be used to find out whether people are related to each other.

The Human Genome Project

A DNA molecule consists of two long chains joined together with pairs of 'bases'. There are only four types of base (called A, C, G and T), and it is the pattern of bases along a section of chromosome that forms a gene.

The Human Genome Project (HGP) was completed in 2003. It produced a 'map' of the bases in the human genome (all the DNA on all the chromosomes in a human cell). This map will help scientists find out what all the different genes do. This will help them to:

- identify certain genes that may make some people more likely to get diseases such as cancer
- develop ways of fixing faulty genes to cure diseases
- develop new 'tailor-made' drugs with fewer side effects.

Not everyone thinks these developments are a good idea. Some objections are:

- mapping a person's DNA is an invasion of privacy
- finding out you may get a genetic disease is no use if there's no cure
- if insurance companies find out you may be more likely to get a disease, you may not be able to get insurance.

Test yourself

1 Genes carry instructions for the characteristics of an organism. What is a gene?
   A an alternative form of an allele   B a unit of inheritance
   C a complete DNA molecule   D an energy-giving molecule

2 Complete these sentences.
   a Genes are made from ...   b Genes are part of ...
   c ... are found in the nucleus of cells.

3 Explain how genetic information can help to solve crimes.

4 a What do the letters HGP stand for?
   b What was the HGP?

5 Explain how knowing about the genes in humans can help to prevent or cure diseases.

6 Why do some people think that knowing about their genes may not be a good idea?

Need more help?
For more on this topic, see pages 34–35, 38–39.

2.2: Reproduction and variation

- B1.a.2.5 Describe how plants reproduce by asexual reproduction; explain how asexual reproduction produces genetically identical organisms called clones
- B1.a.2.6 Outline what sexual reproduction is; discuss how it leads to a mixing up of genes and to variation in the new generation
- B1.a.2.7 State how some characteristics can be changed by changes in environmental conditions, including the food we eat
- B1.a.2.7 Explain that plant growth is influenced by mineral resources in the soil

edexcel key terms

asexual reproduction Reproduction in which genes are passed on from only one parent.
clone A group of genetically identical plants or animals produced asexually from one parent.
diploid Containing two sets of chromosomes.
environment The surrounding conditions in which an organism develops.
fertilisation When the nuclei of two sex cells (such as an egg and sperm) join together.
gamete A sex cell such as an egg or sperm cell.
haploid Containing only one set of chromosomes.
inheritance The passing of genes from parents to offspring.
sexual reproduction Reproduction in which half the genes are inherited from each parent.
variation The differences in a group of organisms of the same species.

ResultsPlus Exam tip

You need to learn the meanings of all the words in the key terms list very carefully. This applies to all parts of the course, but students often have particular difficulty with the meanings of words connected with genetics and reproduction.

Asexual reproduction

Some plants and animals can reproduce without needing a mate of the opposite sex. This is called asexual reproduction (reproduction without sex). Bacteria also reproduce asexually.

All the offspring of asexual reproduction have only one parent, so they have exactly the same genes as the parent (and they also all have the same genes as each other). The offspring are referred to as clones.

Asexual reproduction means that the plants or animals can produce more offspring, as they don't have to find a mate first (or be pollinated, in the case of plants).

Asexual reproduction involves cell division, where one cell divides to form two identical cells. Both these cells have the same, complete set of chromosomes. They are called diploid cells. Cell division that produces diploid cells is called mitosis.

Spider plants can reproduce asexually. So can many crop plants such as potatoes, onions and strawberries.

Sexual reproduction

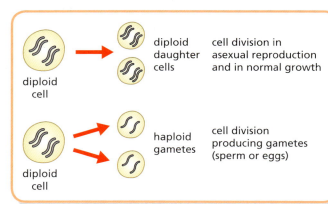

Cell divisions.

Sexual reproduction occurs when two organisms produce offspring. Each parent produces gametes that have half the normal number of chromosomes. Female gametes are eggs, and male gametes are sperm (or pollen in plants). Gametes are referred to as haploid cells, because they have only one set of chromosomes. Cell division that results in haploid cells is called meiosis.

When animals mate (or flowers are pollinated), the male and female gametes join up. This is called fertilisation. When the two gametes join, the resulting cell has pairs of chromosomes again (it has the normal number of chromosomes). Cells with the normal number of chromosomes are called diploid cells.

The offspring produced by sexual reproduction have a mixture of genes from both parents, so sexual reproduction leads to variation.

Genes 2

Exam Question Report

Female bullfrogs lay eggs that the male bullfrogs fertilise externally. This is an example of:
A asexual reproduction
B binary fission
C *in vitro* fertilisation
D sexual reproduction
Answer: The correct answer is D.

How students answered
Nearly half the students answering this question thought the answer was A. The majority of students could tell this is sexual reproduction, because a male and a female are involved, and the eggs are fertilised.

Genes or environment?

There is variation between different organisms in a species. Some of this variation is due to slight differences in the genes that offspring inherit from their parents in sexual reproduction, and some is due to environmental differences. In this context, 'environment' means the availability of food, whether the organism has been affected by a disease, and so on. Characteristics such as eye colour are determined by genes alone, but characteristics such as height or weight are determined by a combination of genes and environmental factors.

Human growth is partly affected by genes, but the availability of food has a big effect too. If children are malnourished (don't get enough food of the right kinds), they won't grow to their full potential size. They will be thin and more likely to suffer from diseases. If children eat too much they may become obese, and will be more likely to suffer from conditions such as heart disease.

Plant growth is also affected by the availability of food and nutrients. Plants manufacture their own food using light energy (photosynthesis), so if a plant doesn't get enough light it will not grow properly. Plants also need nutrients from the soil to grow properly.

A plant lacking:
- phosphates will have poor roots and slow growth
- potassium salts will have poor growth and poor fruits
- nitrates will have stunted growth and yellow leaves
- magnesium salts will have yellow leaves.

Higher tier
For more on this topic, see pages 42–43.

Exam Question Report

A survey found out that 19.8% of overweight or obese children had parents who were either overweight or obese. What can be concluded from these data?
A that obesity is inherited
B that obesity is inherited but there is an environmental influence
C that obesity is influenced only by the environment
D no definite conclusion can be made
Answer: The correct answer is D.

How students answered
The biggest proportion of wrong answers (44%) was for option B and 23% chose option C.

75% 0 marks

Many students don't like to choose an option like D because they assume they wouldn't be asked a question without a definite conclusion. But sometimes the correct answer really is that you can't draw a conclusion from the data you've been given.

25% 1 mark

Test yourself

1. What are the two kinds of gamete called?

2. What do these words mean?
   a gamete   b sperm   c egg   d haploid
   e diploid   f fertilisation g pollination

3. Answer these questions by choosing 'asexual reproduction' or 'sexual reproduction'.
   a Which uses haploid cells?   b Which produces clones?
   c Which produces offspring with variation?

4. Summarise the differences between asexual and sexual reproduction.

5. Explain how human and plant growth can be affected by environmental factors.

edexcel key terms

alleles Alternative forms of the same gene.
dominant An allele that overrides other alleles of a gene so that their effects are hidden.
generation A term used to describe all the organisms in a species at a particular step in a line of descent.
genotype The combination of genes within an organism.
heterozygous Having two different alleles of a particular gene.
homozygous Having two identical alleles of a particular gene.
phenotype The observable characteristics of an organism.
recessive An allele whose effects are hidden by the presence of a dominant allele.

2.3: Passing on the genes

- B1.a.2.6 Outline what sexual reproduction is; discuss how this leads to a mixing up of genes and variation in the new generation
- B1.a.2.8 Explain the difference between dominant and recessive alleles
- B1.a.2.8 Explain how alternative forms of a gene cause variation in a characteristic

An organism that has been produced by sexual reproduction has two copies of each gene, one inherited from each parent. Each gene can have different variants, called alleles. For example, a pea plant with red flowers will have different alleles for flower colour than a plant with white flowers.

When an organism produces gametes, each gamete gets just one copy of each allele. The diagram below shows what happens when two pea plants reproduce. The same information can be shown on a Punnett square. The shaded boxes on the square show the different possible genotypes of the offspring. The genotype is the combination of genes in an organism.

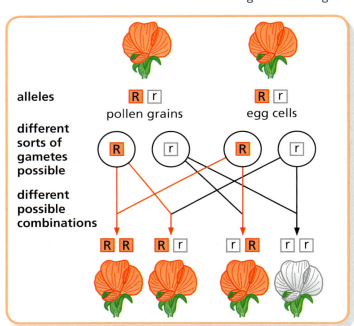

Genetic diagram showing inheritance of flower colour.

The phenotype is the observable characteristics of an organism. The diagram shows that the **RR** and **Rr** genotypes produce phenotypes with red flowers, and only the **rr** genotype produces the phenotype with white flowers.

Alleles can be dominant or recessive. In peas, the allele for red flowers (**R**) is dominant, and the allele for white flowers (**r**) is recessive. A dominant allele does not allow a recessive allele to work. An upper case letter is used to show which allele is dominant.

We also say that an organism with two identical alleles of a gene is homozygous for that gene. An organism with two different alleles is heterozygous. So pea plants with the **RR** or **rr** genotypes are homozygous, and pea plants with the **Rr** genotype are heterozygous.

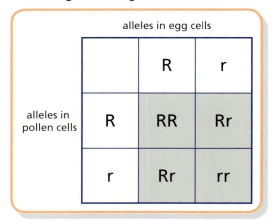

Punnett square showing inheritance of flower colour.

Worked example

A man has the sex chromosomes XY. A woman has the sex chromosomes XX. If their first baby is a boy, what is the chance of their second baby being a girl?

A 25%   **B** 50%   **C** 75%   **D** 100%

The Punnett square shows that there is a 50% chance of having a girl, and a 50% chance of having a boy. These chances apply each time the couple have a baby. The fact that they had a boy the first time makes no difference to the probability of having a girl the second time.

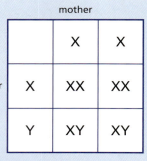

Genes 2

ResultsPlus
Exam Question Report

A dwarf variety of wheat has only recessive alleles for height. Two wheat plants, heterozygous for height, were bred together. What percentage of the offspring would be dwarf wheat plants?

A 0%   B 25%   C 50%   D 100%

Answer: The answer is B.

How students answered

More than half the students got this wrong.

Students who got this right probably drew a Punnett square. You can use **H** and **h** to represent the alleles for height. The question says that the parent plants are heterozygous for height, so they must both be **Hh**. The dwarf offspring will be the ones with the **hh** genotype. The square shows that only one quarter (25%) of the offspring will have this genotype.

	H	h
H	HH	Hh
h	Hh	hh

Test yourself

1. Why do pea plant gametes only have one allele for flower colour?

2. What is:
   a. a genotype
   b. a phenotype?

3. A pea plant has the genotype Rr. What colour flowers will it have?
   A red
   B white
   C pink
   D some red and some white

4. The Punnett square on the right is for pea plants.
   a. Are the parent plants homozygous or heterozygous?
   b. What colour flowers do the parents have?
   c. What proportion of the offspring will have white flowers?
   d. The first generation of offspring are bred with each other. What proportion of the second generation will have white flowers?

5. A gardener buys some pea plants with red flowers. Explain why she may get some white flowers if these plants are bred together.

6. Short pea plants always have short offspring. Tall pea plants can have tall or short offspring.
   a. Is the gene for being tall dominant or recessive?
   b. What genotypes could tall pea plants have?
   c. What is the probability of two short pea plants having tall offspring?

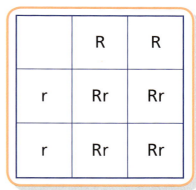

Punnett square for pea plants

29

Need more help?
For more on this topic, see pages 44–45.

edexcel key terms

carrier A person whose cells have a normal and a faulty allele. They do not show any signs of the genetic disease they are carrying.
cystic fibrosis A genetic disorder in which the person produces thick, sticky mucus in their lungs.
gene therapy Replacing faulty alleles with working copies of the affected genes.
genotype The combination of alleles in the cells of an organism.
phenotype The appearance or other characteristic of an organism caused by its particular combination of alleles.

	C	c
C	CC	Cc
C	CC	Cc

	C	c
C	CC	Cc
c	Cc	cc

If only one parent is a carrier, none of their children will have the disease.

If both parents are carriers, there is a 25% chance that each child will have the disease.

Inheritance of cystic fibrosis.

ResultsPlus Exam tip

Remember how to draw Punnett squares, and that a capital letter represents a dominant allele. If a question asks you about the probability of a person having a particular combination of alleles (or having a particular genetic disease), it's best to draw a Punnett square to help you work out your answer.

2.4: Inherited diseases

 B1.a.2.9 Explain how some alleles cause diseases that can be inherited, including sickle-cell anaemia, Huntington's disease and haemophilia

 B1.a.2.4 Describe how gene therapy works

B1.a.2.4 Discuss how the life of a person suffering from cystic fibrosis or breast cancer would change if this disease could be treated genetically

Some diseases are caused by faulty genes. For example:

Disease	Symptoms
cystic fibrosis	sticky mucus that clogs the lungs and affects the digestive system
Huntington's disease	affects the nervous system and the brain
sickle-cell disease	red blood cells change shape, which causes pain and serious complications
haemophilia	blood does not clot normally

Cystic fibrosis (CF) is caused by a recessive allele, so a person only has the disease if they inherit two copies of the faulty allele (genotype **cc**). A person with one normal and one faulty allele (genotype **Cc**) is said to be a carrier. They don't have symptoms of the disease, but they can pass the faulty allele on to their children.

The diagrams on the left show how cystic fibrosis can be inherited.

ResultsPlus
Exam Question Report

The table shows two diseases. Which row of the table correctly shows which of the diseases are genetic?

	haemophilia	sickle-cell anaemia
A	yes	yes
B	yes	no
C	no	yes
D	no	no

Answer: The correct answer is A.

How students answered
Most students couldn't identify that both of these diseases are genetic diseases.

 61% 0 marks

Only 39% realised they were both inherited.

 39% 1 mark

Genes 2

Gene therapy

Someone with cystic fibrosis has to have regular and lengthy physiotherapy sessions to try to clear the mucus from their lungs. They also need to take lots of antibiotics, as the mucus makes them more likely to get infections.

Gene therapy involves putting working copies of the faulty gene into a patient. For example, working copies of the gene that causes cystic fibrosis can be put into tiny droplets called liposomes, which can be inhaled using a nasal spray. The healthy alleles end up in the lung cells, and the cells no longer make the sticky mucus. A person who has had this gene therapy doesn't need physiotherapy or antibiotics. But the therapy isn't permanent because the lung cells are continually renewed, and so the treatment will need to be repeated.

Some forms of breast cancer have genetic causes. At the moment, someone with an allele that makes them more likely to have breast cancer will have more screening and tests than a person without this allele. They will probably also worry a lot about getting the disease. If gene therapy could fix the faulty allele, these people wouldn't have to worry so much.

> **Higher tier**
> For more on this topic, see pages 48–49.

Test yourself

1. A carrier of CF:
   A shows symptoms of the disease but can't pass it to their children
   B shows symptoms of the disease and can pass it to their children
   C shows no symptoms of the disease and can't pass it to their children
   D shows no symptoms of the disease but can pass it to their children

2. Anne has cystic fibrosis. Beth and Calum both have two normal alleles. Dan is a carrier of CF.
   a What is Anne's genotype?
   b What is Beth's genotype?
   c What is Dan's genotype?
   d If Beth and Dan have a baby, what is the chance of the baby having CF?
   e If Anne and Calum have a baby, what is the chance of the baby having CF?

3. CF is caused by recessive alleles. The table shows the phenotype of 400 children born to parents who were both heterozygous for CF.

number of children without CF	number of children with CF
300	100

   How many of the 400 children would you expect to be heterozygous?
   A 100   B 200   C 300   D 400

4. The table shows the number of alleles for CF that are present in different sets of parents. Which row of the table shows the parents whose child would definitely **not** have CF?

	mother number of dominant alleles	father number of recessive alleles
A	2	0
B	0	2
C	1	1
D	0	1

5. a What is gene therapy?
   b How could gene therapy help to improve the life of someone with CF?
   c How could gene therapy help to improve the life of someone with an allele that makes them more likely to get breast cancer?

Need more help?
For more on this topic, see pages 50–51.

2.5: Cloning, transgenic animals and designer babies

- B1.a.2.11 Discuss the social and ethical concerns of cloning mammals
- B1.a.2.11 Discuss the possibility of cloning human body parts for transplant surgery
- B1.a.2.10 Explain how mammals can be cloned
- B1.a.2.10 Describe how transgenic animals can be used for the production of 'designer milk'
- B1.a.2.10 Investigate ways in which we might use transgenic animals
- B1.a.2.12 Describe what is meant by 'designer babies'
- B1.a.2.12 Discuss the contemporary scientific theory of 'designer babies'
- B1.a.2.12 Explain why the idea of 'designer babies' is so controversial

Cloning

All mammals use sexual reproduction. The only way that clones normally occur is when identical twins are born. Identical twins occur when one fertilised egg splits up to form two individuals. Identical twins have exactly the same genes.

Scientists can now also clone animals by taking a nucleus from a body cell of an animal. The nucleus is put into an egg cell from a female animal of the same species from which the nucleus has been removed (enucleated). However, many of the animals that have been cloned so far have suffered from health problems, and some people think that cloning should not be carried out.

It is possible that we may one day be able to grow new cloned body parts to be transplanted into patients. At present, patients who need a new heart or liver have to wait until a donor organ is available. Many patients awaiting transplants die before they get a donor organ. After the transplant is done, the patient will have to take drugs for the rest of their life to stop their bodies rejecting the organs. If organs could be cloned, there would be a greater supply of them. If they were cloned using genetic information from the patient, there would be no need to take drugs to stop the body rejecting the organ.

edexcel key terms

antibody A substance produced by white blood cells in response to an infection.
transgenic An organism containing genes taken from another species.
transplant An organ that has been donated by one organism and inserted into the body of another.

Test yourself

1 What is a clone?
2 Write down two advantages of using cloned body parts for transplants.
3 What is cloning?
   A making identical copies of an individual by replicating a haploid cell
   B making non-identical copies of an individual using a diploid cell
   C making identical copies of an individual by replicating a diploid cell
   D making identical copies of an individual using the HGP

Mammals can be artificially cloned by taking the nucleus from one animal and putting it into an empty egg from another animal. The modified egg is given an electric shock to make it start dividing, and is then implanted into a surrogate mother. The offspring is genetically identical to the animal from which the nucleus was taken.

Cloning could be used to make exact copies of successful racehorses, for example, or cows that produced lots of milk.

Transgenic animals

Genes from animals or plants can be put into other organisms by genetic engineering. An organism with genes added in this way is called a transgenic organism.

Transgenic cows could be made that produce 'designer milk'. For example, the milk could have low cholesterol, could contain an enzyme needed to treat a particular disease, or could contain human antibodies.

Designer babies

Some couples can't have babies normally and use IVF instead. In IVF, eggs are removed from the woman and fertilised in a lab with sperm from the man. The fertilised eggs are allowed to grow into embryos and then one or two of the embryos are implanted in the woman to develop into babies. You will learn more about this on pages 42–43.

It is possible to test all the embryos produced during IVF to see if any of them have faulty genes. This is called embryo screening and it is used to allow parents to make sure they don't pass on genetic diseases such as cystic fibrosis.

When we know more about which genes control different characteristics, it will also be possible to select embryos with particular characteristics, such as being tall or being very intelligent. Babies selected in this way are called 'designer babies'.

Many people object to embryo screening and designer babies on religious or ethical grounds. One objection is that rejected embryos are destroyed (but then spare embryos left over from IVF treatments are also destroyed). Others say that we are 'playing god' and should not meddle.

> **Higher tier**
> For more on this topic, see pages 50–53.

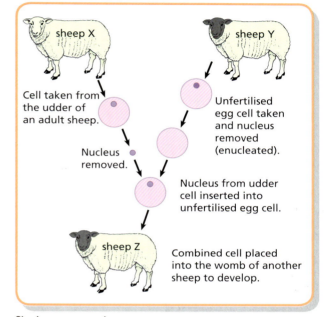

Cloning a mammal.

> **ResultsPlus**
> **Watch out!**
>
> Remember that the cloned animal is genetically identical to the animal from which the nucleus was taken. It's **not** related at all to the surrogate mother in which the egg was implanted.

Test yourself

4 a What is a transgenic animal?
 b What could transgenic animals be used for?

5 a What is a designer baby?
 b Why do some people object to the idea of designer babies?

3.1: The nervous system

- B1.b.3.2 Describe the structure of the central nervous system
- B1.b.3.2 Describe how the central nervous system carries electrical impulses from sense organs to muscles
- B1.b.3.5 Explain that receptors in sense organs detect internal and external changes
- B1.b.3.5 Explain how the body responds to the stimuli of internal and external changes
- B1.b.3.1 Explain what reaction time is
- B1.b.3.1 Suggest why reaction time is important
- B1.b.3.1 State how reaction time can be measured

Need more help?
For more on this topic, see pages 58–61, 64–65.

edexcel key terms

brain An organ that controls the actions of your body.
central nervous system (CNS) The brain and spinal cord.
electrical impulse A signal carried by the nerves in your body.
motor neurone A neurone that carries impulses to an effector (usually a muscle).
muscle Tissue made from cells that can contract, moving parts of the body.
nerve A bundle of cells called neurones, which carry messages between different parts of the body.
peripheral nervous system (PNS) The nerves that are not part of the CNS.
reaction time The time between a sense organ detecting a stimulus and the muscles reacting.
receptor A special cell that detects a stimulus, like light, sound or heat.
relay neurone A neurone found in the central nervous system connecting a sensory neurone and a motor neurone as part of a reflex.
sense organ An organ that contains receptors that detect stimuli (e.g. eyes, ears, skin, etc.).
sensory neurone A neurone carrying impulses between a receptor cell and the central nervous system.
stimulus Something you react to, like a sound, a hot object, or something you see (plural: stimuli).

Your nervous system carries messages between your brain, muscles and sense organs (such as eyes, skin and ears). The central nervous system (CNS) is the brain and the spinal cord. This is connected to the rest of the body by nerves. These nerves make up the peripheral nervous system (PNS).

Each nerve consists of lots of nerve cells, called neurones. The nerve signals travel along the axons of a neurone as electrical impulses. The myelin sheath insulates the axon.

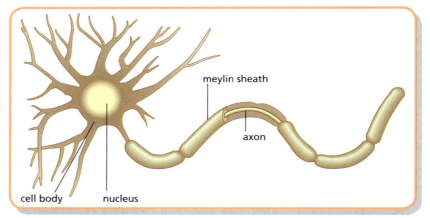

A neurone.

Neurones are joined to one another at synapses. A chemical called a neurotransmitter is produced when an impulse reaches the end of a neurone. The chemical diffuses across the gap to the next neurone, and starts a new impulse in the next neurone.

Sense organs are the parts of the body that detect changes inside and outside the body. Receptors in your ears, eyes and nose detect changes outside the body. Receptors in your skin can also detect internal changes such as changes in body temperature.

Effectors are the parts of the body that *do* things (mostly muscles).

Neurones are given different names, depending on which way they are carrying signals:

- A sensory neurone carries signals *from* receptors (such as the skin, eyes and ears – your senses) *to* the brain.
- A motor neurone carries signals *from* the brain *to* muscles. (Remember **m**otor neurones send messages to **m**uscles.)

A synapse.

Electrical and Chemical Signals 3

Responding to stimuli

A stimulus is a change in your body or in your surroundings. For example, sensors in your skin might detect that your skin is cold. You might respond to this by putting a sweater on. Sensory neurones send messages to the brain, the brain decides what to do, and then it sends messages along motor neurones to make your hands put on the sweater.

Some responses need to be faster than this, such as when an athlete responds to the starting gun. The time between the stimulus arriving at her ears and the moment she moves is her reaction time.

Having a fast reaction time can be very important, as it might save you from injury. The faster you react to seeing a car coming towards you, the more likely you are to be able to get out of the way in time.

The simplest way of measuring reaction time is to ask a friend to drop a special ruler. The slower your reaction time, the further the ruler will fall before you grab it.

ResultsPlus
Exam tip

Students often get questions about impulses and synapses wrong. Remember that when the signal is travelling *along a neurone* it is an electrical impulse. When the signal *crosses the gap* of a synapse between one neurone and the next it is done through the diffusion of a chemical.

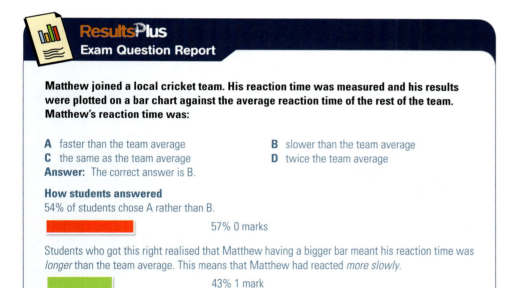

ResultsPlus
Exam Question Report

Matthew joined a local cricket team. His reaction time was measured and his results were plotted on a bar chart against the average reaction time of the rest of the team. Matthew's reaction time was:

A faster than the team average
B slower than the team average
C the same as the team average
D twice the team average

Answer: The correct answer is B.

How students answered
54% of students chose A rather than B.

57% 0 marks

Students who got this right realised that Matthew having a bigger bar meant his reaction time was *longer* than the team average. This means that Matthew had reacted *more slowly*.

43% 1 mark

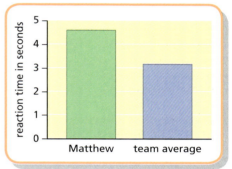

Test yourself

1. a Name the parts of the central nervous system.
   b What forms the peripheral nervous system?

2. a Which part of a neurone carries electrical impulses?
   b What does the myelin sheath do?
   c What is a synapse?

3. Which statement shows how neurones communicate with each other across the synapse?
   A diffusion of chemical messages
   B diffusion of electrical signals
   C conduction of electrical signals
   D conduction of chemical messages

4. What is the difference between a sensory neurone and a motor neurone?

5. a What is reaction time?
   b Why is a fast reaction time important?

3.2: Reflex actions

- B1.b.3.6 Describe the difference between voluntary and reflex responses
- B1.b.3.6 Explain why the iris reflex is useful in helping to protect the body
- B1.b.3.6 Explain how the eye focuses light on the retina
- B1.b.3.6 Suggest some advantages of the accommodation reflex in helping to safeguard the body
- B1.b.3.6 Give examples of the 'ducking' reaction to objects travelling close to the head in helping to safeguard the body

Need more help? For more on this topic, see pages 66–71.

edexcel key terms

iris The coloured ring of muscle in the eye that controls the size of the pupil.
iris reflex A reflex action that controls the size of the pupil.
reflex An automatic response to a stimulus. Also called an involuntary response.
reflex arc The pathway of an impulse during a reflex action.
voluntary response A response to a stimulus that you have to think about and can control.

Voluntary and reflex actions

Actions such as putting on a sweater when it gets cold are voluntary actions. You think and then decide what to do. Other examples are deciding which TV channel to watch, moving into the shade if you are hot, and deciding to drink when you are thirsty.

Some of your reactions are involuntary responses, or reflex actions. These are automatic responses, and you can't control what happens. Examples include sneezing when dust gets up your nose, pulling your hand away from a hot object, and sweating when you are hot.

Reflex actions happen faster than voluntary responses because the brain is not involved. Instead, signals from sensory neurones go to relay neurones in the spinal cord, and then directly to motor neurones. This pathway is called the reflex arc.

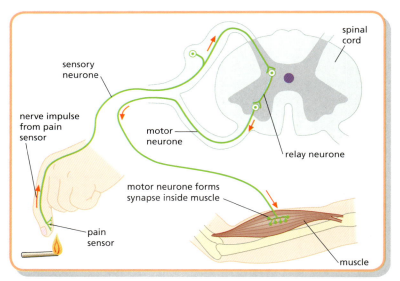

The reflex arc.

The eyes

Light enters your eyes through a hole called the pupil. The coloured part of your eye around the pupil is called the iris. Muscles in the iris can change the size of the pupil, which controls the amount of light that can get into the eye. Smaller pupils let less light in.

There is an involuntary response that reduces the size of the pupil if a bright light shines into the eyes. This protects the cells in the retina from too much light, which could damage them. This is called the iris reflex.

The iris reflex.

Your eyes focus light onto the retina at the back of the eye. Focusing is partly done by the lens. The shape of the lens is controlled by the ciliary muscles. The muscles act to change the shape of the lens, making it fatter when you're looking at close objects and thinner when you're looking at distant objects. This is called the accommodation reflex. It is a reflex because it happens automatically. The accommodation reflex makes sure you can always clearly see what you're looking at, so you can detect danger approaching.

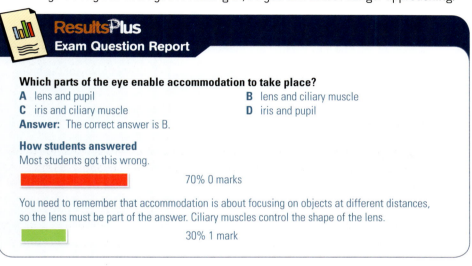

ResultsPlus
Exam tip

Students often call the iris reflex the 'pupil reflex', and lose marks. Although it is the size of the pupil that changes, you need to remember that the pupil is just a hole, and the iris contains the muscles that make the change. It is therefore called the *iris* reflex.

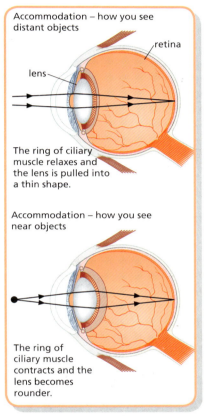

The accommodation reflex.

The 'ducking' reflex

If something moves fast near your head, you 'duck'. This is an involuntary response (you don't need to think about it, your body just does it automatically). It helps to protect your head and brain from injury.

Test yourself

1. Jaya picks up an egg that has just been boiled, and then quickly drops it. Jaya's behaviour is called:
   - **A** a voluntary response
   - **B** an involuntary response
   - **C** a stimulus
   - **D** an impulse

2. Jaya's movement involved neurones passing impulses. Write down the three types of neurone involved, in the correct order, choosing your answers from this list:

   relay, sensory, effector, motor, sensor, synapse

3. a What is the iris reflex?
   b How does the iris reflex help to protect the body?

4. a Which part of the eye focuses light on the retina?
   b How does this part change when you are looking at objects at different distances?
   c Is the changing of this part a voluntary or involuntary response?
   d What is this response called?
   e How does this response help to protect the body?

5. a What is the ducking reflex?
   b How does this reflex help to protect the body?

Need more help?
For more on this topic, see pages 62–63.

3.3: The brain

- B1.b.3.2 Describe the structure of the brain
- B1.b.3.2 Describe the functions of the brain
- B1.b.3.4 Describe how strokes disrupt the functioning of the brain
- B1.b.3.4 Describe how brain tumours disrupt the functioning of the brain
- B1.b.3.4 Describe how Parkinson's disease disrupts the functioning of the brain
- B1.b.3.4 Describe how grand mal epilepsy disrupts the functioning of the brain

The brain controls most of what happens in our bodies. It contains sensory, motor and relay neurones. Different parts of the brain are responsible for different functions.

edexcel key terms

grand mal epilepsy A form of epilepsy where the person loses consciousness and makes jerky movements.
Parkinson's disease A disease where the brain is unable to coordinate muscle actions properly.
stroke A blood clot or bleeding in the brain, which causes brain cells to die.
tumour Cells growing to form an abnormal tissue.

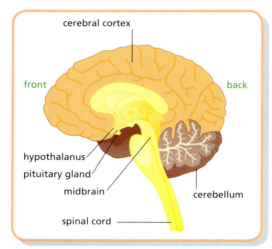

Parts of the brain.

Different parts of the brain have different functions. The table shows just some of the parts of the brain and what they do.

ResultsPlus Exam tip

You need to learn the names of these parts of the brain and what they do.

Part	Function
cerebral cortex	senses, behaviour, consciousness (thinking and feeling)
cerebellum	controls muscles and balance
medulla	controls automatic responses such as breathing, heart rate, digestion, etc.
hypothalamus	helps to keep conditions in the body constant, e.g. helps maintain a steady body temperature
pituitary gland	releases hormones (see pages 40–41) that control many different body functions

3 Electrical and Chemical Signals

When the brain goes wrong

Things can go wrong in the brain that affect its functioning.

A stroke happens when part of the brain does not get enough oxygen. This is usually due to a blood clot or bleeding inside the brain.

- The oxygen supply to part of the brain is cut off.
- If the oxygen supply to the cells is not restored quickly, some brain cells will die (and cannot re-grow).
- Bleeding inside the brain makes pressure build up.
- The pressure may damage brain cells.

A brain tumour (cancer) occurs when cells grow out of control inside the brain.

- The extra cells cause pressure.
- The pressure causes headaches, damage to cells and unconsciousness.
- Brain tumours can interfere with the way impulses travel between cells.
- Brain tumours can cause seizures (when muscles may contract uncontrollably and the patient may lose consciousness).

Parkinson's disease is caused by problems with the transmission of signals from one neurone to another, and from motor neurones to muscles.

- Symptoms include muscle tremors, stiffness, muscle rigidity and slow movement.
- Parkinson's disease can't be cured, but drugs and therapy can help with the symptoms.

In epilepsy, people have sudden bursts of electrical activity in their brains.

- The extra electrical activity disrupts the normal transmission of impulses in the brain.
- Some epileptic seizures are minor and only last for a few seconds.
- In a grand mal seizure, people may fall down, jerk uncontrollably and lose consciousness.

Higher tier
For more on this topic, see page 63.

Test yourself

1. Name four different parts of the brain.

2. Which row of the table shows the correct parts of the brain responsible for body temperature and movement?

	body temperature	body movement
A	hypothalamus	pituitary gland
B	pituitary gland	hypothalamus
C	hypothalamus	cerebellum
D	cerebellum	pituitary gland

3. Which part of the brain:
   a allows you to think
   b controls your breathing?

4. a Write down two different causes of strokes.
   b How does a stroke affect the brain?

5. a What is epilepsy?
   b What happens in a grand mal seizure?

6. a What causes Parkinson's disease?
   b What are the symptoms?

7. a What is a brain tumour?
   b How does a brain tumour affect the functioning of the brain?

Need more help?
For more on this topic, see pages 72–73.

3.4: Chemical messages

- B1.b.3.7 Describe the composition of the blood
- B1.b.3.7 Describe the transport function of the blood
- B1.b.3.8 Explain how hormones act as chemical messengers
- B1.b.3.8 Explain how hormones act as chemical messages affecting target organs
- B1.b.3.8 Explain how hormones act as chemical messages affecting cells
- B1.b.3.13 Explain how insulin produced by the pancreas regulates glucose concentrations in the blood
- B1.b.3.14 Describe the advantages for people with diabetes of the use of human insulin produced by genetically modified bacteria

edexcel key terms

bacteria A type of microorganism. Many are useful but some cause disease.
diabetes A disease where your body can't control the level of sugar in the blood.
genetically modified When something has had specific sections of DNA added to change what it produces.
genetically modified organism (GMO) An organism whose DNA has been modified.
glucose A simple sugar (a type of carbohydrate).
hormone A chemical produced by a gland that is used to carry messages around the body.
insulin A hormone made in the pancreas to control the level of sugar in the blood.
pancreas An organ in the abdomen that produces insulin.
target organ The organ a particular hormone works on.

Blood

Blood consists of a liquid (plasma) that carries lots of different types of cells around the body. Each type of cell has a different function. The table shows the functions of the blood that you need to learn.

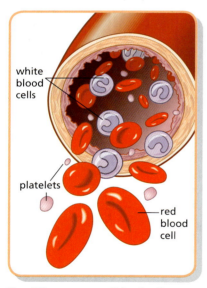

The different types of blood cell.

Part of blood	Description	Function
plasma	straw-coloured liquid	• transports different blood cells around the body • transports the following substances: – carbon dioxide – hormones – glucose and other chemicals taken into the body through the digestive system – waste from cells
red blood cells	red discs, containing haemoglobin	• carry oxygen around the body
white blood cells	white cells of different shapes	• fight infections (you'll learn more about this in topic 4)
platelets	small fragments of cells	• help blood to clot after an injury

Hormones

Hormones are chemicals that are used to send signals around the body. They are carried in the blood plasma. Hormones are produced by organs called endocrine glands. Each hormone affects only one or two organs, called target organs.

Exam tip

Lots of students lose marks on easy questions about the blood – you just need to remember what all the different parts of the blood do.

Electrical and Chemical Signals 3

Controlling glucose

The cells in your body need glucose to provide energy. The level of glucose in the blood needs to be controlled carefully, as too much can damage the body. Glucose enters the blood when carbohydrates in food are broken down. The amount of glucose is controlled by hormones called insulin and glucagon, which are made in the pancreas. The liver is the target organ for insulin and glucagon. Insulin makes the liver convert glucose into a carbohydrate called glycogen for storage. Glucagon makes the liver convert the glycogen back into glucose.

The glucose control system doesn't work properly in people with diabetes. In a diabetic person the pancreas doesn't make enough insulin so blood glucose levels can become dangerously high. This can be treated by injecting insulin.

The insulin needed by diabetics can be made from the pancreases of pigs or cattle, or can be made using genetically modified (GM) bacteria. The GM bacteria have had the human gene for making insulin put into them. This insulin can be made in large quantities, and vegetarians and vegans can use it.

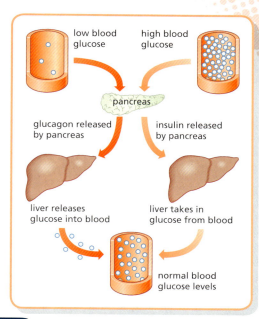

How glucose is controlled.

ResultsPlus — Exam Question Report

People with diabetes cannot lower their blood sugar levels naturally. What is least likely to affect the glucose levels of a diabetic?
- A a diet including high proportions of sweets and cakes
- B a high protein diet
- C daily injections of insulin
- D daily injections of glucagon

Answer: The answer is B.

How students answered
Not many students got the right answer. Some thought it was C or D, but insulin and glucagon are both hormones that affect the amount of glucose in the blood, so injections of these *will* affect glucose levels. To get it right students had to know that sweets and cakes contain carbohydrates and will be broken down to form glucose in the digestive system. Proteins are broken down to form amino acids, not glucose, so a high protein diet will have the least effect on glucose levels.

ResultsPlus — Watch out!

You need to remember the names of the hormones and carbohydrates. This can be a bit tricky because glycogen and glucagon sound quite similar. You can make up a little story to help you remember which is which: **Gluc**ag**on** is made when the **gluc**ose in the blood is **gon**e. G**ly**cogen is **ly**ing around in the liver.

Test yourself

1. The function of red blood cells is to:
   - A carry plasma
   - B transport hormones
   - C carry oxygen
   - D ingest bacteria

2. What part of the blood is involved in clotting?
   - A urea
   - B platelets
   - C haemoglobin
   - D white blood cells

3. Write down three things that the blood plasma carries around the body.

4. What is: a a hormone   b a target organ?

5. a Write down the names of two hormones involved in controlling glucose in the blood.
   b How are these hormones carried around the body?
   c Which of these hormones would be released after eating a big meal?
   d Which would be released if you had been exercising for several hours? Explain your answer.

6. a What causes diabetes?
   b How can GM bacteria be used to help diabetics?

3.5: Hormones and reproduction

GCSE 360 Science

Need more help?
For more on this topic, see pages 74–77.

- ✓ **B1.b.3.11** Explain how manufactured sex hormones can be used for contraception
- ✓ **B1.b.3.11** Explain how manufactured sex hormones can be used to treat infertility in women
- ✓ **B1.b.3.12** Discuss the social and ethical implications of IVF treatment
- ✓ **B1.b.3.12** Discuss the social and ethical implications of IVF treatment in mature clients
- ✓ **B1.b.3.9** Interpret data to explain how oestrogen causes the lining of the uterus to thicken during the early part of the menstrual cycle
- ✓ **B1.b.3.10** Interpret data to explain how progesterone maintains the lining of the uterus during the middle part of the menstrual cycle and during pregnancy

edexcel key terms

contraception A method of preventing pregnancy.
follicle stimulating hormone (FSH) A hormone that stimulates the growth of eggs in the ovaries.
infertility Where a couple are unable to have children.
***in vitro* fertilisation (IVF)** Fertilisation of an egg in the laboratory, using an egg removed from a woman and sperm donated by a man.
luteinising hormone (LH) A hormone that triggers ovulation.
menstrual cycle The cycle of preparing the uterus to receive a fertilised egg after ovulation.
oestrogen A hormone that makes the lining of the uterus thicken and stops eggs from developing.
pregnancy The development of an embryo from fertilisation until birth.
progesterone A hormone that makes the uterus lining thicken after ovulation.

The menstrual cycle

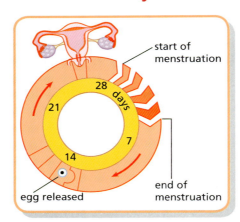

The menstrual cycle.

Adult women have a menstrual cycle. Part of this cycle is menstruation (also called a 'period'). The menstrual cycle is controlled by four hormones: oestrogen, progesterone, follicle stimulating hormone (FSH) and luteinising hormone (LH).

The diagram below shows what happens if the egg released is not fertilised. If the egg *is* fertilised, then oestrogen and progesterone continue to be released. This stops menstruation and stops any more eggs being released. As the placenta develops, it releases oestrogen and progesterone.

Just after menstruation an immature egg starts to develop in an ovary. As it matures a hormone (**follicle stimulating hormone (FSH)**) is released from the pituitary gland. FSH makes the ovary produce a protective covering (follicle) around the egg.

Just before ovulation the pituitary gland secretes a hormone (**luteinising hormone**). This triggers ovulation and turns the follicle into a yellow body.

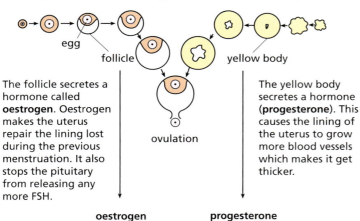

The follicle secretes a hormone called **oestrogen**. Oestrogen makes the uterus repair the lining lost during the previous menstruation. It also stops the pituitary from releasing any more FSH.

The yellow body secretes a hormone (**progesterone**). This causes the lining of the uterus to grow more blood vessels which makes it get thicker.

oestrogen   **progesterone**

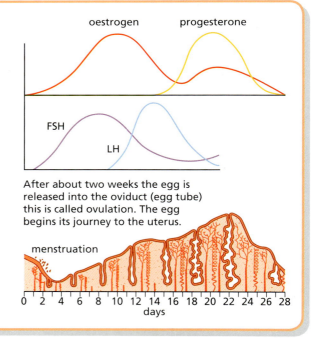

After about two weeks the egg is released into the oviduct (egg tube) this is called ovulation. The egg begins its journey to the uterus.

Hormones in the menstrual cycle.

Contraceptives and IVF

Women who don't want to become pregnant can take pills containing the hormones oestrogen and progesterone. The pills stop eggs being released (this is similar to what would happen if an egg had been fertilised), so the woman can't become pregnant.

Hormones are also used in IVF treatments. This happens when a couple can't have babies in the normal way.

- A woman is injected with a fertility hormone (LH or FSH) to make her produce more eggs.
- Eggs are collected from the woman's ovaries.
- Sperm are mixed with the eggs.
- An egg is fertilised and develops into an embryo.
- The embryo is inserted into the uterus.

IVF treatment has allowed many couples to have children who wouldn't have been able to otherwise. But there are some social and ethical concerns about the method:

- More embryos are produced than are used, so the unused embryos are destroyed.
- There's a low success rate and the treatment is expensive. If more embryos are inserted into the uterus to improve the odds of success, there's a risk of multiple births (twins, triplets, etc.), which is risky for the mother and babies.
- IVF can be used to allow 'mature' (i.e. older) women to become mothers. Some people think this is wrong because they will be very old by the time their child grows up.

Test yourself

1. What is menstruation?
2. Which hormones are produced by the pituitary gland?
3. Which hormone is produced by the follicle?
4. What happens to the levels of progesterone and oestrogen just before a woman has her period?
5. How can LH and FSH be used in medicine?
6. Oestrogen works as a contraceptive because it:
   - A thins the uterus lining
   - B promotes FSH release
   - C thickens the uterus lining
   - D inhibits FSH release
7. Progesterone works as a contraceptive because it:
   - A maintains the uterus lining
   - B prevents ovulation
   - C promotes LH release
   - D thickens the uterus lining

4.1: Stimulants, sedatives and depressants

- **B1.b.4.3** Explain the effects on nerve transmission and reaction times of stimulants, including caffeine
- **B1.b.4.3** Explain the effects on nerve transmission and reaction times of sedatives, including barbiturates
- **B1.b.4.3** Explain the effects on nerve transmission of painkillers, including paracetamol
- **B1.b.4.3** Explain the effects on reaction times of depressants, including alcohol and solvents
- **B1.b.4.5** Describe the uses of paracetamol and the dangers of overdose
- **B1.b.4.4** Discuss the use of opiates and cannabinoids in pain-relief for terminally ill patients, including the dangers of addiction
- **B1.b.4.6** Discuss why medical opinion on the use of cannabis for pain-relief has fluctuated over the years

Need more help?
For more on this topic, see pages 94–97.

edexcel key terms

addiction When someone is dependent on a drug and cannot do without it.
alcohol A drug produced by yeast. Has a sedative effect on the body.
barbiturate A sedative that slows down the nervous system.
caffeine A stimulant drug that increases alertness.
cannabis An illegal drug that may have pain-relief properties.
depressants Drugs that slow down reaction times.
drug A chemical that changes the way your body works.
neurone A single cell that carries impulses.
opiate A drug from the opium family, including opium and heroin.
overdose Taking more of a drug than is recommended. Can cause death.
pain-relief Blocking the impulses that tell the body about pain.
paracetamol A general-purpose painkiller.
reaction time The time it takes your body to react to a stimulus.
sedative A type of drug that can slow down the nervous system.
stimulant A type of drug that increases your alertness and heart rate.
synapse The gap between two neurones.

ResultsPlus Exam tip

Make sure you remember what some of the side-effects of the different types of drugs are – there are often questions on this in exams, which students don't answer very well.

Drugs are substances that affect the way the body works. There are different types of drugs, which have different effects on the body.

Drug type	Examples
stimulants	• caffeine (found in tea, coffee, cola drinks, chocolate) • cocaine • amphetamines
sedatives/depressants	• barbiturates • alcohol • solvents
painkillers	• paracetamol • aspirin • morphine • heroin

Stimulants

The nervous system carries signals around the body. Stimulants increase the speed at which signals cross synapses from one neurone to another (see pages 24–25). This means the speed at which nerve signals are sent increases. This may increase the heartbeat and breathing rate and make the person feel more alert. Stimulants speed up reaction time (make reaction times shorter).

Depressants and sedatives

These drugs slow down the nervous system and may increase reaction time. These drugs can be used to relieve stress and help people to sleep, but people can become addicted to them.

Painkillers

Many pain-relief drugs work by blocking impulses that travel to the part of the brain that deals with pain. Some of these drugs block impulses that lead to pain by slowing down or stopping the movement of neurotransmitters across synapses.

Drugs prescribed by doctors or bought from pharmacies are safe as long as you only take the dose recommended. If you take too much of the drug it may be harmful. This is called an overdose.

Paracetamol is a widely used medicine for relieving headaches and other pains, and for reducing fevers. However, if too much is taken it can damage the liver and lead to death.

Some patients need much stronger painkillers. Morphine and heroin are very strong painkillers. They are called opiates because they are made from the opium poppy. These drugs are addictive, and heroin can also produce tolerance. Tolerance is when you need to take more and more of a drug to get the same effect. This can lead to an overdose. Because of the dangers of addiction, opiates are often only used for terminally ill patients, such as cancer patients.

Cannabis is an illegal drug that can be smoked. It contains chemicals called cannabinoids. Many people use cannabis recreationally (not for medical reasons), as it makes them feel relaxed. Some people with multiple sclerosis use it as a painkiller, even though it is illegal. Cannabis used to be considered safer than tobacco, but now we know that it can lead to cancer, bronchitis and mental health problems (e.g. psychosis). Doctors don't all agree on whether some patients should be allowed to use it.

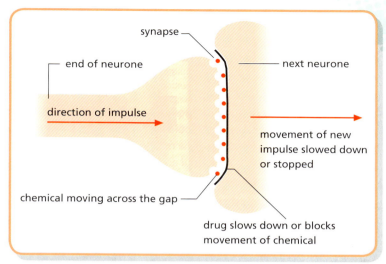

Some painkillers work by stopping neurotransmitters diffusing across synapses.

ResultsPlus Exam tip

Students are often confused about reaction times. Remember that if a reaction time is *slower*, the reaction time *increases* so it takes *longer* for the person to react. If reactions are *speeded up*, it takes *less* time for the person to react and the reaction time is *shorter*.

Test yourself

1. Caffeine is a:
   A painkiller   B sedative   C stimulant   D antibiotic

2. If you drink a lot of coffee with caffeine you are likely to:
   A have a slower heart rate   B take longer to react
   C be more alert   D feel sleepy

3. Write down two drugs that are:
   a depressants   b painkillers

4. Which drugs:
   a speed up the transmission of impulses
   b block impulses
   c slow the transmission of impulses?

5. John drinks some beer. What effect will this have on the following?
   a the speed of his reactions   b his reaction time

6. a Why do some people need to take morphine for pain relief?
   b Why can't you buy morphine to cure your headache?

7. a What is an overdose?
   b What organ is harmed by an overdose of paracetamol?

8. Suggest why the use of cannabis as a painkiller is illegal.

Need more help?
For more on this topic, see pages 98–101.

4.2: Drug misuse and abuse

- **B1.b.4.1** Describe the main mental and physical effects of solvents (including effects on lungs and neurones)
- **B1.b.4.1** Describe the main mental and physical effects of alcohol (including effects on reaction times, the liver and the brain)
- **B1.b.4.1** Describe the main mental and physical effects of tobacco (including effects on the gaseous exchange and circulatory systems)
- **B1.b.4.2** Describe how the use of drugs may affect activities such as driving, produce abnormal behaviour and create the risk of viral infections
- **B1.b.4.8** Explore secondary sources of data about the main physical and mental effects of the misuse of drugs
- **B1.b.4.8** Use data on drug misuse to present information to different audiences

edexcel key terms

gaseous exchange The process by which your lungs take in oxygen and expel carbon dioxide.
infection When microorganisms invade the body.
solvent A chemical used to dissolve other substances. Solvents are found in aerosols, spray paint and thinners, and can be abused by sniffing.
tobacco A drug made from the tobacco plant. Usually smoked. Contains nicotine and tar.
viral infection An infection caused by a virus. Cannot be cured with antibiotics.

Solvents

Solvents are found in many products, including glue, aerosols, thinners, etc. Some people sniff solvents to get high. When it is inhaled, the solvent gets into the blood and reaches the brain. Most solvents are sedatives; they lower the heart rate and breathing rate. They can also cause nausea, vomiting, headaches and blackouts. Sniffing solvents can also cause heart attacks. Solvents attack the myelin sheath around neurones (see pages 34–35), which can lead to memory loss, brain damage and kidney or liver failure.

Alcohol

Many people enjoy drinking alcohol, and it does little harm if used in moderation. However, it can be addictive. It is a sedative, so it increases reaction times (slows reactions). When someone has drunk too much they may have slurred speech and lose coordination. If they have even more, they may pass out. If someone drinks too much over a period of time, the alcohol can damage the brain and the liver.

Tobacco

Some people find smoking tobacco relaxing, but it is addictive. Tobacco smoke contains many different substances that are harmful to health:

- Nicotine increases the heart rate and makes blood vessels narrower. This can lead to high blood pressure and heart disease. Nicotine causes changes in the brain that make smoking addictive.
- Carbon monoxide is produced when tobacco burns. This is a toxic gas. The red blood cells take up carbon monoxide instead of oxygen, so the blood of a smoker doesn't carry as much oxygen as it should.
- Tar is a mixture of many chemicals, which irritate the airways and make them narrower. Chemicals in tar can also cause lung cancer.
- Chemicals in the smoke stop the cilia in the air passages working, so tar, dirt and bacteria stay in the air passages and the lungs. This can lead to bronchitis.
- The smoke damages the air sacs in the lungs, leading to less surface area for gas exchange. This disease is called emphysema.

ResultsPlus Exam tip
You need to remember all these different harmful effects of smoking tobacco. In one exam, nearly half of the students thought that nicotine was the only harmful chemical in tobacco smoke.

Exam Question Report

Smokers are more likely than non-smokers to get lung infections. These lung infections are caused by microbes that are carried:

A in blood   B in food   C by mosquitoes   D in air

Answer: The answer is D.

How students answered

More than half of the students who answered this question thought that the answer was A rather than D. Students who got this right knew that smoking damages the lungs and makes it easier for microbes in the *air* to get into the lungs and cause infection.

Other risks from drugs

You have just read a list of the medical effects of certain drugs. However, misusing drugs can have other, less direct effects:

- Alcohol and other drugs affect reaction times and can affect judgement. This makes someone who has taken drugs or drunk alcohol more likely to have an accident, especially when driving.
- Users of injected drugs such as heroin often share needles. This can allow viral infections such as HIV and hepatitis B to be transmitted.

Presenting data

People need to know about different drugs and their effects so they can make choices. For example, someone might decide to try to give up smoking if they understood all the harm it could do.

There's a lot of information available about the effects of different drugs, but the data need to be presented in different ways depending on the audience. For example, a doctor might want to know all the details of a study, but most members of the public would be confused by all this information. Messages like 'Limit your drinking to 14 units a week' are easier to understand and remember.

Test yourself

1. Which drug (or drugs) on these pages:
   a increases the heart rate
   b slows down reactions
   c can lead to lung infections
   d can lead to cancer and heart disease
   e can lead to liver disease?

2. Nicotine is the addictive substance in cigarette smoke. The receptors responsible for addiction are found in the:
   A heart   B liver   C brain   D lungs

3. Cigarette smoke contains a substance that reduces the amount of oxygen that red blood cells can carry. The name of this substance is:
   A carbon monoxide   B carbon dioxide
   C tar   D nitrogen

4. How can drinking alcohol lead to accidents?

5. Explain why nicotine can lead to heart disease.

4.3: Transmitting disease

> **Need more help?**
> For more on this topic, see pages 86–89.

- ✓ **B1.b.4.7** Describe a pathogen as a disease-causing organism
- ✓ **B1.b.4.9** Explain that microbes can be transmitted by direct contact
- ✓ **B1.b.4.9** Explain that microbes can be transmitted by vertical direct contact from mother to fetus
- ✓ **B1.b.4.9** Explain that microbes can be transmitted by horizontal direct contact
- ✓ **B1.b.4.9** Explain that microbes can be transmitted by indirect contact
- ✓ **B1.b.4.9** Explain how microbes can be transmitted by vehicle-borne mechanisms
- ✓ **B1.b.4.9** Explain how microbes can be transmitted by vector-borne mechanisms
- ✓ **B1.b.4.10** Describe the body's physical barriers as the first line of defence against microorganisms, including skin, nasal hairs and cilia
- ✓ **B1.b.4.10** Describe the body's chemical barriers as the first line of defence against microorganisms (lysozyme in tears)

edexcel key terms

bacteria Tiny single-celled organisms. Most are harmless, some are useful, and some cause disease.
barrier Keeps things out. For example, the skin is a barrier against microorganisms.
cilia Tiny hair-like structures that move mucus out of the lungs and windpipe.
disease When the body isn't working as it should.
foreign body Something that isn't part of the body.
lysozyme An enzyme found in tears that destroys bacteria.
microbe Another word for microorganism.
microorganism Tiny organisms like bacteria, viruses and some fungi.
organism A living thing.
pathogen A microorganism that causes disease.
transmission Passing from one thing to another.
vector-borne Disease carried by animals such as mosquitoes, flies or mammals.
vehicle-borne Disease carried by physical things such as air, water or food.

Organisms such as bacteria and viruses can cause disease in humans. Not all bacteria are harmful. Microorganisms that cause disease are called pathogens.

Pathogens can be transmitted by direct contact or by indirect contact.

Direct contact means that the disease is passed on when a person with the infection touches someone else in some way.

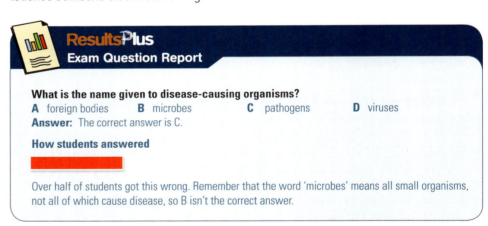

ResultsPlus Exam Question Report

What is the name given to disease-causing organisms?
A foreign bodies   **B** microbes   **C** pathogens   **D** viruses
Answer: The correct answer is C.

How students answered

Over half of students got this wrong. Remember that the word 'microbes' means all small organisms, not all of which cause disease, so B isn't the correct answer.

Horizontal direct contact is from person to person. This contact can be:
- touching
- having sex
- coughing and sneezing
- kissing.

Vertical direct contact is when a disease (such as German measles or HIV) is passed from a mother to her unborn baby.

Indirect contact is when the pathogens are carried from one person to another by something else. Vehicle-borne means that pathogens are spread by physical things such as air, water or food. Vector-borne means that the pathogens are carried by other animals. The tables give some examples.

ResultsPlus Exam tip

Learn the difference between vehicle-borne and vector-borne. Only a third of students got this right in one exam. Remember – ve**ct**ors are often inse**ct**s.

'Vehicle'	Examples of diseases
air	TB, influenza
food	*Salmonella* (which causes 'food poisoning') – can be reduced by storing and cooking food properly
water	cholera (spread when human faeces get into drinking water)
needles, thorns, splinters, etc.	tetanus, HIV

'Vector'	Examples of diseases
flies	various diseases, carried on flies' feet or mouth parts
mosquitoes	malaria (spread when mosquitoes bite people)
dogs or other mammals	rabies (spread when an infected animal bites a human)

Body defences

The body has three lines of defence. The first of these consists of physical and chemical barriers that attempt to stop pathogens getting into the body.

Physical barriers stop the pathogens getting in. They include:

- skin, and the membranes inside your body (in your gut and lungs)
- hairs in the nose, which stop dust and microbes getting into your windpipe
- cilia (hair-like structures inside the windpipe), which carry mucus and trapped microbes up out of the windpipe.

Chemical barriers kill pathogens. They include:

- lysozyme (a chemical found in tears)
- sebum (an oily substance made by the skin)
- hydrochloric acid in your stomach.

Test yourself

1. What do the following terms mean?
   a horizontal direct contact
   b vertical direct contact
   c vector-borne
   d vehicle-borne

2. What type of disease transmission is shown in these examples?
   a *Salmonella* bacteria can be passed on in food.
   b Sleeping sickness is passed on by tsetse flies.
   c You catch flu when someone sneezes on you.
   d A drug user gets HIV after sharing a needle.
   e A mother passes a viral infection to her baby.

3. What is the body's main physical barrier against malaria?
   A the cilia
   B the skin
   C white blood cells
   D vaccination

4.4: More body defences

- B1.b.4.11 Describe how infection can lead to inflammation
- B1.b.4.11 Describe how white blood cells defend against microorganisms
- B1.b.4.11 Describe the second line of defence against infection as non-specific
- B1.b.4.12 Describe how the immune system works
- B1.b.4.12 Describe the difference between antibodies and antigens
- B1.b.4.12 Describe the third line of defence as the specific immune system

Need more help? For more on this topic, see pages 90–93.

edexcel key terms

antibody A protein produced by white blood cells to destroy a pathogen.
antigens Protein markers on the surface of every cell, which identify a cell as belonging to the body or being a foreign body.
circulatory system Your heart, blood vessels and blood.
immune system The system inside the body for destroying invading microorganisms.
inflammation One of the body's responses to infection.
white blood cell A special type of cell in the blood that is part of the immune system.

The second line of defence

If pathogens get through the physical and chemical barriers, the body has a second line of defence. This is non-specific, which means that the body's defence is the same for all pathogens.

When pathogens get into the blood, white blood cells move towards them and ingest them (surround them). The white blood cells then destroy the pathogens by digesting them.

Pathogens can enter the body through a cut or other wound. The area around the wound becomes inflamed (red, warm and swollen). The response to an infection caused by damage to the skin is called the inflammatory response.

The damaged skin releases chemicals that make the blood vessels widen, so more blood can flow to the area. This is what makes the skin feel warm and look red. The pus that sometimes forms contains white blood cells, living and dead bacteria, dead tissue and blood plasma.

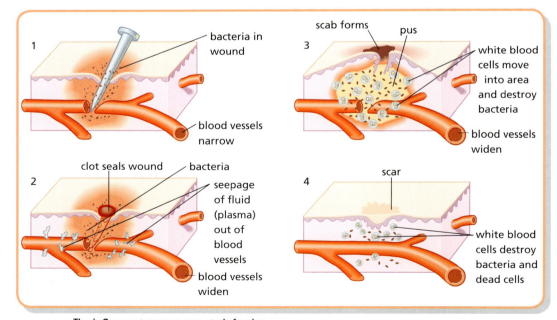

The inflammatory response to infection.

The third line of defence

The third line of defence is the specific immune system. It is called 'specific' because the response depends on the type of pathogen that has got into the body.

When a pathogen gets through the first two lines of defence, white blood cells called lymphocytes produce antibodies. Pathogens have antigens on their surface. Each type of pathogen has its own type of antigen. The lymphocytes make antibodies that attach themselves to the particular antigens on the invading pathogens. Other white blood cells then destroy the pathogens.

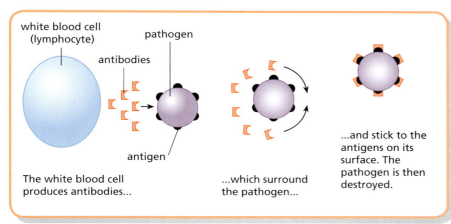

Antibodies and antigens.

ResultsPlus
Watch out!

There are several different kinds of white blood cell. Some engulf pathogens (in the second line of defence), some make antibodies, and some destroy pathogens once the antibodies have surrounded them. You also need to remember the difference between antibodies (things made by lymphocytes) and antigens (chemical markers on pathogens). It is important to learn the meaning of all the words used to describe the body's defence systems. Every year students lose marks because they cannot remember the meanings.

Vaccination

It takes a little while for lymphocytes to make enough antibodies to destroy pathogens. In that time you can be very ill. Your body can be prepared for diseases it might get by vaccination.

Vaccination involves injecting a small, harmless dose of the pathogens into you. These can be dead pathogens, or they can be made harmless in other ways. These pathogens still have the same antigens on them, and so your lymphocytes make antibodies against them.

Once your lymphocytes have made a particular kind of antibody, they can make the same kind much more quickly if they are needed again. This means that if the pathogens you have been vaccinated against get into your body, your white blood cells will kill them without you becoming ill.

Test yourself

1. How is the structure of white blood cells suited to their function?
   - A they are large and can block the walls of arteries
   - B they contain fibrin to seal cuts
   - C they can change shape to engulf bacteria
   - D they have a large surface area to carry oxygen

2. What is another function of white blood cells?
   - A the production of antibodies
   - B the production of antigens
   - C the production of pathogens
   - D the production of cilia

3. What is:
   - a an antigen
   - b a lymphocyte
   - c an antibody?

4. What causes inflammation?

5. White blood cells are involved in both the second and third lines of defence. Explain the similarities and differences in what they do in these two types of defence.

6. How does a vaccination work?

Need more help?
For more on this topic, see pages 82–84.

edexcel key terms
tuberculosis A disease caused by a bacterium that causes severe damage to the lungs and can lead to death.

ResultsPlus Watch out!
Some questions ask you to read values from a graph and then do a calculation based on these values. Many students get these answers wrong because they don't read the values off the graph correctly.

Higher tier
For more on this topic, see pages 83–85.

4.5: Tuberculosis and new drugs

- B1.b.4.13 Explain what causes tuberculosis (TB)
- B1.b.4.13 Explain how tuberculosis (TB) is spread
- B1.b.4.14 Describe the prevention and control of TB
- B1.b.4.14 Explain why the emergence of drug-resistant TB is a problem
- B1.b.4.15 Interpret data on the number of cases of TB in the UK over a period of time
- B1.b.4.16 Use secondary data to explore the costs of developing new drugs

Tuberculosis

Tuberculosis (TB) is a disease caused by a bacterium. It is spread through the air in droplets produced when an infected person coughs or sneezes. Sunlight kills the bacteria quite quickly, so most people who become infected have caught the disease because they have spent time indoors with an infected person. TB is often referred to as a 'disease of poverty', which means that it spreads easily among people who live in overcrowded conditions.

TB mainly affects the lungs, but can also affect bones, joints and the kidneys. It can be treated with antibiotics. It can be fatal if it is not treated. There is a vaccine for TB, but it is not very effective in adults or against all forms of TB.

Preventing and controlling TB

The best way of preventing TB is to try to cure those people who already have it, to stop them passing it on. The TB bacterium can survive for many years in people without causing symptoms, so it is not easy to eradicate.

TB can be treated with antibiotics, which are drugs that kill bacteria. However, some bacteria can develop resistance to antibiotics. This happens because:

- people stop taking antibiotics as soon as they feel better
- there will be a few bacteria with mutations that make them resist the antibiotics, and these will be the ones most likely to survive
- these resistant bacteria reproduce and may infect another person.

The development of drug-resistant bacteria can be reduced if people take the whole course of antibiotics that their doctor gives them.

The development of drug-resistant bacteria (of any kind) is a problem, because it may lead to the development of bacteria that we can't kill at all using drugs.

Some strains of TB have developed resistance to various antibiotics, so 'multi-antibiotics' (several different antibiotics used at the same time) are used to treat them. Treatments are given for six months. A system called Directly Observed Treatment, Short Course (DOTS) is used, where a nurse watches the patient take their antibiotics each day, to make sure that they complete their treatment.

New drugs

Scientists are continually trying to develop new drugs to treat diseases. This can be a long and expensive process because every new drug has to be tested for safety. The drug company:

- identifies possible chemicals that might be useful as a drug
- tests the potential drug on cells and modifies it if necessary
- registers the new drug with the regulatory authority
- tests the drug on animals
- tests the drug on human volunteers.

Exam Question Report

The cost of developing a new drug to treat TB may be £500 million or more.
This is because drug development has to go through several stages. Put the stages in the correct order.
1 human volunteers trial the drugs
2 chemicals are tested and developed
3 animals trial the drugs
4 the drug is registered with the regulatory authority
5 possible chemicals are identified

A 5-2-4-3-1   B 5-2-4-1-3
C 5-4-2-3-1   D 5-2-3-1-4

Answer: The correct answer is A.

How students answered
Many students didn't get the correct answer because they weren't able to put the stages involved in the development of a drug into the correct order. Remember that new drugs are registered before testing on animals and humans starts — a lot of students thought this was the last stage.

Clinical trials

Clinical trials are designed to find out if a new drug works, and if it works better than any existing treatment. The more patients that can be used in the trial, the more reliable the results will be.

In many trials, half of the patients are given a placebo. This is a pill that doesn't contain any of the drug. This is done because often if a patient *thinks* they are getting a treatment that will work, they get better. Doctors don't fully understand why this happens. Placebos are used as a control in drug trials, to make sure that if the new drug seems to work it really is because of the chemicals in the drug, and not just due to the placebo effect.

If there is already an existing treatment for a condition, it is not ethical to give patients with the condition a placebo because then they would be getting no treatment at all. Instead, half the patients are given the existing treatment, and half are given the new one.

Test yourself

1. a What kind of organism causes TB?   b How is TB spread?
   c Why is TB sometimes called a 'disease of poverty'?

2. a What is a placebo?   b Why is it used?

3. TB can now be cured using drug therapy and DOTS.
   a What is DOTS?   b Why is it needed?
   c Why is this treatment likely to be expensive for the health service?

4. Since 1960 the incidence of TB has increased dramatically in some parts of the country. What is the most likely reason for this increase?
   A the development of multi-antibiotics to treat sufferers
   B the use of DOTS (Directly Observed Treatment, Short Course)
   C a greater amount of food is imported from abroad
   D the emergence of a drug-resistant form of the TB bacteria

5. These statements are about TB. Which are true?
   A TB is increasing in the UK because there are drug-resistant forms of the bacteria.
   B TB is increasing in the UK because there is more global travel.
   C TB is increasing in the UK because there are no effective antibiotics.

5.1: The periodic table

- C1.a.5.5 Use the periodic table to find the symbol of an element
- C1.a.5.6 Identify and recall the position of metals and non-metals in the periodic table
- C1.a.5.7 Identify and recall the positions of the alkali metals, halogens, noble gases and transition metals in the periodic table
- C1.a.5.8 Recall that elements in the same group have similar properties
- C1.a.5.9 Recall that a row in the periodic table is called a period and that a column in the periodic table is called a group
- C1.a.5.9 Use secondary data to explore the arrangement of elements in the periodic table
- C1.a.5 Recall the symbols of elements in topic 5 and identify their positions in the periodic table

Need more help?
For more on this topic, see pages 106–107 of the main student book (ISBN 978-1-903133-68-2).

edexcel key terms

alkali metal An element found in group 1 of the periodic table. Alkali metals include lithium, sodium and potassium.
element A substance made of only one type of atom. An element cannot be split up into a simpler substance using chemical reactions.
group A vertical column of the periodic table.
halogen An element found in group 7 of the periodic table. Halogens include chlorine, bromine and iodine.
noble gas An element found in group 0 of the periodic table. Noble gases include helium, neon and argon.
period A horizontal row of the periodic table.
symbol A way of representing something. Elements are represented by symbols consisting of one or two letters.
transition metal An element found between groups 2 and 3 of the periodic table. Transition metals include copper, iron and gold.

The periodic table is a chart of all the known elements. The elements are divided into metals and non-metals. The metals are shown on the left of the table and the non-metals on the right.

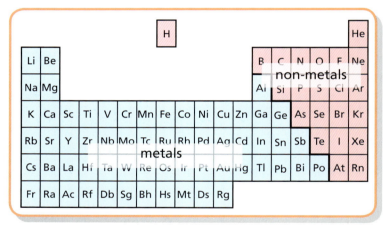

Metals and non-metals in the periodic table.

Some elements have properties in common, and the periodic table groups these elements together.

A group is a vertical column, and elements in the group have similar properties. The horizontal rows on the table are called periods.

ResultsPlus Watch out!

Exam questions often ask you for an element in period 3, or period 4. Students frequently get these wrong because they forget that the very top row, with only hydrogen and helium in it, is period 1.

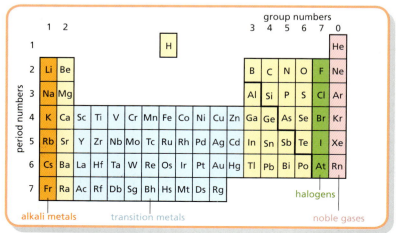

Groups and periods in the periodic table.

Patterns in Properties

You will need to remember the names and the positions in the periodic table of four of these groups. You also need to remember the names and symbols of some of the elements in these groups.

Group	Elements to learn	Symbols
alkali metals	lithium	Li
	sodium	Na
	potassium	K
transition metals	iron	Fe
	copper	Cu
	silver	Ag
	gold	Au
halogens	fluorine	F
	chlorine	Cl
	bromine	Br
	iodine	I
	astatine	At
noble gases ('inert' gases)	helium	He
	neon	Ne
	argon	Ar
	krypton	Kr
	xenon	Xe

ResultsPlus
Watch out!

If you look at all the symbols for elements on these pages, you'll see that every symbol is either just one capital letter (such as H), or a capital letter followed by a small letter (such as He). The symbol for chlorine is Cl, and *never* CL. Students often lose easy marks by forgetting this simple rule.

Symbols for elements

As well as learning the names and symbols of the elements in the table above, there are a few other elements whose names and symbols you need to be able to recognise and use. They are:

- barium, Ba
- hydrogen, H
- oxygen, O
- calcium, Ca
- magnesium, Mg
- sulphur, S
- carbon, C
- nitrogen, N
- zinc, Zn

Test yourself

1. The symbol for an atom of iron is:
   A I   B Fe   C Ir   D FE

2. The diagram shows the periodic table. Which letter shows:
   a a noble gas
   b an element in period 1
   c a halogen
   d an alkali metal
   e a transition metal
   f a non-metal
   g hydrogen?

3. Write down three elements that are:
   a noble gases   b alkali metals   c transition metals   d halogens

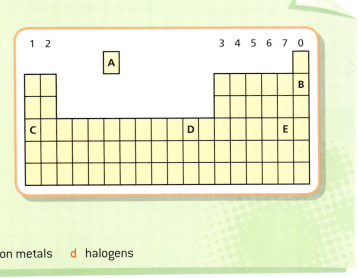

5.2: Atoms, elements and molecules

> **Need more help?**
> For more on this topic, see pages 112–113, 122–123.

✓ **C1.a.5.10** Describe how an atom consists of neutrons and positively charged protons in a nucleus surrounded by negatively charged electrons

✓ **C1.a.5.11** Explain how the periodic table was used to predict the discovery of new elements

✓ **C1.a.5.13** Recall that all atoms of the same element have the same number of protons and that this is the atomic number

✓ **C1.a.5.12** Use secondary data to explore the use of atomic number in the periodic table

✓ **C1.a.5** Identify and recall the formulae of simple compounds in topic 5

Atomic structure

All atoms are made of different combinations of three types of smaller particles. These smaller particles are protons, electrons and neutrons.

You need to remember:

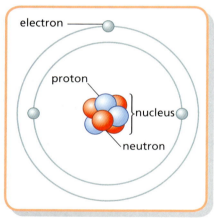

- the nucleus contains protons and neutrons
- electrons are outside the nucleus
- protons have a positive charge
- neutrons have no charge
- electrons have a negative charge.

Atomic structure.

All the atoms of a particular element have the *same* number of protons in their nucleus. So all hydrogen atoms have just one proton. All helium atoms have two protons. The number of protons in the atoms of an element is the atomic number.

Atoms are electrically neutral, so they have the same number of electrons as protons (the positive and negative charges balance each other).

The total number of protons and neutrons in an atom is its mass number.

edexcel key terms

atomic number The number of protons in the nucleus of an atom.
atoms Particles that are the smallest part of an element that can exist.
compound Two or more different elements chemically joined together.
electron A negatively charged particle outside the nucleus in an atom.
formula The chemical code for a substance, which shows how many atoms of different elements make up a molecule of the compound.
molecule A particle made from atoms joined together by chemical bonds.
negative A type of electric charge.
neutral An object with no electric charge, or with equal numbers of positive and negative charges.
neutron An electrically neutral particle found in the nucleus of most atoms.
positive A type of electric charge.
proton Positively charged particle found in the nucleus of all atoms.

ResultsPlus Watch out!

Lots of students lose marks because they forget that atoms of the same element all have the same number of *protons*.

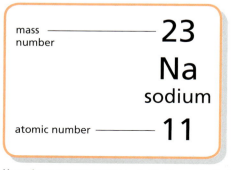

How elements are represented in the periodic table.

Predicting new elements

The periodic table that we use today was developed by a Russian chemist called Dmitri Mendeleev. Scientists didn't know about atomic numbers at that time, so he arranged the elements in order of their atomic masses. He also grouped them according to properties they had in common. Using atomic masses didn't quite allow all the patterns to match up, so Mendeleev swapped a few elements around. We still use the same pattern today, which gives us a table with the elements in order of their atomic numbers.

Mendeleev's pattern also had gaps. He predicted that new elements would be discovered that would fill these gaps, and predicted their properties. These elements *were* discovered a few years later.

ResultsPlus Watch out!

Remember that the elements in the periodic table are in order of *atomic number*, not mass number.

Elements and compounds

In an element, all the atoms have the same number of protons and have the same properties. Elements can join together to make compounds. In a compound, two or more elements are chemically joined together in a molecule. Some elements can also form molecules, but when you have a molecule of an *element*, all the atoms in the molecule are the same.

The formula for a compound shows how many atoms of different kinds are joined together to form one molecule.

Formula	What it shows
Ar	An atom of argon. This is an atom, not a molecule, because only one atom is shown.
H_2	A molecule of hydrogen gas, consisting of two hydrogen atoms joined together. This is a molecule of an *element*, because both atoms are the same.
H_2O	A molecule of water (a compound). Two hydrogen atoms are joined to one oxygen atom.
CO_2	A molecule of carbon dioxide (another compound). There is one carbon atom, with two oxygen atoms joined to it.

ResultsPlus Exam tip

You need to remember the formulae for all the compounds you learn about in this topic (and the other chemistry topics).

ResultsPlus Exam Question Report

The formula of carbon dioxide is:
A CO^2 B CO C CO_2 D Co_2
Answer: The correct answer is C.

How students answered
Many students put A. Remember, the little number has to be at the bottom of the formula, not at the top.

63% 0 marks

To get it right you also had to realise that B shows the formula for carbon monoxide, not carbon dioxide. D actually shows the symbol for cobalt!

37% 1 mark

Test yourself

1. **a** Write down the names of the three types of particles found in atoms.
   b Say what charge each one has, and where it is found in an atom.
2. What does the atomic number of an element show?
3. Is the periodic table arranged in order of mass number or atomic number?
4. What is the formula for:
   a water
   b hydrogen gas
   c oxygen gas (two oxygen atoms joined together)
   d sulphur dioxide (one atom of sulphur joined to two atoms of oxygen)?
5. Which of these two statements about the periodic table are correct?
   (i) The modern periodic table lists all elements in order of increasing mass number.
   (ii) Gaps were left in the early versions of the periodic table so that known elements could be placed in their correct group.
   A (i) only
   B (ii) only
   C both (i) and (ii)
   D neither (i) nor (ii)

GCSE 360 Science

Need more help?
For more on this topic, see pages 111, 115, 120.

5.3: Word and symbol equations

 C1.a.5 Represent chemical reactions in topic 5 by word equations

 C1.a.5.22 Explain the use of the endings -ide and -ate in chemical names

C1.a.5 Represent a range of chemical reactions by balanced equations, including state symbols

Word equations

New substances are produced in chemical reactions. A word equation uses the names of the elements or compounds involved to show what happens.

This word equation shows what happens when oxygen and hydrogen combine to form water.

hydrogen + oxygen ⟶ water

You need to be able to use word equations to show all the reactions you learn about in this topic (and in the other chemistry topics).

Higher tier
For more on this topic, see pages 121.

State symbol	Meaning
(s)	solid
(l)	liquid
(g)	gas
(aq)	aqueous (dissolved in water)

State symbols.

Naming compounds

The names of most compounds tell you which elements are in the compound. There are some exceptions (like water!). In some cases, you need to know what the ending of a name means:

- Sodium chlor**ide** (NaCl) contains only sodium and chlorine atoms.
- Sodium chlor**ate** ($NaClO_3$) contains oxygen as well as sodium and chlorine.

The '-ide' ending shows that only the elements in the name are present. The '-ate' ending shows that oxygen is in the compound as well.

Symbol equations

A balanced symbol equation shows more information than a simple word equation. Here is the full symbol equation for the reaction that forms water:

$$2H_2(g) + O_2(g) \rightarrow 2H_2O(l)$$

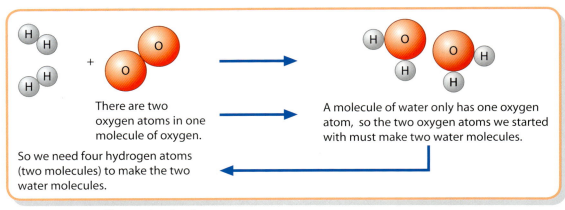

There are two oxygen atoms in one molecule of oxygen.

A molecule of water only has one oxygen atom, so the two oxygen atoms we started with must make two water molecules.

So we need four hydrogen atoms (two molecules) to make the two water molecules.

The reaction that forms water.

Patterns in Properties 5

The symbol equation shows us:

- that hydrogen and oxygen are diatomic molecules (the atoms 'go around in pairs')
- the formula of water
- that hydrogen and oxygen are gases, and the water produced is a liquid
- that two molecules of hydrogen are needed to react with each molecule of oxygen, and that two molecules of water are produced.

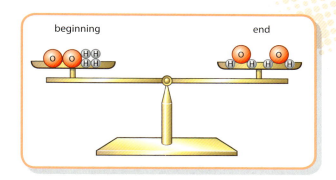

In a balanced equation, there are the same number of atoms of each element on each side of the equation.

Worked example

The equation for a reaction can be represented by: $wKI + xBr_2 \rightarrow yI_2 + zKBr$

Which row of the table on the right shows values of w, x, y and z that give a balanced equation?

First look at the formulae for the molecules present. Br_2 means two atoms of bromine joined together.

Then count up the atoms on each side for each possible answer:

Row A – left: 1 × K, 1 × I and 4 × Br   right: 2 × I, 2 × K, 2 × Br   not balanced

Row B – left: 1 × K, 1 × I, 2 × Br   right: 2 × I, 1 × K, 1 × Br   not balanced

Row C – left: 2 × K, 2 × I, 2 × Br   right: 2 × I, 2 × K, 2 × Br   balanced

(but check the final answer anyway, just in case you've made a mistake!)

Row D – left: 2 × K, 2 × I, 2 × Br   right: 4 × I, 1 × K, 1 × Br   not balanced

So the correct answer is C.

	w	x	y	z
A	1	2	1	2
B	1	1	1	1
C	2	1	1	2
D	2	1	2	1

Test yourself

1. Write word equations to show the following reactions.
   a. When methane burns it combines with oxygen. It forms carbon dioxide and water.
   b. Sodium chloride is produced when sodium is reacted with chlorine.
   c. In photosynthesis, glucose is produced when carbon dioxide and water combine. Oxygen is a waste product.

2. A compound of selenium, Se, has the formula Na_2SeO_4. The most likely name for this compound is:
   - A sodium selenium oxide
   - B sodium selenide
   - C sodium selenate
   - D sodium oxyselenide

3. Potassium sulphate is used in fertilisers. What elements does it contain?

4. Sodium (a metal) reacts with chlorine (a gas) to form sodium chloride (common salt). This symbol equation is not complete:

   $Na + Cl_2 \rightarrow NaCl$

   Complete the symbol equation by balancing it and adding state symbols.

ResultsPlus Exam tip

Because the Science exams are multiple choice, you won't need to be able to balance equations yourself. However, you are likely to be given four different options and asked to choose which one is balanced. Sometimes these questions will give you four options that are all balanced, but only one of them will contain the correct formulae for the compounds. It is important to learn the formulae for the compounds you learn about in this course.

> **Need more help?**
> For more on this topic, see pages 108–109, 116–117.

5.4: Noble gases and transition metals

- C1.a.5.3 Interpret data describing the properties of helium, neon and argon
- C1.a.5.3 Give examples of the uses of helium, neon and argon
- C1.a.5.3 Interpret data describing the properties of iron, copper, silver and gold
- C1.a.5.3 Give examples of the uses of iron, copper, silver and gold
- C1.a.5.17 Recognise the gradual change in the properties of elements from the top to the bottom of each group
- C1.a.5.20 Describe the noble gases as chemically inert compared with other elements

edexcel key terms

inert Unreactive.

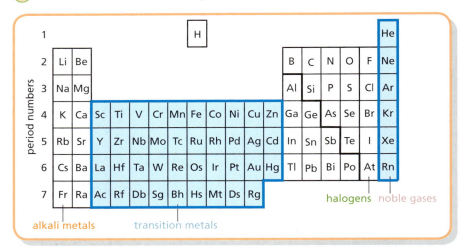

The positions of the noble gases and transition metals on the periodic table.

Noble gases

The noble gases are all inert non-metal elements. 'Inert' means that it is very difficult to make them react with anything. The noble gases are in group 0, on the right-hand side of the periodic table.

For all groups of elements in the periodic table, the properties of the elements change as you go down the group. The bar chart shows how the density of the noble gases changes as you go down the group.

You need to know the properties and uses of helium, neon and argon. These are all colourless gases. The table shows which property is important for each use.

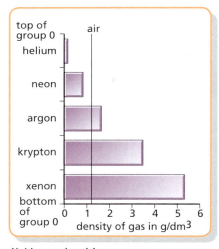

Noble gas densities.

Gas	Uses (and properties)
helium, He	• used to fill party balloons and airships (it is lighter than air)
neon, Ne	• used in coloured light in advertising signs (it glows red when an electric current passes through it)
argon, Ar	• used in welding to stop the hot steel reacting with oxygen in the air • used in old-fashioned light bulbs to stop the filament burning up

Transition metals

All metals have certain properties. They are all:

- shiny
- solid at room temperature (except for mercury)
- good conductors of heat and electricity
- malleable (can be hammered into shape)
- ductile (can be drawn into wires).

Some metals corrode (react with water and air). When iron corrodes it forms rust. Rust can damage the metal. Rusting is a slow chemical change.

The transition metals are the metals in the central block of the periodic table. They include iron, copper, silver and gold. You need to remember the properties and uses of these metals. The table shows which property is important for each use.

Metal	Appearance	Uses (and properties)
iron, Fe	grey metal	- making steel for use in buildings and bridges (cheap and widely available, strong, malleable) - making steel for use in cars (thin sheets of steel can be pressed into shape)
copper, Cu	shiny reddish metal	- electric wires (very good conductor of electricity, ductile, cheaper than better conductors such as silver) - water tanks and water pipes (doesn't corrode much when in contact with water and air, malleable and ductile) - saucepans (very good conductor of heat)
silver, Ag	shiny grey metal	- jewellery (doesn't corrode easily, so it stays shiny for longer than most other metals) - circuit boards and electrical contacts (better electrical conductor than other metals)
gold, Au	shiny yellow metal	- jewellery (doesn't react with air or water at all, so it stays shiny) - electrical contacts and computer chips (nearly as good as copper at conducting electricity, doesn't corrode at all)

Test yourself

1. a Write down the names and symbols of three noble gases.
   b Where are the noble gases in the periodic table?
   c What do the noble gases look like?

2. How does the density of the noble gases change as you go down the group?

3. Give one use of:
   a argon
   b helium
   c neon

4. a Where are the transition metals in the periodic table?
   b Write down the names and symbols of four transition metals.

5. Some rings were made from a shiny, yellow metal. This metal is:
   A iron
   B sodium
   C gold
   D silver

6. What properties of each metal are most important for the given use?
   a copper used for electrical wiring
   b iron used for buildings and bridges
   c gold used for jewellery
   d silver used for electrical contacts

5.5: Alkali metals

Need more help?
For more on this topic, see pages 114–115.

- ✓ **C1.a.5.14** Describe the reactions of alkali metals with water
- ✓ **C1.a.5.14** Recall that the alkali metals' reactivity with water increases with increase in atomic number
- ✓ **C1.a.5.16** Recall that chemical reactions that give out heat are exothermic
- ✓ **C1.a.5.16** Recall that chemical reactions that take in heat are endothermic
- ✓ **C1.a.5.16** Recall that chemical reactions happen at different rates
- ✓ **C1.a.5.21** Recall that elements in the same group of the periodic table have similar chemical properties
- ✓ **C1.a.5** Represent a range of chemical reactions by balanced equations, including state symbols

edexcel key terms

endothermic A reaction that takes in energy from its surroundings.
exothermic A reaction that gives out energy, usually in the form of heat energy.

The alkali metals are in group 1, on the left of the periodic table. Because they are metals, they all have the following properties:

- shiny (when freshly cut)
- solid at room temperature
- good conductors of heat and electricity.

The alkali metals share some other properties that are different from other metals:

- they are all very reactive metals
- they are very soft (they can be cut with a knife)
- they have low densities (they float on water).

The alkali metals react very quickly with oxygen in the air. If you cut a piece of an alkali metal, it looks shiny at first but then very quickly goes dull as a metal oxide forms on the surface. Alkali metals are stored in oil to stop this reaction.

ResultsPlus Exam tip

You need to remember that exothermic reactions give out heat. Reactions that take in heat are called endothermic. All the reactions of the alkali metals are exothermic.

Reactions with water

All the alkali metals react with water to form a metal hydroxide and hydrogen gas. These are all exothermic reactions (they give out heat). The heat is enough to melt the metals and they form a molten ball that floats on the water. The hydrogen given off often catches fire. The flame is yellow when sodium reacts and lilac when potassium reacts. (These are the same colours as you see in flame tests – pages 66–67).

This is the equation for lithium reacting with water:

lithium + water $\rightarrow$ lithium hydroxide + hydrogen

ResultsPlus Exam Question Report

Hydrogen is produced when potassium reacts with water. The word equation for the reaction is:
A potassium + water + oxygen $\rightarrow$ potassium oxide + hydrogen
B potassium + water $\rightarrow$ potassium chloride + hydrogen
C potassium + water $\rightarrow$ potassium sulphate + hydrogen
D potassium + water $\rightarrow$ potassium hydroxide + hydrogen
Answer: D is the correct answer.

How students answered
Lots of students got this wrong. You need to memorise the word equations for reactions of alkali metals with water to make sure you get the marks.

Patterns in Properties

Higher tier

The balanced symbol equation for this reaction is:

$$2Li(s) + 2H_2O(l) \rightarrow 2LiOH(aq) + H_2(g)$$

The equations for the reactions of the other alkali metals are similar:

$$2Na(s) + 2H_2O(l) \rightarrow 2NaOH(aq) + H_2(g) \qquad 2K(s) + 2H_2O(l) \rightarrow 2KOH(aq) + H_2(g)$$

ResultsPlus
Exam Question Report

Which of these is the correct balanced equation for the reaction of potassium with water?
A $K + H_2O \rightarrow KOH + H$
B $K + 2H_2O \rightarrow K(OH)_2 + H_2$
C $2K + 2H_2O \rightarrow 2KOH + H_2$
D $2K + 2H_2O \rightarrow K_2O + 2H_2$
Answer: The correct answer is C.

How students answered
Most students got this wrong. They failed to spot that A has the wrong formula for hydrogen gas, B has the wrong formula for potassium hydroxide, and D has potassium oxide in it, not potassium hydroxide.

70% 0 marks

You can actually work this out without even having to think about whether or not the equation is balanced, just by looking at the formulae!

30% 1 mark

Changes down the group

Chemical reactions happen at different rates. There are many things that affect the rate of the reaction. One factor is the reactivity of the elements involved.

Lithium is the least reactive alkali metal. When you put lithium in water it fizzes (as hydrogen gas is given off) and moves around on the surface of the water.

As you go down the group (and the atomic number increases) the metals get more reactive. Sodium reacts more vigorously than lithium. Francium is at the bottom of group 1. If you were to put a piece of francium in water the container would explode!

Test yourself

1. All of the elements in group 1:
   A have similar chemical properties
   B are non-metals
   C have identical physical properties
   D only react with water

2. Write a word equation to show the reaction of sodium with water.

3. Which is the most reactive, lithium or potassium?

4. a Describe what you would see when potassium reacts with water.
   b Is this an exothermic or endothermic reaction? Explain your answer.

5. Write a balanced symbol equation (including state symbols) for the reaction of sodium with water.

Need more help?
For more on this topic, see pages 118–121.

5.6: Halogens

- C1.a.5.3 Interpret data describing the properties of chlorine and iodine
- C1.a.5.3 Give examples of the uses of chlorine and iodine
- C1.a.5.18 Describe the variation in colour of the halogens
- C1.a.5.18 List the physical states at room temperature of the halogens
- C1.a.5.18 Recall the trends in boiling points of the halogens
- C1.a.5.19 Describe how the reactivity of the halogens decreases as the group descends
- C1.a.5.19 Describe the displacement reactions of halogens with solutions of other halides

The halogens are in group 7, next to the noble gases on the right of the table. They are all reactive non-metals. They all exist as diatomic molecules (two atoms joined together).

Element	Formula of gas	State and appearance at room temperature	Reactivity	Melting and boiling points
fluorine	F_2	pale yellow gas	greatest ↓	lowest ↓
chlorine	Cl_2	yellow-green gas		
bromine	Br_2	red-brown liquid		
iodine	I_2	grey solid	least (but still reactive)	highest
astatine	At_2	black solid		

The boiling points of fluorine and chlorine are below room temperature, which is why these elements are gases at room temperature.

Fluorine is the most reactive of the halogens, and iodine is the least reactive.

edexcel key terms

diatomic molecule A molecule made from two atoms chemically joined together.
solution The mixture formed when a substance dissolves in water.

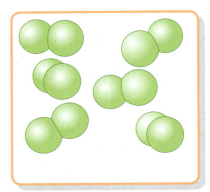

Chlorine and the other halogens exist as diatomic molecules.

ResultsPlus Exam tip

You need to learn the appearances and properties of the halogens, and also how their properties change down the group. There are usually questions on these things.

Worked example

The table shows information about the physical and chemical properties of four elements, A, B, C and D.

element	melting point (°C)	boiling point (°C)	electrical conductivity	reactivity
A	−101	−35	poor	reactive
B	−189	−186	poor	unreactive
C	98	890	good	reactive
D	114	184	poor	reactive

1. Which element could be in group 0 of the periodic table?
2. Which element could be chlorine?
3. Which element could be sodium?
4. Which element could be iodine?

A and B are gases (as their boiling points are below room temperature). C and D are solids.

B is the only one that is unreactive, so it is a noble gas (group 0). The answer to Q1 is B.

Chlorine is a gas. The only gas left is A, so the answer to Q2 is A.

C is the only one that conducts electricity, so it is a metal (sodium). The answer to Q3 is C.

Iodine is a solid. The answer to Q4 is D.

ResultsPlus
Exam tip

Questions of this type come up very often so you need to remember the properties of the different groups in the periodic table.

Uses of the halogens

The halogens are toxic, so they can be used to kill harmful bacteria. Chlorine is used to sterilise drinking water and water in swimming pools. Iodine is used in antiseptics to treat wounds.

Displacement reactions

The halogens form salts when they react with metals. Examples of these salts include sodium chloride (common salt), potassium bromide and lithium iodide.

Some halogens will react with salts of other halogens. Whether or not a reaction happens depends on the reactivity of the two halogens.

Chlorine is more reactive than bromine, so chlorine will 'push' bromine out of a compound. This is called a displacement reaction, as chlorine is displacing bromine.

chlorine + potassium bromide → potassium chloride + bromine

If you add chlorine water (water with chlorine dissolved in it) to potassium bromide solution you'll see an orange colour in the solution as bromine is formed.

If you mix iodine with potassium bromide, nothing will happen. This is because bromine is more reactive than iodine, and bromine is already part of the compound.

iodine + potassium bromide → NO REACTION

ResultsPlus
Exam Question Report

Hashim added halogens to solutions of sodium halides. Which of these reacted?
A iodine and sodium chloride
B bromine and sodium chloride
C bromine and sodium iodide
D iodine and sodium bromide
Answer: The correct answer is C, as bromine is more reactive than iodine.

How students answered
Many students thought that bromine would react with sodium chloride. It won't, because chlorine is more reactive than bromine.

 69% 0 marks

You need to be able to remember the order of reactivity to get this right (the most reactive halogens are at the top of the group).

31% 1 mark

Test yourself

1. Write down the names and symbols for each of the halogens.
2. Where are the halogens in the periodic table?
3. a Are the most reactive elements at the top or bottom of the group?
   b Are the elements with the highest boiling points at the top or bottom of the group?
4. Write down one use for:
   a chlorine
   b iodine
5. Which halogen is:
   a a yellow-green gas
   b a grey solid
   c a red-brown liquid?
6. Which of these salts in solution would you expect to react with bromine?
   A potassium bromide
   B potassium fluoride
   C potassium chloride
   D potassium astatide

Need more help?
For more on this topic, see pages 110–111, 124–125.

5.7: Identifying substances

- **C1.a.5.1** Explain how flame tests are used to identify the presence of a particular metal
- **C1.a.5.1** Use the result of a flame test to identify the presence of a particular metal
- **C1.a.5.2** Use results of analysis to identify substances found at a crime scene
- **C1.a.5.4** Describe how to identify iron, copper and zinc using sodium hydroxide solution

Forensic scientists often need to identify chemicals found at the scene of a crime. Some metals can be identified using flame tests, or by using sodium hydroxide solution.

edexcel key terms

analytical Analytical tests are experiments to find out which chemicals a substance contains.
flame test An analytical test to find out which metal is present in a substance. Different metals produce different colours when held in a Bunsen flame.
precipitation A reaction in which a solid (precipitate) is formed when two solutions are mixed together.

Flame tests

A flame test can be used to identify the metal present in a solution of a compound. For example, to find out whether a solution is made of potassium chloride or sodium chloride.

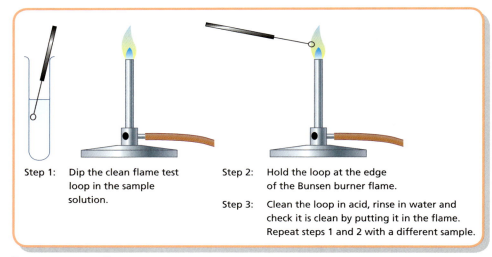

Step 1: Dip the clean flame test loop in the sample solution.
Step 2: Hold the loop at the edge of the Bunsen burner flame.
Step 3: Clean the loop in acid, rinse in water and check it is clean by putting it in the flame. Repeat steps 1 and 2 with a different sample.

How to carry out a flame test.

ResultsPlus Exam tip

You need to learn these colours. There's often a question asking about the results of flame tests and many students get these wrong.

The table shows the flame test colours produced by several different metals.

Metal	Flame test colour
lithium	red
sodium	yellow
potassium	lilac (a pale purple colour)
calcium	yellow-red
barium	pale green
copper	green-blue

Testing with sodium hydroxide

Iron(II) compounds form green precipitates that gradually turn brown.

Some metal compounds, such as sodium chloride, are soluble in water. Other metal compounds are insoluble. The solutions of transition metal compounds form coloured solutions. If sodium hydroxide is mixed with one of these solutions, an insoluble compound may be formed. This will give a precipitate.

The colour of the precipitate formed can help to identify the metal in the compound.

Transition metal in compound	Colour of precipitate when mixed with sodium hydroxide
copper	pale blue
iron(II)	green (turns brown when left standing)
iron(III)	red-brown
zinc	white

ResultsPlus Exam tip

This is another table that you just have to learn. There are often questions on this, too – and they are simple marks to get if you can remember the colours.

Higher tier

This symbol equation shows what happens when copper sulphate is mixed with sodium hydroxide:

$$CuSO_4(aq) + 2NaOH(aq) \rightarrow Cu(OH)_2(s) + Na_2SO_4(aq)$$

Worked example

Jane carried out two tests on separate samples of the salt copper(II) chloride. Which of the following statements are true?

(i) A yellow flame was produced in a flame test.

(ii) When sodium hydroxide solution was added to a solution of the salt, it produced a green precipitate.

A (i) only   B (ii) only
C both (i) and (ii)   D neither (i) nor (ii)

Copper produces green-blue flames in a flame test, so (i) is not correct.

Copper produces a pale-blue precipitate when solutions of its compounds are mixed with sodium hydroxide, so (ii) is not correct either.

The correct answer is D.

ResultsPlus Exam tip

Don't be afraid to pick the option that says neither statement is right, if this is what you think the answer is. Some students think that this type of question is a trick – but sometimes the correct answer *is* that none of the statements given are correct!

Test yourself

1. Which of the following metals, in one of its compounds, can be identified using a flame test on the compound?
   A iron   B copper   C silver   D gold

2. Some white powder was discovered at a crime scene. In a flame test the powder produced a yellow flame. This was because the white powder was a compound of:
   A carbon   B neon   C sodium   D copper

3. a Describe how to carry out a flame test.
   b Why is it important that a clean loop is used?

4. What is a precipitate?

5. Jan wants to test a compound to find out if it contains iron or zinc. Which of the two tests described on these pages should he use? Explain your answer.

6.1: Neutralisation reactions and salts

Need more help?
For more on this topic, see pages 136–140.

- ✓ C1.a.6.1 Describe how neutralisation can be used to make salts
- ✓ C1.a.6.1 Recall that some salts are used in fertilisers and that some salts can be used to produce colours in fireworks
- ✓ C1.a.6.2 Recall the reactions of metal oxides, hydroxides and carbonates with dilute sulphuric and hydrochloric acids
- ✓ C1.a.6.3 Describe the preparation of pure, dry samples of insoluble salts from solutions of soluble salts
- ✓ C1.a.6 Represent chemical reactions in topic 6 by word equations
- ✓ C1.a.6 Represent chemical reactions in topic 6 by balanced simple formulae equations

edexcel key terms

combustion Burning.
dilute A substance that has been mixed with water to make it less concentrated.
insoluble salt A salt that doesn't dissolve in water.
neutralisation The reaction between an acid and an alkali (or other base) to form a neutral solution.
precipitate The insoluble solid formed in a precipitation reaction.
salt One of the substances produced in a neutralisation reaction.
soluble salt A salt that dissolves in water.

Acids can be neutralised by reacting them with:

- metal oxides
- metal hydroxides
- metal carbonates.

These reactions produce salts. Salts are compounds consisting of a metal and a non-metal (such as sodium chloride – common salt).

Equations for neutralisation reactions

You need to remember these word equations and be able to apply them to real compounds.

> metal oxide + acid → salt + water
> metal hydroxide + acid → salt + water
> metal carbonate + acid → salt + water + carbon dioxide

Examples:

copper oxide + sulphuric acid → copper sulphate + water
sodium hydroxide + hydrochloric acid → sodium chloride + water
calcium carbonate + hydrochloric acid → calcium chloride + water + carbon dioxide

ResultsPlus Exam tip

Exam questions often ask which chemicals you should use to get a particular salt. Remember that hydrochloric acid will produce chloride salts, and sulphuric acid will produce sulphates.

Higher tier

You also need to be able to write balanced symbol equations for these reactions, and other similar ones. You can find out more about this on pages 58–59).

$$CuO(s) + H_2SO_4(aq) \rightarrow CuSO_4(aq) + H_2O(l)$$
$$NaOH(aq) + HCl(aq) \rightarrow NaCl(aq) + H_2O(l)$$
$$CaCO_3(s) + 2HCl(aq) \rightarrow CaCl_2(aq) + H_2O(l) + CO_2(g)$$

ResultsPlus Watch out!

It is only metal oxides, hydroxides and carbonates that can be used to prepare salts by neutralising an acid. If the name of a compound ends in 'chloride', 'nitrate', etc., then it's not a base and can't be used in a neutralisation reaction.

Preparing salts

The diagram shows how to make copper sulphate in the lab. 'Excess' copper oxide means that more copper oxide than you need is put in, to make absolutely sure that all the acid is neutralised.

Some salts are insoluble. If a reaction produces an insoluble salt, a precipitate will form in the test tube or beaker.

Insoluble salts are prepared by mixing solutions of two soluble salts. A precipitate forms because one of the combinations that can be formed from all the chemicals present in the mixture is insoluble. For example:

lead nitrate + potassium iodide
(soluble)   (soluble)
↓
lead iodide + potassium nitrate
(insoluble)   (soluble)

$$Pb(NO_3)_2(aq) + 2KI(aq) \rightarrow PbI_2(s) + 2KNO_3(aq)$$

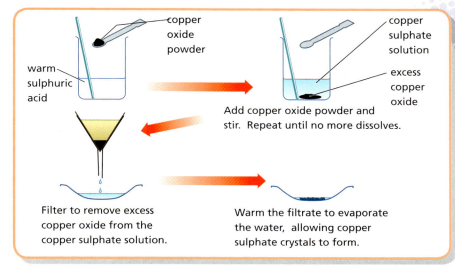

Preparing a soluble salt.

When an insoluble salt is made in this way it is separated from the mixture by filtering. Water is run through the filter paper to wash the salt, and then the paper and salt are dried in an oven.

Uses of salts

There are many uses of salts:
- Salts such as ammonium phosphate, potassium sulphate and ammonium nitrate are used in fertilisers.
- Salts such as copper chloride, barium chloride and lithium carbonate are used to produce colours in fireworks.
- Salts such as potassium nitrate and potassium chlorate are used as oxidising agents (they help things to burn).

Higher tier

ResultsPlus Watch out!

Remember the procedure for making insoluble salts – students often get this wrong in exams.

Test yourself

1. Write down three different compounds of copper that can be used to neutralise an acid.
2. Write a word equation for the reactions of:
   a calcium oxide with hydrochloric acid
   b copper carbonate with sulphuric acid
3. Why do you need to add excess copper oxide when you make copper sulphate?
4. What is a precipitate?
5. Barium sulphate is an insoluble salt. What is the best method of preparing this salt?
6. Once you have carried out the reaction in question 5, how do you obtain a dry sample of barium sulphate?
7. Write balanced symbol equations for the reactions of:
   a calcium oxide (CaO) with hydrochloric acid   b copper carbonate ($CuCO_3$) with sulphuric acid

6.2: Hazards and reactions

> **Need more help?**
> For more on this topic, see pages 130–131, 139–140, 142, 148–149.

- C1.a.6.6 Explain that the addition of oxygen to a substance is oxidation
- C1.a.6.7 Explain that the loss of oxygen from a substance is reduction
- C1.a.6.11 Describe the use of sodium hydrogencarbonate in baking powder
- C1.a.6.12 Recall that heating carbonates and hydrogencarbonates produces carbon dioxide gas and that this is an example of thermal decomposition
- C1.a.6.13 Describe hydration and dehydration
- C1.a.6.14 Recall that cooking involves chemical changes leading to new products
- C1.a.6.18 Describe the uses of hazard labels in the chemistry laboratory

edexcel key terms

carbohydrate A compound of carbon, hydrogen and oxygen.
decomposition A reaction in which a substance breaks down into two or more new substances.
dehydration A reaction in which water is removed from a substance.
hydration A reaction in which water is added to a substance.
oxidation A chemical reaction in which oxygen is added to a substance.
thermal decomposition A reaction in which a substance is broken down using heat energy.

ResultsPlus Exam tip

There are often questions about the dehydration of sugar or other carbohydrates using concentrated sulphuric acid. You don't need to work out what kind of reaction it is from the equations they give you – just remember that if the question asks about concentrated sulphuric acid producing carbon, it's a dehydration reaction.

ResultsPlus Watch out!

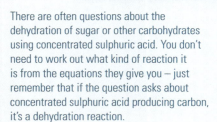

The salt in baking powder is sodium *hydrogen*carbonate, not sodium carbonate. Remember that baking powder also contains a dry acid.

Different types of reaction

You need to be able to describe different types of reaction.

Type of reaction	What it does	Example
oxidation	oxygen is added to a substance	• combustion (burning) • rusting
reduction	oxygen is removed from a substance	• obtaining iron from iron oxide by heating it with carbon (the iron is reduced, the carbon is oxidised)
neutralisation	'cancels' an acid	• adding an acid to an alkali • adding a metal oxide, hydroxide or carbonate to an acid • the reaction when baking powder is used
thermal decomposition	a compound breaks up into smaller molecules when it is heated	• heating carbonates (carbon dioxide is given off) • heating hydrogencarbonates (carbon dioxide and water are given off)
hydration	when water is chemically joined to a substance	• blue copper sulphate crystals have water as part of the crystal (hydration does *not* mean just mixing something with water)
dehydration	when water is removed from a substance	• sugar changing to carbon when bread is cooked • adding concentrated sulphuric acid to sugar or other carbohydrates

Cooking reactions

Cooking involves making chemical changes in foods. Some of the ingredients react together to form new products. Cakes are light and fluffy because of bubbles of gas in them. Baking powder contains sodium hydrogencarbonate ($NaHCO_3$) and tartaric acid powder. When these get wet a neutralisation reaction occurs that releases bubbles of carbon dioxide gas. This is an example of a neutralisation reaction.

The brown crust on bread is partly due to a decomposition reaction, when sugar breaks down to form carbon and water. This is called a thermal decomposition reaction (because heat makes the sugar break up into smaller molecules).

The decomposition of sugar is also a dehydration reaction, because one of the products of the reaction is water. The chemical doesn't have to be wet for a dehydration reaction to happen!

Safety in the lab

Many chemicals are dangerous if they are not used properly. These are labelled to show the dangers. You need to learn the hazard labels and meanings in the diagram.

Toxic
These substances can cause death.

Highly flammable
These substances catch fire easily.

Corrosive
These substances destroy living tissue.

Harmful
Similar to toxic substances but less dangerous.

Oxidising
These provide oxygen for other substances to burn.

Irritant
Not corrosive but may cause blisters or red skin.

Hazard symbols.

Test yourself

1. What do these hazard symbols mean?
   a a skull
   b flames coming from a circle
   c flames with no circle

2. a What are the two important ingredients in baking powder?
   b Why does baking powder only produce carbon dioxide when it is used in a recipe and cooked?
   c What kind of reaction produces the carbon dioxide from baking powder?

3. Carbon dioxide can be made by heating copper carbonate. The word equation for the reaction is:

   copper carbonate → copper oxide + carbon dioxide

   This reaction is an example of:
   A dehydration
   B reduction
   C oxidation
   D thermal decomposition

4. Zinc oxide can be converted into zinc by mixing it with carbon and heating the mixture. This is:
   A neutralisation
   B reduction
   C dehydration
   D thermal decomposition

5. The equation shows the effect of heat on copper sulphate crystals:

   $CuSO_4.5H_2O(s) \rightarrow CuSO_4(s) + 5H_2O(l)$

   Which row of the table describes the type of change occurring when copper sulphate crystals are heated and shows what is formed?

	type of change	what is formed
A	hydration	copper sulphate solution
B	dehydration	copper sulphate and water
C	hydration	copper sulphate and water
D	dehydration	copper sulphate solution

6.3: Extracting metals

Need more help?
For more on this topic, see pages 132, 134–135.

- C1.a.6.4 Explain that most metals have to be extracted from their ores
- C1.a.6.4 Recall that metal ores are found in the Earth's crust
- C1.a.6.5 Recall that some metals occur as their oxides
- C1.a.6.5 Recall how metals can be extracted from oxides by reaction with carbon
- C1.a.6.8 Recall that the least reactive metals are found uncombined in the Earth's crust
- C1.a.6.9 Recall that the more reactive metals have more stable ores
- C1.a.6.9 Describe how the method of extraction of a metal depends on the stability of its ore

Metals are found in the Earth's crust. Some metals, such as gold and platinum, are very unreactive and are found uncombined. Most other metals are found as ores (compounds of the metal with other elements). Many ores are oxides of the metal. These metals have to be extracted from their ores before they can be used. The way they are extracted depends on how reactive they are.

	metal	Extraction method
most reactive	potassium	
	sodium	
	calcium	Extracted using electricity
	magnesium	
	aluminium	
	carbon	
	zinc	
	iron	
	tin	Extracted by reacting with carbon
	lead	
	copper	
	silver	
least reactive	gold	Found uncombined in Earth's crust
	platinum	

The reactivity series.

The reactivity series

If you react metals with acid, you'll find that some react faster than others. If you compare the speeds of reaction of different metals with water, you'll find that the metals come out in the same order. If one metal is more reactive than another with acid, it is also more reactive with oxygen, or water.

The table shows the reactivities of some common metals. Carbon isn't a metal but it is included so you can see why some metals can be extracted using carbon and some cannot.

The more reactive a metal is, the more stable its compounds are. In other words, it is much harder to separate sodium oxide into sodium and oxygen than it is to separate copper oxide into copper and oxygen.

If you mix a more reactive metal with a compound of a less reactive one, the more reactive metal will end up in the compound. It displaces the less reactive metal.

Extraction using carbon

Metals that are less reactive than carbon can be extracted from their ores by heating them with carbon. The carbon is more reactive than the metal, so it ends up with the oxygen. The metal is reduced, and the carbon is oxidised.

Example:

lead oxide + carbon → lead + carbon dioxide

Higher tier

$$2PbO(s) + C(s) \rightarrow 2Pb(s) + CO_2(g)$$

Iron oxide is also reduced using carbon. The carbon is first oxidised to form carbon monoxide. It is the carbon monoxide that reduces the iron oxide. The carbon monoxide is oxidised to form carbon dioxide.

iron oxide + carbon monoxide → iron + carbon dioxide

$$Fe_2O_3(s) + 3CO(g) \rightarrow 2Fe(s) + 3CO_2(g)$$

Higher tier

Results Plus
Exam Question Report

Iron can be obtained from iron(III) oxide. Three mixtures were heated.
1 carbon and iron(III) oxide
2 copper and iron(III) oxide
3 magnesium and iron(III) oxide
Iron would be formed in mixture:

A 1 only   B 2 only   C 1 and 3 only   D 1, 2 and 3

Answer: The correct answer is C.

How students answered
Iron would be formed in mixture 1, because carbon is more reactive than iron (this is how iron is extracted from its ore). Most students understood this, and put A as their answer. Less than half of students realised that mixture 3 will also react, because magnesium is more reactive than iron.

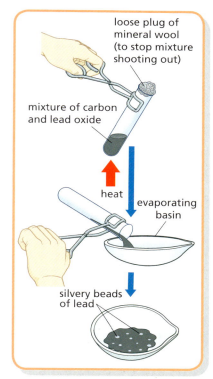

Reducing lead oxide in the lab.

Extraction using electrolysis

Metals that are more reactive than carbon cannot be extracted from their ores using carbon. Instead they are obtained using electrolysis. Electricity is used to separate the different elements in the ore.

Electrolysis can also be used to separate ores of metals that are less reactive than carbon, but it is more expensive than using carbon.

Example:

aluminium oxide → aluminium + oxygen $2Al_2O_3 \rightarrow 4Al + 3O_2$

Higher tier

Test yourself

1 What is an ore?

2 a Name two metals that are found as metals, not as their ores.   b Why are these metals found uncombined?

3 a Write down two different ways in which metals can be extracted from their ores.
   b What decides which method is used for a particular metal ore?

4 Explain what is meant by a 'stable' compound.

5 Tin can be obtained from tin oxide by electrolysis or by heating with carbon.
   a Explain why heating with carbon is likely to be used.
   b Write a word equation for the reaction.   c Which substance is reduced and which is oxidised?

6 The word equation for the formation of iron is: iron(III) oxide + carbon monoxide → iron + carbon dioxide
   Which substance is reduced and which is oxidised?

7 Write a balanced symbol equation for the extraction of tin from tin ore (SnO_2).

6.4: Collecting and testing gases

- C1.a.6.17 Describe how to collect gases by upward delivery
- C1.a.6.17 Describe how to collect gases by downward delivery
- C1.a.6.17 Describe how to collect gases over water
- C1.a.6.17 Describe how to collect gases using a gas syringe
- C1.a.6.17 Relate the method used to collect a gas to the solubility and density of the gas
- C1.a.6.16 Describe how to test for hydrogen, oxygen, carbon dioxide, ammonia and chlorine

Need more help? For more on this topic, see pages 131, 133, 141, 146.

Chemists often need to identify the gas given off in a reaction. To do this they must collect samples of the gas.

Collecting gases

There are different ways of collecting gases, and the method you choose depends on the properties of the gas.

Method	Use for collecting...	Examples
upward delivery	gases that are less dense than air	hydrogen, ammonia
downward delivery	gases that are more dense than air	carbon dioxide
over water	insoluble gases (gases that don't dissolve in water)	hydrogen, carbon dioxide (carbon dioxide dissolves slightly)
gas syringe	any gases, but particularly soluble gases (gases that do dissolve in water)	any

Gases are collected over water or in a gas syringe if you need to measure the volume of gas produced in a reaction.

Exam tip

You need to remember the reasons why the different methods are used. For example, soluble gases can't be collected over water, as the gas would just dissolve in the water. Only 11% of students got a question on how hydrogen is collected right.

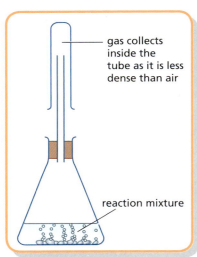

Upward delivery.

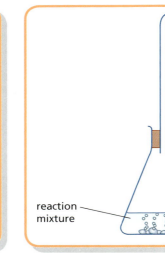

Downward delivery.

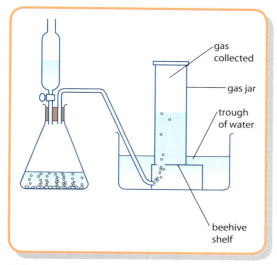
Collection over water.

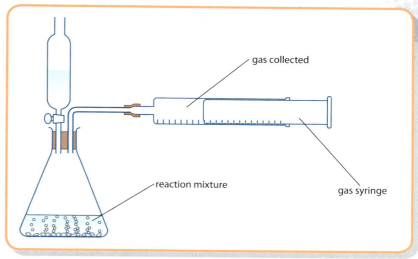
Using a gas syringe.

Testing gases

Gas	Test	What you see if the gas is present
hydrogen	Hold a lighted splint near the mouth of the test tube.	The gas explodes with a squeaky 'pop'.
oxygen	Put a glowing splint into the test tube.	The splint will relight (bursts into flame).
carbon dioxide	Bubble the gas through limewater.	The limewater will turn a cloudy (or milky) white.
	Put a lighted splint into the test tube.	The splint will go out (other gases do this too, so this only shows that the gas *might* be carbon dioxide).
ammonia	Hold damp red litmus paper in the gas.	The litmus paper turns blue.
chlorine	Hold damp blue litmus paper in the gas.	The litmus paper turns red (as chlorine is an acidic gas) and then white (as the chlorine bleaches the colour from the paper).

Test yourself

1. Hydrogen gas can be collected over water, or by upward delivery. What does this tell you about hydrogen's:
   a density
   b solubility?
2. Why is collecting carbon dioxide in a gas syringe a better method than collecting it over water?
3. Look at the table on page 74. Is ammonia more or less dense than air? Explain your answer.
4. Saida says 'This gas is carbon dioxide, because it put out a lighted splint.'
   a What is wrong with this statement?
   b How could Saida show that the gas *is* carbon dioxide?
5. You can test for hydrogen and oxygen using a splint. Explain what you would do for each gas, and what you would see.
6. You only have some red litmus paper. How could you use this as a test for chlorine?

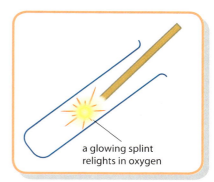
Oxygen will relight a glowing splint.

6.5: Uses of chemicals and artificial additives

Need more help?
For more on this topic, see pages 144–147, 149.

- ✓ C1.a.6.10 Discuss the differences between 'natural' and 'artificial' substances
- ✓ C1.a.6.10 Discuss the impacts on health of artificial food additives
- ✓ C1.a.6.19 Give some examples of the uses of ammonia, carbohydrates, carbon dioxide, caustic soda, sodium chloride and water
- ✓ C1.a.6.19 Give some examples of the uses of acids, including citric acid, ethanoic acid, hydrochloric acid and phosphoric acid
- ✓ C1.a.6.15 Interpret data linking a chemical in food with a health impact, and recognise that a correlation does not imply a cause

edexcel key terms

caustic soda The common name for sodium hydroxide.
citric acid A weak acid found naturally in oranges and lemons.

'Artificial' additives

Food manufacturers put lots of substances in foods to make them taste and look good, and to make sure they can be stored safely. Some of these are natural (like sugar), and some are chemicals manufactured in chemical factories. These are referred to as 'artificial' additives. Artificial flavours are often stronger (so less is needed) and cheaper than the natural versions.

Some people are concerned that artificial additives might be harming our health. However, some additives are useful, such as artificial sweeteners that don't contain as many 'calories'.

Higher tier

Sometimes people find a correlation (a link) between things, such as 'people who use a lot of artificial sweeteners have more heart attacks'. However, this doesn't necessarily show that the artificial sweeteners *cause* the heart attacks. There could be some other reason why these two things are linked. For example, it might be that people who are overweight often use sweeteners instead of sugar to try to lose weight, and it is the fact that they are overweight that increases their risk of heart attacks, not the fact that they use sweeteners.

ResultsPlus
Exam Question Report

Which of the following statements about ammonia are correct?
1 It is a gas that is soluble in water and turns moist red litmus paper blue.
2 It is less dense than air.
A 1 only
B 2 only
C both 1 and 2
D neither 1 nor 2
Answer: The correct answer is C – both statements are correct.

How students answered
Most students (77%) knew that the first statement is correct, but some thought that ammonia was denser than air.

 49% 0 marks

Even if you are unsure about part of an answer, you can use your knowledge about other parts to narrow down the possible options.

51% 1 mark

Uses of chemicals

Ammonia is a compound of nitrogen and hydrogen (NH_3). It is a gas at room temperature, with a sharp smell. It makes damp red litmus paper turn blue and is less dense than air. It is used in household cleaning products, and to make nitric acid and fertilisers such as ammonium sulphate.

Ammonia reacts with acids in a similar way to metals, producing an ammonium salt and water. Ammonium sulphate can be produced by reacting sulphuric acid with ammonia.

Carbohydrates are compounds containing only carbon, hydrogen and oxygen. They include sugar and starches (such as flour), and are important parts of wood and cotton. Carbohydrates are found in many foods, and the fibres from wood and cotton are used in paper, building materials and clothing.

Carbon dioxide is a gas at room temperature. It dissolves slightly in water. Carbon dioxide is the 'fizz' in fizzy drinks. Carbon dioxide released when sodium hydrogencarbonate reacts with acid is what makes cakes rise.

Caustic soda is another name for sodium hydroxide, an alkali. It is used in drain cleaners, because it reacts with the fatty and greasy substances that are usually responsible for blocking sinks and drains.

Sodium chloride is the chemical name for common salt — the stuff you put on your food. Food manufacturers put it into many ready-meals to improve the taste. It is also used in dishwashers to make the water 'soft' and stop it leaving marks on the glasses and cutlery.

Water is a very good solvent and is used in many foods and household products. It is listed as 'aqua' on some labels.

Citric acid is found naturally in citrus fruits such as oranges and lemons. This acid is what gives some fizzy drinks their 'tangy' taste. It is used as an ingredient in sherbet, sweets, ice cream and many other foods. It is also used in limescale removers.

Ethanoic acid is the acid in vinegar (it is sometimes called acetic acid). It is used in crisps and sauces, and also in window cleaning liquids.

Hydrochloric acid is used in toilet cleaners. It is also used in the chemical industry to make certain plastics and in making steel products.

Phosphoric acid is a strong acid, used in rust removers. Dilute phosphoric acid is used in cola, jams, jelly and cheese.

ResultsPlus Exam tip

Make sure you remember that table salt (or common salt) is sodium chloride. There's often a question on this!

ResultsPlus Exam tip

Make sure you remember the uses of these chemicals — there is often a question on what the uses of these chemicals are.

Test yourself

1. a What is an artificial additive?
   b Give two reasons why manufacturers often prefer to use artificial additives.
   c Suggest why some people prefer to buy food without artificial additives.

2. Sugar is a natural sweetener. Natural means:
   A manufactured   B safe
   C pure   D not man-made

3. How do you know that ammonia is a compound, not an element?

4. a Which acids on these pages are used in foods?
   b Which acids are used to clean things?

5. What gives lemonade:
   a its fizz   b its tangy taste?

7.1: Burning fuels

- C1.b.7.2 Recall that energy is released when fuels burn
- C1.b.7.2 Recall that the products of the complete combustion of hydrocarbons are carbon dioxide and water
- C1.b.7.18 Explain why incomplete combustion can occur in faulty appliances
- C1.b.7.19 Describe how incomplete combustion can produce carbon and carbon monoxide
- C1.b.7.20 Explain why carbon monoxide is a toxic gas
- C1.b.7.21 Interpret data relating respiratory diseases to atmospheric pollutants
- C1.b.7 Represent chemical reactions in topic 7 by word equations
- C1.b.7 Represent chemical reactions in topic 7 by balanced simple formulae equations

Need more help?
For more on this topic, see pages 154–157.

edexcel key terms

combustion Another word for burning. The chemical reaction between a fuel and oxygen that gives out heat.
complete combustion When a fuel burns with a good supply of oxygen to produce carbon dioxide and water.
incomplete combustion When a fuel burns without enough oxygen. Carbon monoxide and/or soot can form as well as carbon dioxide and water.
sootiness The amount of soot (carbon) produced by a burning fuel.
toxic Poisonous.

Fuels are a store of energy. We transfer this energy when fuels burn. Most of the fuels we use are hydrocarbons. A hydrocarbon is a molecule made of carbon and hydrogen atoms only.

Complete combustion

The diagram shows what happens to the atoms when methane burns with plenty of oxygen. This is called complete combustion (there is plenty of oxygen to allow all the fuel to burn completely).

Complete combustion.

You can show this using a word equation:

methane + oxygen → carbon dioxide + water

Higher tier

You can also show it using a balanced symbol equation:

$$CH_4(g) + 2O_2(g) \rightarrow CO_2(g) + 2H_2O(l)$$

ResultsPlus
Exam Question Report

A water heater uses liquefied petroleum gas, LPG, which contains propane, C_3H_8. Which equation correctly represents the complete combustion of propane?

A $C_3H_8 + 4O_2 \rightarrow 3C + 4H_2O$
B $2C_3H_8 + 7O_2 \rightarrow 6CO + 8H_2O$
C $C_3H_8 + 3O_2 \rightarrow 3CO_2 + 4H_2$
D $C_3H_8 + 5O_2 \rightarrow 3CO_2 + 4H_2O$

Answer: The correct answer is D.

How students answered
Some students got this wrong, even though you don't need to know anything about balancing equations to get it right. If you look at the right-hand side of each equation, you'll see that D is the only one that has both carbon dioxide and water as products of the reaction.

Incomplete combustion

Incomplete combustion happens when there is not enough oxygen to combine with the hydrogen and carbon atoms in the burning fuel. This can happen when appliances such as gas boilers or gas fires are faulty, particularly if the part that lets air in gets blocked. As air and waste gases usually both go through the same vent in the wall, such a blockage will also make it more likely that waste gases will get into the room.

ResultsPlus
Watch out!

The products of *complete* combustion of *any* hydrocarbon are always just carbon dioxide (CO_2) and water. The products of *incomplete* combustion still include water, and can include a mix of carbon, carbon monoxide and carbon dioxide.

You also need to remember that carbon *mon*oxide has the formula CO. Carbon *di*oxide has the formula CO_2.

There is nearly always a question on the products of combustion, and every time over half of the students get it wrong!

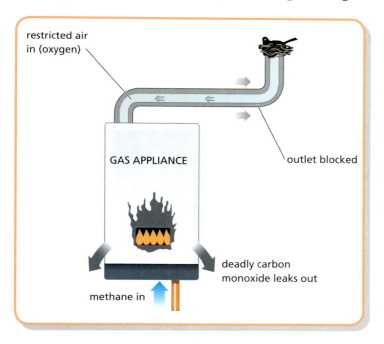

A faulty gas boiler.

Incomplete combustion of a hydrocarbon produces water and a mixture of solid particles of carbon (called particulates or soot), carbon monoxide and carbon dioxide. Some signs that this is happening are a yellow flame and sooty marks around an appliance.

Carbon monoxide is a toxic gas, because it binds to the haemoglobin in your red blood cells better than oxygen does. It stops your red blood cells carrying oxygen.

GCSE 360 Science

ResultsPlus
Exam Question Report

Condensation in a room containing a gas central heating boiler suggests that:
A carbon dioxide is being formed
B carbon monoxide is being formed
C the fumes from the burning gas are leaking into the room
D the supply of oxygen is insufficient
Answer: The correct answer is C.

How students answered
Condensation is formed by water in the waste gases. The presence of condensation doesn't tell you whether the boiler has enough air or not, as some students thought.

75% 0 marks

Water vapour is formed in both complete and incomplete combustion. It can only tell you that the waste gases are leaking into the room.

25% 1 mark

Higher tier

edexcel key terms

acid rain Rain with dissolved pollutants such as sulphur dioxide that make the rain acidic. Acid rain can kill trees and make rivers acidic, which harms wildlife.

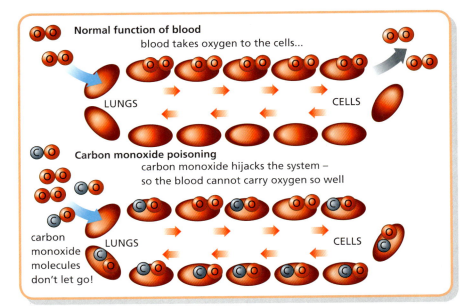

Carbon monoxide 'hijacks' your red blood cells.

Fuels and air pollution

The fuel in some vehicles doesn't always undergo complete combustion, and tiny particles of soot can be put into the air. These are called 'particulates' and can cause respiratory diseases. Other chemicals that are sometimes found in fuel also cause air pollution.

Test yourself

1. Write a word equation for the complete combustion of propane (a hydrocarbon fuel).

2. Write down the names and formulae for the four different things that can be formed in incomplete combustion.

3. Write down a word equation for the incomplete combustion of propane.

4. Why is carbon monoxide toxic?

5. Write down a balanced symbol equation for the complete combustion of propane gas (C_3H_8). Include state symbols.

6. Methane, CH_4, is used as a fuel. Which of these are balanced equations for reactions occurring in the incomplete combustion of methane?
   A $2CH_4 + 3O_2 \rightarrow 2CO + 4H_2O$
   B $2CH_4 + O_2 \rightarrow 2CO + 4H_2$
   C $CH_4 + O_2 \rightarrow C + 2H_2O$

   Explain your answer.

7.2: Products from oil

- C1.b.7.15 Describe the fractional distillation of crude oil
- C1.b.7.16 Give examples of the uses for the main fractions of crude oil
- C1.b.7.17 Explain where the main fractions are produced on the fractionating column
- C1.b.7.17 Outline the relationship between boiling point, the size of molecules, viscosity, ease of ignition and uses of the main fractions of crude oil

Need more help?
For more on this topic, see pages 168–169.

Fractional distillation

Petrol, diesel, kerosene (jet fuel) and many other substances are obtained from crude oil. Crude oil is a mixture of many different hydrocarbon molecules. The different molecules are separated by fractional distillation. This takes place in a fractionating column. Each fraction (such as petrol or diesel) is a mixture of hydrocarbon compounds.

The crude oil is heated and turned into a gas before being put into the bottom of the column. The vapour moves up the column and gradually cools. As it cools, different molecules condense.

edexcel key terms

crude oil The natural form of the fossil fuel oil. Crude oil is a mixture of hydrocarbons.
fractional distillation A form of distillation that separates many different parts of a mixture.
fractionating column A tall tower used to separate the different fractions in crude oil.
ignition Catching fire.
residue Something that is left behind.
viscosity How thick or runny a liquid is. High viscosity is thick, like treacle.

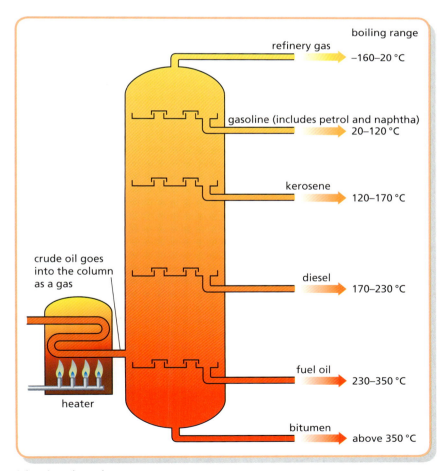

A fractionating column.

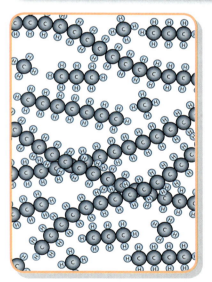

Crude oil is a mixture of hydrocarbons with different carbon chain lengths.

ResultsPlus Watch out!

Hydrocarbons are *compounds* of hydrogen and carbon. Crude oil is a *mixture* of different hydrocarbon compounds.

Uses of the fractions

The table shows some of the uses of the different fractions. You need to learn these!

Fraction	Uses
gases (including Liquid Petroleum Gas, LPG)	bottled gas for campers and caravans, and some cars also run on LPG
petrol	fuel for cars
naphtha	used to make synthetic materials and other chemicals
kerosene (also called paraffin)	fuel for jet engines in aircraft and central heating systems
diesel	fuel for cars, lorries, trains and other large vehicles
fuel oil	fuel for ships and power stations, and used to lubricate engines
bitumen	tar for roads, waterproofing materials used on flat roofs

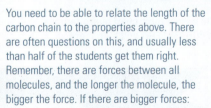

Higher tier
For more on this topic, see page 169.

Properties and molecules

The different fractions have different properties, which are related to the lengths of the carbon chains. Remember that each fraction is still a mixture of different chain lengths.

The shorter the chain of carbon atoms:

- the less viscous (more runny) the liquid
- the lower the boiling point
- the easier it is to ignite (set alight).

The lower the boiling point, the further up the fractionating column the molecules get before they condense. The fractions with the shortest chain lengths are produced at the top of the column, and the fractions with the longest chain lengths are produced at the bottom.

ResultsPlus Exam tip

You need to be able to relate the length of the carbon chain to the properties above. There are often questions on this, and usually less than half of the students get them right. Remember, there are forces between all molecules, and the longer the molecule, the bigger the force. If there are bigger forces:

- it is harder for a molecule to escape from the liquid (so the boiling point is higher)
- it is harder to light (because it is evaporated liquid that actually burns)
- the substance is more viscous (think about the long molecules getting tangled up).

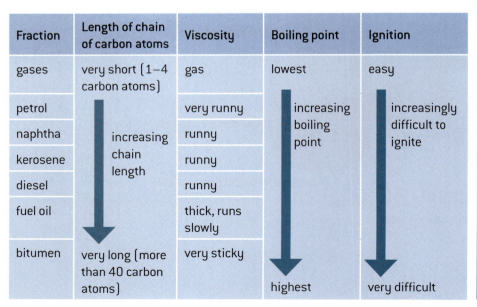

7 There's One Earth

ResultsPlus
Exam Question Report

Two fuels that can be used for cars are petrol and diesel. Which of the following statements is *false*?
A The waste products produced during complete combustion are the same for both fuels.
B Loss of diesel from the fuel tank by evaporation in warm weather would be greater than for petrol.
C Diesel is more likely to solidify in very cold weather than petrol.
D Diesel is more difficult to ignite than petrol.

Answer: The correct answer is B.

How students answered
Well over half of students got this wrong.

69% 0 marks

Diesel fuel consists of longer carbon chains than petrol, so it has a higher boiling point and evaporates *less* easily. C and D are therefore correct and B is false. A is also correct (see pages 77–80).

31% 1 mark

Test yourself

1. a What is crude oil?
   b How is it separated into different 'fractions'?

2. Is the crude oil a solid, a liquid or a gas when it goes into the fractionating column?

3. What are the main uses of these fractions?
   a gas   b bitumen   c kerosene
   d petrol   e diesel   f fuel oil

4. Which of the following statements are correct?
   A Crude oil enters the bottom of the fractionating column as a liquid.
   B When crude oil is vaporised, petrol and fuel oil vaporise at the same time.

5. Some petrol and some diesel are spilled on the ground.
   a Which puddle will evaporate first?
   b Which is most likely to catch fire if someone has a naked light nearby? Explain your answer.

Need more help?
For more on this topic, see pages 158–163.

7.3: Global warming

- C1.b.7.1 Recall what is meant by global warming
- C1.b.7.1 Recall that the idea of global warming started as a single scientist's idea
- C1.b.7.1 Explain how the idea of global warming became a widely accepted theory
- C1.b.7.3 Explain how burning fossil fuels may lead to global warming
- C1.b.7.4 Describe how the composition of the Earth's atmosphere and the Earth's temperature have varied over time
- C1.b.7.5 Recall that predictions about global warming use computer models, which carry uncertainties
- C1.b.7.6 Suggest what could be done to combat global warming

edexcel key terms
fossil fuel A fuel that formed millions of years ago from the remains of plants and tiny animals. Includes coal, oil and natural gas.
global warming A rise in the average temperature of the Earth that could lead to climate change.
hydrocarbon A compound made from carbon and hydrogen atoms only.

Atmosphere and temperature

When the Earth first formed, the atmosphere was mostly carbon dioxide. The chart shows how this changed as life evolved. Plants produce oxygen as a waste product in photosynthesis. Today the atmosphere is approximately 78% nitrogen, 21% oxygen, and 0.035% carbon dioxide.

The temperature of the Earth has also changed over time. Scientists think that this is linked to the amount of carbon dioxide in the air. The graph shows how the amount of carbon dioxide in the atmosphere affects the temperature.

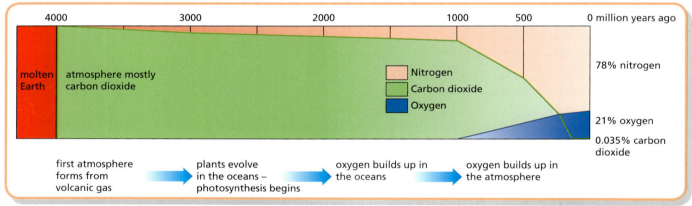

How the Earth's atmosphere has changed.

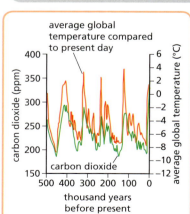

Carbon dioxide and temperature over the last 500 000 years.

Global warming

A Swedish scientist called Svante Arrhenius (1859–1927) was the first to suggest that there might be a link between the amount of carbon dioxide in the atmosphere and the temperature of the Earth. He also suggested that burning fossil fuels could result in the temperature of the Earth increasing.

Since then, many scientists have gathered more data, and now it is generally agreed that the carbon dioxide (and other greenhouse gases such as methane) that humans are putting into the atmosphere is making the Earth warmer. This happens because greenhouse gases trap heat in the atmosphere.

Increases in temperature will lead to changes in climate, with some places becoming warmer and others cooler. Rainfall patterns will be affected, and there may be more storms. All of this could lead to food shortages, increases in diseases, and flooding of low-lying countries.

Greenhouse gases include methane and water vapour, as well as carbon dioxide. Scientists have predicted the effects of greenhouse gases in the atmosphere using computer models. The predictions made by these models are not certain because the processes involved are so complicated, but they give a good idea of what may happen.

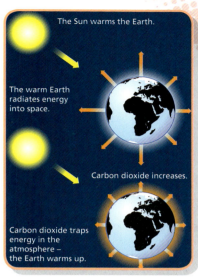

How carbon dioxide may cause global warming.

ResultsPlus
Exam Question Report

Which of the following, present in the atmosphere, is least likely to contribute to global warming?

A carbon dioxide B hydrogen C water vapour D methane

Answer: The correct answer is B.

How students answered
Nearly three-quarters of students got this one wrong.

72% 0 marks

You should know that carbon dioxide, methane and water vapour are 'greenhouse gases' that are thought to contribute to global warming. Hydrogen is a reactive gas and will react with oxygen to form water.

28% 1 mark

What can be done?

The link between burning fossil fuels and global warming has not been *proved*. However, scientists think the link is likely enough that we should try to prevent it happening. This 'playing safe' is called the precautionary principle.

The main way we can try to slow the increase of carbon dioxide in the atmosphere is to reduce our use of fossil fuels, which means using energy more efficiently.

Higher tier

Test yourself

1. a What was the main gas in the atmosphere when the Earth was first formed?
   b What caused oxygen to be added to the atmosphere?
   c What are the two main gases in the atmosphere today?

2. Which of these activities is least likely to increase global warming?
   A burning coal   B growing trees
   C combustion of petrol   D aeroplane flights

3. One theory is that global warming is caused by greenhouse gases. All greenhouse gases:
   A allow extra heat to reach us from the Sun
   B are less dense than air and escape from the Earth's atmosphere
   C reduce the amount of heat escaping from the Earth
   D damage the ozone layer and allow extra UV radiation to reach the Earth

4. Scientists make predictions about global warming. Why are these predictions not certain?

Need more help? For more on this topic, see pages 164–165.

7.4: Other fuels

- C1.b.7.11 Describe the properties of a useful fuel
- C1.b.7.12 Explain why bio-fuels are sometimes an attractive alternative to fossil fuels
- C1.b.7.13 Discuss the benefits and drawbacks of hydrogen as a fuel
- C1.b.7.14 Recall that alcohol obtained from crops is a useful bio-fuel
- C1.b.7.14 Recall that large areas of fertile land are needed to produce bio-fuels

edexcel key terms

bio-fuel A fuel made from living things.

Many different substances can be used as fuels, but some make better fuels than others. A useful fuel:

- releases a lot of energy when it burns (so a smaller volume of fuel is needed to release the same amount of energy)
- does not make soot or smoke (these cause pollution and show that not all the energy stored in the fuel is being released as heat energy)
- does not leave a solid residue behind after burning
- is easy to store and transport.

Wood and coal both burn with smoky flames and leave ash behind. Fuels such as hydrocarbons and alcohols don't leave any residue when they burn. All of the fuel is converted into carbon dioxide and water when these fuels burn. Hydrogen produces water when it burns, and leaves no residue.

Most of the fuels we use (except for hydrogen) release carbon dioxide into the atmosphere when they burn. Most scientists agree that this is causing global warming, and we need to try to reduce the amount of carbon dioxide emitted. This means we need to find alternatives to fuels obtained from oil. Oil is also a non-renewable resource, and will run out one day.

ResultsPlus Watch out!

All fuels produce waste products when they burn (carbon dioxide and water, except for hydrogen, which just produces water). *Not* all fuels leave a solid residue.

Bio-fuels

Bio-fuels are fuels made from living things – plant or animal waste, or plants specially grown to turn into bio-fuels. Bio-fuels are a renewable energy resource.

As plants grow they take carbon dioxide out of the air. This carbon dioxide is released again when the fuels burn. Bio-fuels are referred to as carbon-neutral, because they don't add to the amount of carbon dioxide in the atmosphere overall. (This is only true if all the fuel used in manufacturing and transporting the fuel is also carbon-neutral.)

ResultsPlus Watch out!

Bio-fuels *do* release carbon dioxide into the atmosphere. They are called carbon-neutral because they only release carbon dioxide that they have just taken in, so overall they don't affect the amount of carbon dioxide in the air.

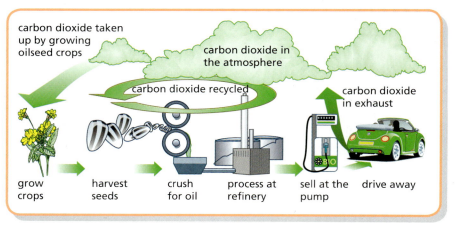

Bio-fuels.

Plants can be grown to make bio-diesel, or sugar cane can be grown to make ethanol (a kind of alcohol). This is used in car engines. Growing crops for bio-fuels takes up large areas of land, and can lead to cutting down rainforests or food shortages (as land gets used for bio-fuel crops instead of for growing food).

Hydrogen

Hydrogen is used as a fuel in some buses in the UK. Hydrogen only produces water vapour when it burns. Water vapour is a greenhouse gas, but the concentration of water vapour in the atmospheres varies so much with changes in the weather that the extra water added by burning hydrogen isn't likely to have an overall effect on the Earth's temperature. However, hydrogen is usually made from water using electricity, so it is only really a 'green' fuel if the electricity used to make it comes from renewable resources. Hydrogen has to be compressed to store it, and it can be dangerous if it's not stored properly.

Bio-butanol is a new fuel that the producers intend to market. Bio-butanol has a higher energy content per litre than bio-ethanol. An advantage of bio-butanol compared to bio-ethanol is:

A it is produced from renewable resources
B under the same conditions a car will use less fuel
C it can be used instead of petrol
D it produces different waste products
Answer: The answer is B.

How students answered

Two-thirds of students got this wrong. Only about one-third of students gave the correct answer. Statements A and C are correct, but they aren't advantages of bio-butanol *compared to* bio-ethanol, as they apply to bio-ethanol as well.

Fuels summary

The table shows the properties of some different fuels.

Fuel	Waste products	Advantages	Disadvantages
wood	carbon dioxide, water, ash	• renewable if from sustainable resource	• produces smoke and ash • not much energy per kg
coal	carbon dioxide, water, ash	• cheap	• produces smoke and ash • produces CO_2 • non-renewable • less energy per kg than other fossil fuels
oil (petrol, diesel etc.)	carbon dioxide, water	• cheap • easy to store and transport	• produces CO_2 • non-renewable
natural gas	carbon dioxide, water	• cheap • easy to store and transport	• produces CO_2 • non-renewable
bio-fuels	carbon dioxide, water	• renewable • can be carbon-neutral if produced properly	• takes large areas of land to produce the plants used
hydrogen	water	• doesn't produce CO_2 • can be renewable if made using electricity from renewable resources	• difficult and possibly dangerous to store

Test yourself

1. Write down three properties of a useful fuel.

2. What waste products do the following fuels produce?
   a. hydrogen
   b. bio-diesel
   c. coal
   d. petrol
   e. fuel oil

3. Which fuels on this page can be produced in a renewable way?

4. John says: 'Bio-fuels do not put carbon dioxide into the air, so they do not contribute to global warming.' Explain what is wrong with this statement.

5. Which of these is an advantage of using bio-ethanol instead of petrol as a fuel?
   A. bio-ethanol is non-biodegradable
   B. bio-ethanol is non-renewable
   C. growing crops to make large quantities of bio-ethanol uses only small areas of land
   D. use of bio-ethanol conserves oil supplies

6. Ethanol is used as a fuel in some countries. Which of these statements are correct?
   A. Growing crops to produce ethanol reduces the land available for food production.
   B. Growing plants use carbon dioxide.
   C. Burning ethanol produces carbon dioxide.

7.5: Products from air, rocks and the sea

> **Need more help?**
> For more on this topic, see pages 170–173.

✓ **C1.b.7.22** Describe how nitrogen and oxygen can be obtained from liquid air

✓ **C1.b.7.23** Give examples of useful substances obtained from sea water and rock salt

Gases from the air

The air is a mixture of gases. It is about 78% nitrogen and 21% oxygen. The remaining 1% is a mixture of many different gases.

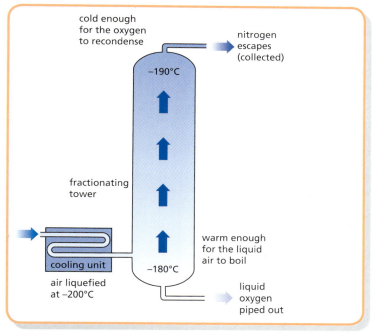

Fractional distillation of air.

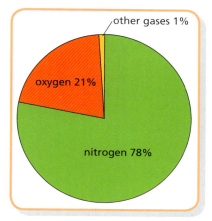

The gases in air.

Exam tip

Remember the gases in the air and their percentages. Many students get questions on the gases in air wrong.

Nitrogen and oxygen (and other gases) are obtained from air using fractional distillation. Air is cooled down to −200°C, when the carbon dioxide and water vapour in it become solid and can be removed. The liquid air is then allowed to boil in the fractionating column. The temperature changes up the column. The different gases in air have different boiling points, so they condense at different points and are removed. Distillation relies on physical changes, *not* a chemical reaction.

Products from rock salt and sea water

The chemical name for common salt is sodium chloride. It can be obtained from sea water (which has a lot of sodium chloride dissolved in it) or from rock salt (which is dug out of the ground).

Drinking water can be obtained from sea water in countries that don't have enough rainfall. This is called desalination. In one method, the processes involved are:

- filtering (to remove any solids in the sea water)
- evaporation (only the water evaporates, leaving the salts behind)
- condensation (to turn the water vapour back into a liquid).

If filtered sea water (or salty water made from rock salt) is evaporated, the sodium chloride is left behind. Sodium metal can be obtained from molten sodium chloride by electrolysis.

Other chemicals can be obtained from salty water (called 'brine') using electrolysis. Chlorine and hydrogen gases are given off at the electrodes, and sodium hydroxide remains dissolved in the solution.

The table below shows some of the uses of the chemicals from sea water.

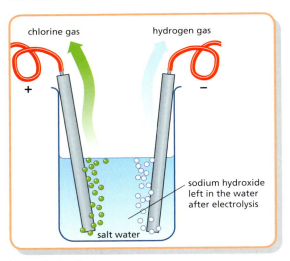

Electrolysis of salt water.

Chemical	Uses
sodium	- streetlamps - chemical industry
chlorine	- killing bacteria - purifying drinking water and swimming pools - used in chemical industry to make PVC and other chemicals - making bleach (with sodium hydroxide)
sodium chloride	- used in food - making sodium
hydrogen	- fuel - making ammonia - making margarine
sodium hydroxide	- oven cleaner - making soaps and detergents - making bleach (with chlorine) - in fabric and paper production

Exam Question Report

Bleach and oven cleaners are two products used in the home. The table shows some substances that may be in these products and from where they are obtained. Which row of the table is correct?

	product	substance in product	this substance is obtained from
A	bleach	chlorine	liquid air
B	bleach	sodium	rock salt
C	oven cleaner	sodium hydroxide	rock salt
D	oven cleaner	sodium	sea water

Answer: The correct answer is C.

How students answered

Nearly one-third of students put B or D. Remember that sodium is a reactive metal. There are *compounds* of sodium in bleach and oven cleaner, but this isn't the same as saying that sodium is used.

Test yourself

1. What is the approximate percentage in air of:
   a oxygen   b nitrogen?

2. Nitrogen can be obtained from liquid air. The process involves:
   A a chemical reaction   B nanotechnology
   C fractional distillation   D a high temperature

3. Fractional distillation of air works because the gases in air have different:
   A melting points   B numbers of protons in their atoms
   C densities   D boiling points

4. Write down five substances that can be obtained from sea water or rock salt.

5. Many oven cleaners contain sodium hydroxide. Sodium hydroxide can be made from:
   A sea water or rock salt   B sea water only
   C rock salt only   D neither sea water nor rock salt

6. Write down two uses of:
   a chlorine   b sodium hydroxide

Need more help?
For more on this topic, see pages 166–167.

7.6: Sustainable living

- C1.b.7.7 Explain the importance of recycling waste products such as glass, metal and papers
- C1.b.7.8 Evaluate economic and environmental reasons for recycling
- C1.b.7.8 Evaluate economic and environmental reasons for the desalination of sea water
- C1.b.7.9 Explain what we mean by sustainable development
- C1.b.7.10 Describe how the Internet can be used to obtain information about environmental change
- C1.b.7.10 Recognise the need to check the reliability of information from the Internet

edexcel key terms

desalination Turning salt water into fresh water by removing the salt.
recycle Use the same material again.
sustainability Being able to keep doing the same thing over and over again without causing harm to the environment or using up resources.

ResultsPlus Watch out!

Remember that plastics are **not** biodegradable. This means that they don't break down and some plastics can last for hundreds of years.

Recycling

Many of the resources we use are non-renewable (they will run out one day). We throw away many items and materials that could be reused. As well as using up non-renewable resources, throwing things away can cause pollution and takes up lots of land in landfill sites. We can avoid some of these problems by recycling.

For many materials, like aluminium drinks cans, it is cheaper to make new cans from old ones than it is to use new aluminium obtained from rocks. For other materials, such as paper, recycling avoids the need to cut down more trees.

Material	Features
paper	• biodegradable, so can be used in compost bins • can be recycled to make cardboard or toilet paper
metals	• non-biodegradable • recycling saves money or conserves scarce raw materials
plastics	• non-biodegradable • difficult to separate the different types for recycling • can be burned (but this can cause pollution)
glass	• non-biodegradable

Drinking water from sea water

In some countries, water is recycled from sea water in a process called desalination. If this wasn't done, these countries would not be able to support as many people, or they would have to import fresh water. This would be expensive, and transporting the water would use fuel, which would be bad for the environment.

Sustainable development

We have a very high standard of living in the UK in comparison to many other countries. Most people in these other countries would like to have our standard of living. These countries are developing their industries, and some of them may soon be richer than us! However, this kind of development uses up natural resources and can cause pollution.

We (and other countries) must try to develop sustainably, without harming the environment or wasting resources. This will help to make sure that there are still resources left for future generations to use, and the Earth will not be too polluted for our children or grandchildren to live on.

Using the Internet

The Internet is a huge source of information, and can be used to find out about many kinds of environmental change. The governments of lots of different countries gather information about pollution, energy resources, etc. in their own countries, and put this on the Internet for anyone to look at. These tend to be reliable sources of information.

However, not all sources of information on the Internet are reliable. For example, information about global warming may be put on the Internet by oil companies, who want people to carry on using lots of oil so they can make a profit! Campaigners for environmental causes sometimes put up biased information on their websites to try to persuade more people to join their campaign. In fact, anyone can put their opinions on the Internet, whether or not they have any scientific knowledge. You need to think carefully about *who* has put the information on the Internet before you decide whether or not to trust it.

Test yourself

1 Paper is recycled. Recycling is carried out because:
   A fewer trees are destroyed
   B it increases the amount of waste
   C it is difficult to carry out
   D paper cannot be disposed of by burning

2 It is difficult to recycle plastic. An advantage of recycling plastic is that:
   A it wastes energy
   B it increases landfill
   C most plastics are biodegradable
   D the amount of plastic waste is reduced

3 Empty glass bottles can be recycled. The main raw material for making glass is sand. It is important to recycle glass because:
   A sand is a very expensive material
   B glass cannot be put in landfill sites
   C making glass from raw materials uses large amounts of energy
   D glass decomposes to produce methane

4 Manchu looks on the Internet for information about global warming. Which of these websites is most likely to provide him with reliable, unbiased information?
   A a car manufacturer's website
   B a petrol company's website
   C the 'prevent global warming' website
   D the Royal Society of Chemistry's website

5 a What is sustainable development?
   b How is recycling part of sustainable development?

8.1: Modern materials

- **C1.b.8.1** Relate properties to uses of materials in clothing and sports equipment, including carbon fibres, Thinsulate® and Lycra®
- **C1.b.8.2** Explain that smart materials change their properties in response to changing conditions
- **C1.b.8.3** Describe how scientists create new materials with special properties; suggest why some new materials have unexpected novel properties
- **C1.b.8.3** Suggest why uses for some new materials are only discovered after they have been made
- **C1.b.8.4** Explain the breathability of fabrics like Gore-Tex® in terms of their structure
- **C1.b.8.5** Suggest how the properties of a material such as Kevlar® might be used in everyday life
- **C1.b.8.12** Design a list of properties for a product, based on its end use

Need more help? For more on this topic, see pages 178–181, 196–197

edexcel key terms

breathability The ability to let water vapour from sweat through without letting liquid water through.
carbon fibre Fibres made from carbon atoms only.
Gore-Tex® A special fabric that can 'breathe' but keeps liquid water drops out.
Kevlar® A very strong fibre that can be used for bullet-proof vests.

Materials have different properties (such as strength, stiffness, etc.), which make them suitable for different uses. The table shows some modern materials, their properties and their uses.

Material	Properties	Uses
Lycra®	• very stretchy • stronger than rubber • not affected by sunlight or sweat	• sports clothing such as cycling shorts or running clothes
Thinsulate®	• very good insulator • light weight	• jackets, gloves and other clothing used in cold conditions
carbon fibre composite materials	• carbon fibres are very stiff and strong • light weight	• sporting equipment such as tennis racquets • helicopter rotor blades and other parts of aircraft
Gore-tex®	• lets water vapour through but not liquid water drops ('breathable')	• waterproof clothing that allows sweat to escape
Kevlar®	• strong and light • can be woven into cloth	• bullet-proof vests • skis • brake pads
Teflon®	• very slippery, so doesn't stick to things well (and things don't stick to it)	• coating for non-stick pans • the microporous membrane in Gore-tex® • coating fibres used to make clothes, so that dirt will not stick to them
smart materials	• materials that change their properties when the conditions change (shape-memory alloys are an example of smart materials)	• sunglasses that darken when the light gets brighter
shape-memory alloys	• metal alloys that change their shape when the temperature changes	• 'superelastic' glasses that spring back into shape if they are bent • stents (used in medicine to expand blood vessels) • braces for teeth

Designer Products 8

Materials scientists can design materials to help to solve different problems, or sometimes a new material is discovered by chance and scientists think up uses for it later. Gore-tex® and Kevlar® are examples of materials that were specially designed. Teflon® and the weak glue on Post-It® notes are examples of materials that were discovered by accident, and uses found for them later.

Why they work

Kevlar® is very strong because it is made of long molecules with strong bonds between each atom, and the molecules are lined up next to each other with very strong bonds between them.

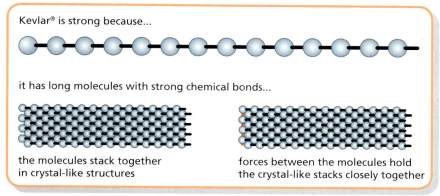

Structure of Kevlar®.

Gore-tex® is breathable because it has very tiny holes in it that are big enough for molecules of water vapour to go through, but not big enough for drops of water to go through.

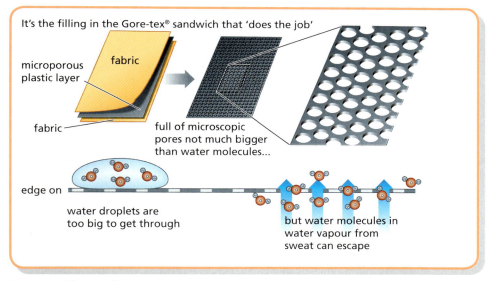

Structure of Gore-tex®.

edexcel key terms

Lycra® A brand of very stretchy polymer fibre.
smart material A material that can change its properties as conditions change.
Teflon® A non-reactive material used to coat 'non-stick' pans and as a lubricant.
Thinsulate® A brand of insulating material that is made from very fine polypropene fibres.

ResultsPlus Exam tip

Remember the meaning of 'breathable' – it lets water vapour through but not liquid water drops. This means it keeps rain out, but lets sweat go through it. A question might not mention breathability, but if it mentions sweating, or any activity where a person might sweat, the answer is to do with breathability!

95

ResultsPlus Exam Question Report

Some frying pans have a coloured spot in the centre of the base. This spot shows when the pan is hot enough to cook food by changing colour. The material used for the spot:

A is smart   B is toxic
C melts at 30°C   D burns at 60°C

Answer: The answer is A.

How students answered
Some students got this one wrong. The key part of the question here is that the spot *changes its properties* (colour) when the conditions (temperature) change.

ResultsPlus Exam Question Report

Coolmax is a fabric that allows moisture from the surface of the skin to pass through it. Which of these is probably not made using coolmax?

A swimming shorts   B sports shirt
C motor cycle helmet lining   D socks

Answer: The correct answer is A.

How students answered
Two-thirds of students got this one wrong.

67% 0 marks

The question tells you that coolmax allows sweat to pass through it, so it is likely to be used when a person might get hot and sweaty. The only application in the list where people don't usually get sweaty is while swimming.

33% 1 mark

Test yourself

1. Write down the names of two modern materials that were:
   a. designed for their purpose
   b. discovered accidentally

2. Sympatex is a 'breathable' membrane used in many types of clothes. Sympatex is useful for these clothes because it:
   A allows oxygen to pass in and carbon dioxide to pass out
   B allows water vapour to pass out but stops water passing in
   C allows carbon dioxide to pass out but stops water passing in
   D allows oxygen to pass in and water vapour to pass out

3. a. What is the important property of a 'breathable' material?
   b. Why is Gore-tex® breathable?

4. Which material mentioned in this section would you use to make:
   a. gloves for wearing outdoors in the winter
   b. a rain-proof jacket
   c. a close-fitting gymnastics costume
   d. protective trousers for people using chain-saws?

5. Clare uses a lightweight tent on some of her walks. The poles of the tent are reinforced with fibres. Which of these fibres is likely to be used?
   A steel fibres that are strong and dense
   B Nomex fibres that are flame resistant
   C carbon fibres that are strong and light
   D Dacron fibres that provide good thermal insulation

8.2: Nanoparticles

- C1.b.8.6 Compare sizes of nanoparticles with conventionally produced materials
- C1.b.8.6 Describe the special properties nanoparticles have because of their size
- C1.b.8.6 Relate the size of nanoparticles to their uses
- C1.b.8.7 Discuss the risks and uncertainties of nanotechnologies
- C1.b.8.7 Discuss how nanotechnology is presented in the media

Need more help?
For more on this topic, see pages 182–185.

Nanoparticles are extremely small particles. They are particles that are less than 100 nanometres (nm) across. (A nanometre is one-billionth of a metre.) They are a little bigger than atoms, but not much. They are too small to see, even with the most powerful microscopes.

Nanoparticles of various substances have always existed, but today scientists are making nanoparticles out of many different materials, because of their useful properties.

Words that include 'nano' are referring to very small particles. So nanotechnology is the use of nanoparticles to make things. A 'nanocomposite' is a material that combines nanoparticles with other materials.

A material may have different properties when it is made into nanoparticles from when it is used in bigger pieces. The molecules that make up the material are still the same – it is only the fact that the material is in much smaller pieces that makes the properties different.

edexcel key terms

nanocomposite A material that has nanoparticles used in combination with other materials.
nanoparticle A particle with a diameter of between 10 and 100 nanometres.
nanotechnology Technology built around the use of nanoparticles.

ResultsPlus Watch out!

Nanoparticles are *not* smart materials. They don't change their properties when the conditions change.

Sunscreens

Sunscreens are chemicals that you can apply to your skin to protect you from the ultraviolet rays in sunlight. They work because they contain chemicals such as titanium oxide, which reflects sunlight. Ordinary sunscreens contain particles up to 50 000 nm in diameter, and these particles make you look white when you put the sunscreen on. New versions of the sunscreens use nanoparticles of titanium oxide or zinc oxide. These don't reflect visible light, so they don't make your skin look white. However, they do still reflect or absorb UV light, so you are protected from sunburn.

Other uses

Some other uses of nanoparticles are:

- using iron nanoparticles to speed up the breakdown of oil spills and other pollutants
- using silver nanoparticles to clean kitchen surfaces or babies' bottles
- embedding clay nanoparticles in nylon fibres to make a nanocomposite material that is stronger than the nylon it is made from
- using carbon nanotubes in electronic devices.

Higher tier

Exam Question Report

A number of people are concerned about the risks of using nanoparticles. This is because:
A the particles are too small to see
B nanoparticles can behave differently to conventional-sized particles of the same substance
C nanoparticles did not exist until chemists invented them
D nanoparticles can make copies of themselves
Answer: The correct answer is B.

How students answered
Some students got this wrong because they picked A. A is a correct statement, but it doesn't explain why some people are concerned about using nanoparticles.

Risks and uncertainties

Nanoparticles of a substance have different properties from larger pieces of the substance. This means that even if a material is safe to use, nanoparticles made from that material may not be safe and need to be tested thoroughly before they are used.

Stories about nanoparticles sometimes appear in the media, usually as 'scare stories'. Such stories should give both sides of the argument, listing the benefits of nanotechnology as well as the possible risks. However, scare tactics tend to sell more newspapers than balanced stories, so often the coverage is not balanced.

Test yourself

1. Which of these statements about nanoparticles is true?
   A nanoparticles are more than 1 cm in diameter
   B nanoparticles do not contain atoms
   C nanoparticles are less than 100 nm in diameter
   D nanoparticles are smaller than individual atoms

2. Nanoparticles mixed with other materials are called:
   A emulsifiers   B nanocompounds
   C nanotubes   D nanocomposites

3. Why are nanoparticles of titanium oxide used in some sunscreens?

4. Nanotechnology is used to produce very small particles called nanoparticles. Nanoparticles of a given substance often have different properties from larger particles of the same substance. Which of these statements are correct?
   A Nano-sized particles existed before scientists started to make them using nanotechnology.
   B Scientists fully understand the risks involved in the use of nanotechnology.

5. Some glass has a metallic coating of nanoparticles that reflects heat from the Sun. Which statement is true?
   A The nanoparticles in the coating have the same properties as larger particles of the same metal.
   B The coating is transparent to visible light and to infrared radiation.
   C The coating lets through infrared radiation and reflects visible light.
   D The coating reflects infrared radiation and is transparent to visible light.

8.3: Alcoholic drinks

- C1.b.8.8 Describe how beer and wine can be made by fermentation
- C1.b.8.8 Describe how fermentation uses yeast to convert sugars to alcohol
- C1.b.8.9 Describe the effects of ethanol in alcoholic drinks on the human body
- C1.b.8.9 Discuss the social issues of drinking alcohol

Making alcoholic drinks

Alcoholic drinks are made by a process of fermentation. This process uses yeast to turn sugar into alcohol and carbon dioxide. The sugar must be in solution, and the mixture must be kept at a temperature of around 30°C. The carbon dioxide is given off as bubbles of gas. The type of alcohol found in alcoholic drinks is called ethanol.

sugar → alcohol + carbon dioxide

$$C_6H_{12}O_6 \rightarrow 2C_2H_5OH + 2CO_2$$

The taste of the alcoholic drink depends on what provided the sugar. For beers, the sugar is provided by boiling up barley with water. For wines, grape juice is used.

Fermentation eventually stops when all the sugar in the solution is used up. Wine has a higher concentration of alcohol than beer, because grape juice contains more sugar than the solution of barley in water. However, even with lots of sugar, a fermented drink will never get stronger than about 15% alcohol. This is because this concentration of alcohol kills off the yeast. Drinks (such as whisky) that have a higher percentage of alcohol than this have been made by distillation.

Alcoholic drinks are stored in sealed bottles or barrels, as oxygen can react with chemicals in the drink to spoil the taste.

Alcohol and the body

The short-term effects of drinking ethanol are to slow the reactions and affect judgement. If you drink more, it may make you:

- become emotional or aggressive
- lose your balance and coordination
- vomit
- faint (pass out)
- die (if you drink too much in one go).

Ethanol makes the body produce more urine, so you usually end up dehydrated after drinking. This gives you a hangover the next morning, with a headache and sometimes nausea and vomiting.

Long-term damage from drinking alcohol includes liver damage, heart disease and strokes, and an increased risk of some cancers.

Need more help?
For more on this topic, see pages 186–191.

edexcel key terms

alcohol A family of chemicals that can be made by fermenting sugars.
ethanol The chemical name of the type of alcohol in alcoholic drinks.
fermentation The process in which yeast turns sugar into alcohol and carbon dioxide. Used to make beer and wine.
sugar A sweet-tasting chemical found naturally in fruits.

Higher tier

ResultsPlus Watch out!

All alcoholic drinks are made by fermentation. For wine and beer, fermentation is the *only* process used. For stronger drinks such as whisky, vodka, etc., distillation is used *as well*.

GCSE 360 Science

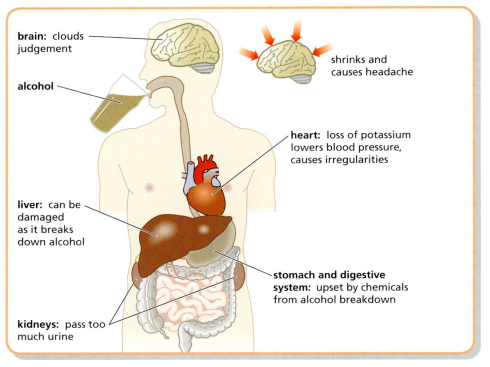

Safe drinking

Health advice for safe levels of drinking is based on 'units' of alcohol. One unit of alcohol is the amount contained in a small glass of wine, half a pint of beer, a single pub measure of spirits, or two-thirds of an alcopop bottle. The limits are 3–4 units per day for men, and 2–3 units per day for women. These limits are per day, and you cannot 'save them up' (for example, by having no alcohol for a week, then drinking 14 units in one go). Drinking a lot of alcohol at once is called binge drinking.

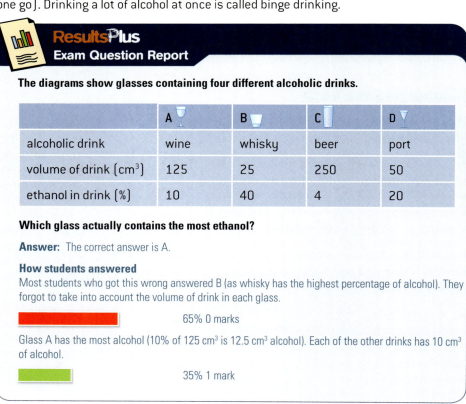

Designer Products 8

Social effects of drinking

People who binge drink are damaging their own health, but they also affect other people in different ways:

- city centres are littered and vandalised
- people can be attacked by drunks
- police are needed to keep order
- hospital casualty departments are overworked dealing with people suffering from the effects of alcohol
- drink-driving accidents kill or seriously injure over 3000 people every year.

Test yourself

1. **a** Write down three substances needed for fermentation.
   b Name the two products of fermentation.

2. **a** What is the maximum strength of a fermented drink such as beer or wine?
   b Why is this the maximum strength?
   c What process is used to make stronger drinks such as whisky?

3. Different alcoholic drinks contain different amounts of ethanol. The amount of ethanol in drinks can be measured in units of ethanol. Which of these drinks contains the smallest number of units in 290 cm^3 of the drink?

Type of drink	beer	whisky	lager	wine
Volume of drink (cm^3)	290	25	290	175
Units of ethanol	1	1	2	2

4. Bio-ethanol is a bio-fuel produced by fermentation of some crops. Three possible conditions for the production of bio-ethanol by fermentation are:

   A a temperature of 80°C
   B presence of yeast
   C presence of oxygen

   Which one or more of these conditions are necessary for a successful fermentation?

5. Write down three ways in which ethanol affects the human body.

6. What is meant by 'the social cost of drinking'?

8.4: Technology and food

> **Need more help?**
> For more on this topic, see pages 192–195.

- ✓ **C1.b.8.10** Explain what intelligent packaging is
- ✓ **C1.b.8.10** Explain how intelligent packaging can show whether food is fresh
- ✓ **C1.b.8.11** Describe how emulsifiers work
- ✓ **C1.b.8.11** Give examples of the use of emulsifiers in foods like mayonnaise

Emulsions

An emulsion is a mixture of two different liquids. Some liquids such as ethanoic acid and water mix together readily. A solution of ethanoic acid in water is vinegar. Other liquids (such as oil and vinegar) do not mix well. This is why you often have to shake a bottle of salad dressing before you use it.

Mayonnaise is a mixture of oil and vinegar, plus an emulsifier that stops the oil and vinegar separating after they have been mixed. Milk is another emulsion, of oil droplets in water.

An emulsifier consists of long molecules with a hydrophilic ('water-loving') end and a hydrophobic ('water-hating') end. In the mayonnaise example, the hydrophilic end is attracted to the vinegar droplets, and the hydrophobic end sticks out into the surrounding oil. This stops the droplets of vinegar combining, and so it stops the mixture separating. Soaps work in a similar way.

> **edexcel key terms**
>
> **emulsifier** A chemical that stops the oil and water parts of an emulsion from separating.
> **hydrophilic** 'Water-loving' – chemicals that dissolve or mix completely with water.
> **hydrophobic** 'Water-hating' – chemicals that do not mix with water.

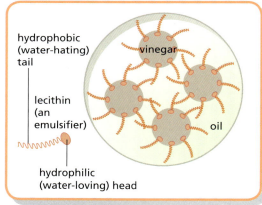

How an emulsifier works.

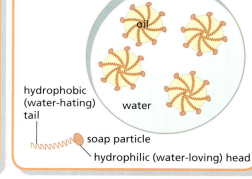

How soap works.

Storing food

Food goes bad when microbes grow in it. Microbes need a supply of oxygen to allow them to grow, so if oxygen can be kept away from the food, the food will last for longer. This is why some foods, such as crisps, are packed in bags filled with nitrogen. Nitrogen is an inert gas, so it won't react with any of the ingredients in the food. Carbon dioxide can also be used. Keeping oxygen away from the fats in food stops the fat going rancid.

Food can also be kept fresh for longer by keeping it cold, or drying it. Microbes need warmth and water, as well as oxygen, for growth. We can stop them growing by removing any one of these three requirements.

Intelligent packaging

Intelligent packaging is packaging that changes depending on how the food is kept. For example, many fresh foods need to be kept cool to make sure that any microbes in them do not reproduce. A spot made of a material that changes colour permanently if it gets to a temperature of 10°C could be stuck onto the packaging. If the spot had changed colour, a shopper would know not to buy the food because it had not been kept cold.

Fruits and vegetables give off various gases as they ripen. Intelligent packaging could be made from a material that changes colour if these gases are detected, showing that the food is ready to eat.

Eventually we may be able to have microchips on food packaging, which could continuously monitor the condition of the food, and even transmit details to a special microwave oven so that the oven can automatically cook the food properly.

ResultsPlus
Exam Question Report

Food packaging that has a spot that changes colour when the food is no longer fresh enough to eat is being developed. The use of this spot means the packaging is:
A colour fast
B microbe resistant
C cool
D intelligent
Answer: The correct answer is D.
How students answered

Over half of the students thought that the spot made the packaging microbe-resistant (B). All the spot does is tell the user *when* the food is no longer fit to eat. It doesn't stop the food going bad.

ResultsPlus
Exam tip

Remember that 'intelligent' packaging, just like 'smart' materials, *changes* when the conditions change.

Test yourself

1. a What is an emulsion?
   b What are the two main ingredients in mayonnaise?
   c Why is an emulsifier needed in mayonnaise?
2. What do the words 'hydrophobic' and 'hydrophilic' mean?
3. Decayed food can cause illness. Scientists have developed a food-wrapping material that will remove a gas from the contents of the package. The gas that must be removed to prevent the food decaying is:
   A nitrogen   B oxygen   C argon   D carbon monoxide
4. Why is some food packed in sealed bags filled with nitrogen?
5. Why is some food refrigerated to make it keep longer?
6. Why does a moist cake go mouldy faster than a packet of dry biscuits?

9.1: Current and voltage

- **P1.a.9.5** Explain how a change in the resistance in a series circuit changes the current
- **P1.a.9.5** Explain how a change in the resistance in a parallel circuit changes the current
- **P1.a.9.8** Recall that current is a rate of flow of negatively charged electrons, which can be measured by an ammeter placed in series in a circuit
- **P1.a.9.10** Use data to explain how current varies with voltage for fixed value resistors and filament lamps
- **P1.a.9.10** Describe how to investigate how the current varies with the voltage for fixed value resistors of filament lamps
- **P1.a.9.11** Use the relationship between the voltage, current and resistance: $V = I \times R$

Need more help? For more on this topic, see pages 204–205, 208–209.

edexcel key terms

ammeter A device used to measure electrical current.
current The flow of charge around a circuit. The units are amps (A) or milliamps (mA).
parallel circuit A circuit with two or more branches that split up and join up again.
potential difference Another name for voltage.
resistance A measure of how difficult it is for electricity to flow around a circuit. The unit is the ohm (Ω).
resistor An electrical component that restricts the flow of current.
series circuit A circuit where all the components are connected together in one loop.
voltage The difference in electrical energy between two points, which makes a current flow. The units are volts (V) or millivolts (mV).

Electric current is a flow of negatively charged particles called electrons. These flow from the negative terminal of a cell or battery, and back into the positive terminal.

When electricity was first discovered, people didn't know that electrons existed, and said that the current flows from the positive terminal of a cell to the negative terminal. This is called 'conventional current', and is the 'direction' of the current used when you are thinking about generators or motors.

Measuring electricity

The size of a current is measured using an ammeter. This is placed in series with other components in a circuit. The unit for current is the amp (A).

The voltage is a measure of the energy carried by each amp of current, and is measured using a voltmeter. This is connected in parallel with a component. The unit for voltage is the volt (V).

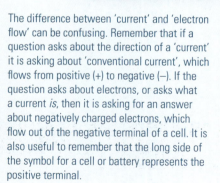

ResultsPlus — Watch out!

The difference between 'current' and 'electron flow' can be confusing. Remember that if a question asks about the direction of a 'current' it is asking about 'conventional current', which flows from positive (+) to negative (−). If the question asks about electrons, or asks what a current *is*, then it is asking for an answer about negatively charged electrons, which flow out of the negative terminal of a cell. It is also useful to remember that the long side of the symbol for a cell or battery represents the positive terminal.

ResultsPlus — Watch out!

Remember that an ammeter is always placed in the main part of a series circuit, so the same current flows through the ammeter as through all the other components.

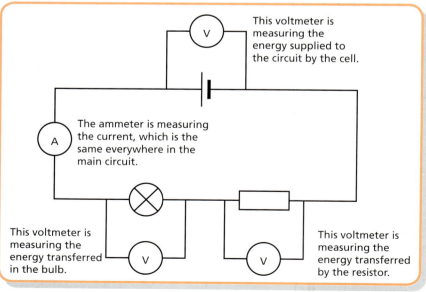

Ammeters and voltmeters.

Resistance

The size of the current in a circuit depends on the voltage of the cell and on the resistance in the circuit. The resistance is a measure of how hard it is for current to flow around a circuit. The unit for resistance is the ohm (Ω).

- The higher the voltage of the cell, the higher the current.
- The bigger the resistance in a circuit, the lower the current.

ResultsPlus
Watch out!

A lot of students get this wrong. Remember: resistance up, current down!

Higher tier

In any circuit, if the total resistance increases the current goes down. Adding a resistor to a series circuit increases the resistance. However, adding a resistor in parallel decreases the overall resistance of the circuit, as the current now has an alternative path to flow through.

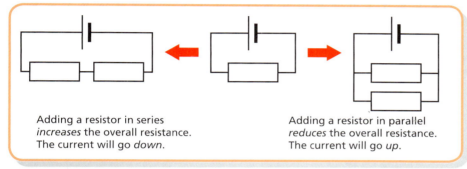

Adding a resistor in series *increases* the overall resistance. The current will go *down*.

Adding a resistor in parallel *reduces* the overall resistance. The current will go *up*.

Adding resistors to a circuit.

In a parallel circuit, the current splits up, so the current through the individual branches of the circuit will depend on the resistance in each branch.

For a fixed resistance, a graph of current against voltage is a straight line.

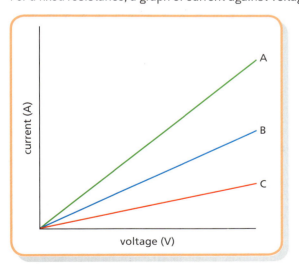

ResultsPlus
Watch out!

Remember that a straight line on a current/voltage graph shows that the resistance is *constant*.

A has the lowest resistance. C has the highest resistance. The shallower the line, the higher the resistance.

You can calculate the current, voltage or resistance in a circuit using this formula:

voltage (V) = current (A) × resistance (Ω)

ResultsPlus — Exam tip

You don't need to remember any formulae, as they will be given to you in the exam if you need them. But you *do* need to be able to use them, and you may be asked to rearrange them. Memorising formula triangles will help you with this.

I stands for current, V for voltage and R for resistance.

ResultsPlus — Watch out!

Be careful with the units. If you are given a current in milliamps (mA), you must convert it to amps first by dividing by 1000. Or you may be given a resistance in kilo-ohms (kΩ). Convert this to ohms first by multiplying by 1000.

Worked example

A current of 2 A flows through a 6 Ω resistor. What is the voltage across the resistor?

$$V = I \times R$$
$$= 2\,A \times 6\,\Omega$$
$$= 12\,V$$

Worked example

A circuit has a cell that provides 12 V, and a resistor with a resistance of 2 kΩ. What current flows in the circuit?

Convert kΩ into Ω: 2 kΩ = 2000 Ω

Rearrange the formula: $I = \dfrac{V}{R}$

$$= \dfrac{12\,V}{2000\,\Omega}$$
$$= 0.006\,A \text{ (or 6 mA)}$$

Test yourself

1. Draw a circuit diagram showing a cell, a bulb, an ammeter and a voltmeter, all in the correct places.
2. What is the unit for:
   a current
   b voltage
   c resistance?
3. Look at the first circuit diagram on page 104. Explain why only one ammeter is needed, but three voltmeters are useful.
4. Rajiv sets up a circuit like the first one on page 104. What will happen to the current if he:
   a increases the voltage of the cell
   b adds another resistor in series
   c adds a resistor in parallel to the one already there?
5. What voltage does Leanne need to use to make a 3 A current in a circuit with a total resistance of 12 Ω?
   A 0.25 V   B 3 V   C 4 V   D 36 V
6. A circuit is connected to the 230 V mains supply. The current in the circuit is 5 mA. What is the resistance of the circuit?

9.2: Changing resistance

- P1.a.9.6 Describe how the resistance of a light-dependent resistor (LDR) changes with light intensity
- P1.a.9.6 Describe how the resistance of a thermistor changes with a change of temperature
- P1.a.9.7 Describe applications depending on resistance change, such as controlling the exposure time of a digital camera
- P1.a.9.10 Use data to explain how current varies with voltage for fixed value resistors and filament lamps
- P1.a.9.10 Describe how to investigate how the current varies with the voltage for fixed value resistors or filament lamps

Need more help?
For more on this topic, see pages 210–211, 214–217.

The relationship $V = IR$ applies when the resistance of a component does not change. The resistance of some components *can* change. These components are used to control the current in electric circuits.

edexcel key terms

light-dependent resistor (LDR) A resistor whose resistance changes with light intensity.
thermistor A resistor whose resistance changes with temperature.

Investigating resistance

You can use a circuit like this to investigate the change in current and voltage for different kinds of resistor. You use the variable resistor to change the voltage, and write down the current at different voltages.

The graph shows the results of an investigation into the resistance of a filament lamp.

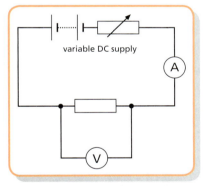

A circuit used to investigate resistance.

The point at 6 V has been ignored when drawing the line. It is an anomalous result (it doesn't fit the pattern), and is probably due to a mistake in reading the ammeter.

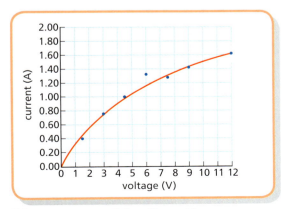

Voltage–current graph for a filament lamp.

107

You may be asked to calculate the resistance of a component from a graph. You do this by reading values from the graph and then using the formula V = IR to work out the resistance (see page 106).

Worked example

What is the resistance of the filament lamp when the voltage is 2 V?

At 2 V the current is approximately 0.55 A.

$$V = I \times R, \text{ so } R = \frac{V}{I}$$
$$= \frac{2 \text{ V}}{0.55 \text{ A}}$$
$$= 3.6 \text{ }\Omega$$

Filament lamp

The resistance of a filament lamp (such as a normal light bulb) increases as the voltage across it increases. This is because a higher voltage makes a larger current flow, which makes the wire in the lamp get hotter. The hotter the wire, the higher the resistance.

Light dependent resistor (LDR)

An LDR is a type of resistor that responds to changes in light intensity. The brighter the light that falls on it, the more energy is available to release electrons within the material, and the lower the resistance.

LDRs can be used in many types of equipment where there is a need to monitor the light intensity, such as in digital cameras or automatic systems that turn lights on when it gets dark. The flow diagram shows how an LDR can be used to make a buzzer get louder when the light gets brighter.

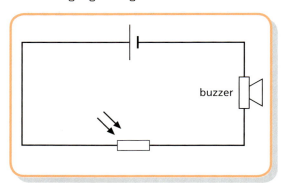

An LDR in a circuit with a buzzer.

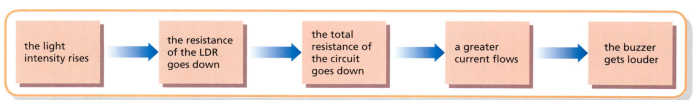

Flow diagram to show why the buzzer gets louder.

ResultsPlus Exam tip

In an exam, over half of higher-tier students got a question like this wrong. It is just a matter of reading numbers from the graph and remembering how to rearrange the formula (which will be given to you in the exam).

ResultsPlus Watch out!

Over 60% of students in one exam didn't know how the resistance of an LDR is affected by intensity of light. Remember: brighter light = lower resistance.

Thermistor

A thermistor is a type of resistor that responds to temperature. The higher the temperature, the lower its resistance. Thermistors can be used as sensors anywhere where the temperature needs to be monitored.

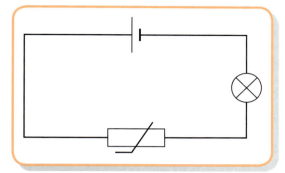

A thermistor in a circuit with a lamp.

There are actually two types of thermistor. In one type, the resistance gets lower when the temperature gets higher. In the other type, the resistance gets higher when the temperature gets higher (just like in a filament lamp). You only need to know about the first kind for the exam.

Test yourself

1. Look at the graph for the filament lamp on page 107. How can you tell just by looking at the graph that the resistance increases as the voltage increases? Pick the best answer.
   A The graph is curved.
   B The slope of the line is shallow at low voltages.
   C The slope of the line is shallow at higher voltages.
   D The slope of the line is steep at higher voltages.

2. Why does the resistance of a filament lamp increase when the voltage is increased?

3. What happens to the resistance of:
   a a thermistor when it gets colder
   b an LDR when the light gets dimmer?

4. Look at the flow diagram for the LDR. Draw a similar diagram for the circuit with a lamp and thermistor, to explain what will happen if the temperature of the thermistor rises.

5. Look at the graph for the filament lamp. What is the resistance of the lamp when the voltage is 12 V?

Need more help? For more on this topic, see pages 212–213.

9.3: Cells

- P1.a.9.9 Recall that a battery's stated capacity is given in terms of amp-hours
- P1.a.9.9 Use the capacity in amp-hours to predict the number of hours a battery should last when supplying a given current
- P1.a.9.12 Identify different battery types
- P1.a.9.12 Investigate the voltage and current output from dry or rechargeable cells
- P1.a.9.12 Discuss the advantages/disadvantages of battery technology including considerations of their cost, performance and impact on the environment

edexcel key terms

ampere-hours (amp-hours) The units for measuring battery capacity.
battery A collection of more than one cell connected together.
battery capacity A measure of the amount of energy that a cell or battery can store. The unit for capacity is the ampere-hour (or amp-hour).
dry cell The most common type of cell, which cannot be recharged. The voltage is produced by a chemical reaction inside the cell.
rechargeable A type of cell or battery that can be used many times.

Cells are very useful for powering portable appliances such as mobile phones and cameras. Two or more cells used together in series is called a battery. You can work out the voltage of the battery by adding up the voltages of the cells.

There are different types of cell and battery:

- A 'dry cell' is a normal cell that you might use in a torch or bicycle lamp. Chemicals inside the cell produce electricity when the cell is part of a circuit.
- Rechargeable batteries can be recharged, so they can be reused over and over again.
- 'Wet cell' batteries (or 'lead-acid' batteries) are used in cars. They contain acid and metal plates. These batteries can be recharged many times.

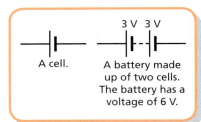

Cells and batteries.

Battery capacity

Different appliances need different amounts of current. The time a battery will last inside an appliance depends on the current used. The capacity of a battery is measured in amp-hours.

A battery with a capacity of 20 amp-hours will last for:

- 20 hours if the current used is 1 A
- 10 hours if the current used is 2 A
- 40 hours if the current used is 0.5 A.

You can work out how long a battery will last using this formula:

$$\text{time (hours)} = \frac{\text{battery capacity (amp-hours)}}{\text{current (amps)}}$$

Remember that when connecting cells to produce a higher voltage, you connect them end to end as shown in the diagram of the 6 V battery.

Worked example

A fully charged battery runs down in 6 hours. It supplies an average current of 0.3 A. What is the capacity of the battery?

capacity = time × current
= 6 hours × 0.3 A
= 1.8 amp-hours

Make sure you learn the unit for battery capacity. In a recent exam only 29% of students could remember that the unit is the amp-hour.

A battery cannot provide the same voltage throughout its 'life'. The voltage of a dry cell decreases gradually as the chemicals inside are used up. The voltage of a rechargeable cell stays constant for most of its life but then drops quickly as the charge runs out.

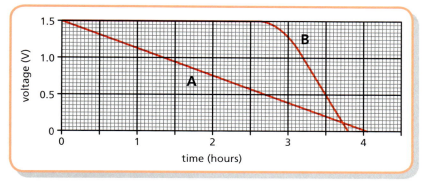

Voltage provided by a dry cell (A) and a rechargeable cell (B).

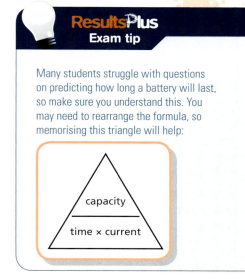

Exam tip

Many students struggle with questions on predicting how long a battery will last, so make sure you understand this. You may need to rearrange the formula, so memorising this triangle will help:

Advantages and disadvantages

The table shows some of the advantages and disadvantages of the two main types of cell.

Cell	Advantages	Disadvantages
Dry cell	• can often store more energy than a rechargeable cell • cheaper than rechargeable cells	• can only be used once • can cause pollution if not disposed of properly
Rechargeable cell	• provides a constant voltage for most of its life • can be reused many times	• often can't store as much energy as a dry cell • needs a recharging unit • costs more than dry cells • can cause pollution if not disposed of properly

Test yourself

1. Draw the symbol for a cell and mark the positive side.

2. Bilal has some 1.5 V cells. He needs a 6 V supply for his circuit. How can he use his cells to produce 6 V? Draw a diagram to illustrate your answer.

3. What kind of cell is usually used inside mobile phones?

4. What is meant by the 'capacity' of a battery?

5. A battery has a capacity of 15 amp-hours. How long will it last if the current is 0.5 A?
   A 3 hours   B 7.5 hours   C 30 hours   D 75 hours

6. An 80 amp-hour battery runs down in 25 hours. What current has it been supplying?

7. Polly says: 'Rechargeable cells are cheaper in the long run.' Explain this statement.

Need more help?
For more on this topic, see pages 202–207.

9.4: Generating current

- **P1.a.9.1** Describe the difference between alternating current and direct current
- **P1.a.9.2** Recall that batteries and solar cells are both sources of direct current
- **P1.a.9.3** Describe how to produce an electric current by rotating a magnet in a coil of wire, as in a dynamo
- **P1.a.9.4** List the factors that affect the direction of an induced voltage
- **P1.a.9.4** List the factors that affect the size of an induced voltage

Cells and solar cells produce direct current (DC). The current is in the same direction all the time. The mains electricity supply is alternating current (AC), where the direction of the current changes many times each second.

edexcel key terms

dynamo A device used to generate electricity by rotating a magnet inside a coil of wire.
magnet Any object that has a magnetic field around it.
solar cell Something that converts energy from light into electricity.

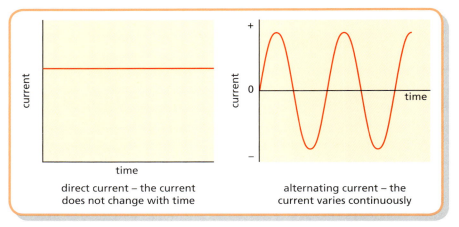

Direct current and alternating current.

Generating current

There is a current whenever a coil is moved relative to a magnetic field. The diagram below shows the simplest way this can happen. It doesn't matter if the magnet is moving or the coil. There is only a current while the magnet and coil are moving relative to one another.

The direction of the current will change if:

- the direction of the magnetic field is changed (e.g. by turning the magnet around)
- the magnet is moved in the opposite direction.

A larger current can be induced by:

- using a magnet with a stronger magnetic field
- moving the magnet (or the coil) faster
- putting more turns of wire on the coil
- adding a soft iron core.

ResultsPlus Watch out!

Lots of students lose marks because they can't remember that solar cells and batteries are sources of direct current. Even more lose marks because they can't interpret graphs of current against time. Remember, a *horizontal line* means *direct current*, which must have come from a *solar cell* or a *battery*.

ResultsPlus Watch out!

The important feature of alternating current is that it changes direction, so a graph showing alternating current will have positive and negative sections. The line on the graph may not always be a smooth curve, but it will *always* go above and below the horizontal axis.

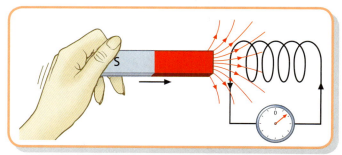

Generating a current with a coil and magnetic field.

Producing and Measuring Electricity

Generators have a moving coil of wire inside a magnetic field. This has the same effect as moving a bar magnet in and out of a coil. Generators produce alternating current. They convert kinetic energy into electrical energy.

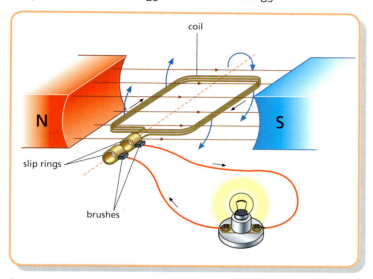

A generator.

Exam Question Report

The useful energy change in a generator is:
A electrical energy → kinetic energy
B electrical energy → sound and thermal energy
C kinetic energy → sound and thermal energy
D kinetic energy → electrical energy
Answer: The correct answer is D.

How students answered
Two-thirds of students got this wrong.

67% 0 marks

The generator is moving so it has kinetic energy. The useful energy produced by a generator is electrical energy. This gives you a choice between A and D, and the form of energy you start with is always on the left.

33% 1 mark

Test yourself

1 Describe the difference between direct current and alternating current.

2 Name two things that produce direct current.

3 The graph shows the current produced by a dynamo (a small generator used on a bicycle). The voltage at 0.028 is about:
  A −1.6V   B −1.3V
  C 1.3V   D 1.6V

4 The type of voltage shown in the graph is alternating because:
  A the voltage decreases at first
  B the greatest time shown is 0.05 s
  C the voltage goes above and below 0 V
  D the pattern repeats regularly with time

5 The bicycle with the dynamo speeds up. Describe how the graph of current against time will look different (or make a sketch to explain). (*Hint:* there are two things that will change.)

6 Write down three ways of increasing the size of the current produced by a generator.

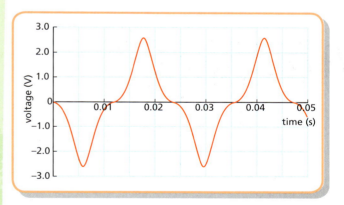

GCSE 360 Science

> **Need more help?**
> For more on this topic, see pages 202–203, 211, 218–219.

9.5: Computers and new technologies

- P1.a.9.13 Discuss the impact that electricity has had on making the modern world
- P1.a.9.13 Discuss the impact that the electric telephone has had on making the modern world
- P1.a.9.15 Use data relating the size of electric circuits to the processing speed of computers
- P1.a.9.16 Explain how to use ICT to collect and display data from electric circuits for analysis
- P1.a.9.16 Compare the use of ICT to collect and display data with traditional methods in terms of reliability and validity of data
- P1.a.9.15 Suggest future applications of computers
- P1.a.9.14 Explain what is meant by superconductivity
- P1.a.9.14 Explain how a new technology, such as Maglev trains, develops as a result of scientific advances, such as the discovery of superconductivity

edexcel key terms

superconductivity The property of conducting electricity very well because of an extremely low resistance.

Electricity and the modern world

The first cell was built in about 1800 but it wasn't until power stations were built and electricity was supplied to homes that it had a big effect on people's lives. Before the availability of mains electricity there were no electric lights, and no labour-saving devices such as electric washing machines and vacuum cleaners. People had to shop for food nearly every day because there were no fridges to keep food fresh. Electricity also made telephones possible. Before telephones were invented many messages had to be carried from place to place by hand.

ResultsPlus Exam tip

Students often have difficulty with the meanings of words used to evaluate data. Remember these definitions:
accurate – a value that is close to the true or accepted value (an accepted value is one found and checked by many scientists and published in data tables or textbooks).
reliable – data you can trust, that would be the same (or very close) if you repeated the experiment (you can improve reliability by repeating your measurements).
valid – data that are relevant to the investigation you are doing, and obtained using a fair test (only changing one variable).

Using ICT in science

Many science investigations use ICT to improve their accuracy and reliability. Computers and sensors can be used to make measurements very quickly or over long periods of time, and can also record values more accurately than a human reading a dial and writing the number down.

For example, computers can be used to:

- record the voltage in a component 100 times a second, to see how the voltage changes with time
- record the voltage provided by a cell in a circuit over a period of 10 hours (a human *could* do this, but it would be very boring!).

Data recorded using ICT can easily be displayed as a graph, making it easier to see patterns in the data. The data can also be transferred to a spreadsheet, so that calculations can be carried out.

Producing and Measuring Electricity

Computers and the future

The size of computers has got smaller and smaller as computer technology has developed. The very first computers filled whole rooms, and had less processing power than a modern mobile phone. Today, the 'chips' that do the processing inside a computer are smaller than a fingernail. This small size means that it doesn't take as long for signals to travel from one part of the processor to another, so computing speeds have also increased greatly.

Today, computers are in many different machines, including:

- washing machines
- cars, to control fuel use, automatic wipers, etc.
- TVs and digital radios.

In the future, computers may also be used to monitor all sorts of things, from health to the stocks of food in your cupboard or fridge.

Superconductivity

Scientists are investigating new materials all the time. Sometimes this is to find a new material for a particular purpose, but sometimes it is just to find out more about how materials work or to investigate other aspects of physics or chemistry.

One such discovery was superconductivity. This happens when certain materials are cooled to almost absolute zero and their electrical resistance becomes zero. The first superconducting materials discovered were not very practical, as materials in everyday use can't be made so cold. However, other materials have been discovered that are superconductors at higher temperatures.

Superconducting materials have made it possible to produce very powerful electromagnets. These can be used in things like Maglev trains (which hover just above the track, making them faster, quieter and smoother than ordinary trains).

Higher tier

Test yourself

1. Write down three ways in which electricity has had an impact on our lives.
2. Suggest two different ways in which ICT can help in collecting data from an investigation.
3. How can using ICT in an investigation give you better results? Explain in as much detail as you can.
4. Write down three different things that would not be possible without computers.
5. Give one reason why computers work faster today than they did 30 years ago.
6. Suggest one new thing that computers might be used for in the future.
7. What is a superconductor?
8. How have superconductors made Maglev trains possible?

10.1: Renewable energy resources

- P1.a.10.1 Describe some different forms of renewable energy
- P1.a.10.1 Evaluate whether solar power can meet the UK's future electricity needs
- P1.a.10.1 Evaluate whether wind power can meet the UK's future electricity needs
- P1.a.10.8 Interpret data about the efficiency of solar cells
- P1.a.10.8 Suggest why solar cells are not yet in widespread use

Need more help? For more on this topic, see pages 226–227, 242–243.

edexcel key terms

efficiency A measure of how good something is at turning energy from one form into another useful form.
electricity The energy involved when charged particles flow from one point to another.
solar cell Something that converts energy from light into electricity.
solar power The energy that comes to us from the Sun.
wind power The energy that can be obtained from the wind using wind turbines.

Renewable energy resources will not run out, and produce far less pollution than non-renewable resources such as fossil fuels. There are many different forms of renewable energy resources, most of which produce electricity.

Solar panels are used to heat water. In some places, giant solar power stations use mirrors to focus sunlight and produce steam, which can then be used to drive generators.

Wind turbines use kinetic energy in the wind to turn generators.

Water can be used as a renewable resource in many ways:

- hydroelectricity is generated using water falling from reservoirs in the hills
- tidal barrages can be built across estuaries to trap water at high tide and then let it run out through turbines, which drive generators
- waves can be used to generate electricity
- turbines can be put under water where tidal currents flow (a bit like wind turbines, but using moving water instead of moving air).

Geothermal power uses water pumped into hot rocks beneath the ground. The hot water can be used for heating or, if it is hot enough, to drive generators to produce electricity.

Biomass fuels are either crops grown to be burned in power stations, or gases produced when animal or plant waste rots or ferments. The gases can be burned to provide heat or to generate electricity.

Using wind and solar power

At present only a very small percentage of the UK's electricity is generated using renewable resources. There are two reasons for this:

- at present we can't generate *enough* electricity to meet the demand
- the supply of electricity from renewable resources is not continuous, as the Sun doesn't shine at night or in bad weather, and the winds vary.

We would need huge areas of land or sea to be covered in wind turbines and/or solar cells to produce enough electricity to meet our needs. Even if we did this, there's no easy way to store electricity, so wind and solar power would have to be backed up by other resources.

Solar cells available today only convert around 20% of the light energy falling on them into electrical energy. Scientists are developing new materials that will make solar cells more efficient, so that more electricity can be produced from the same area of cells.

Solar cells are expensive, and it would take a very large area to produce enough electricity for a house. The householder would also need to buy equipment to convert DC to AC to allow them to sell spare electricity to the National Grid. All this means that the payback time after installing solar panels is many years. The payback time is how long it takes to save the amount of money on electricity bills that you spent on buying the panels and other equipment. You would still need to buy electricity at night, or invest in rechargeable batteries that would be charged up during the day.

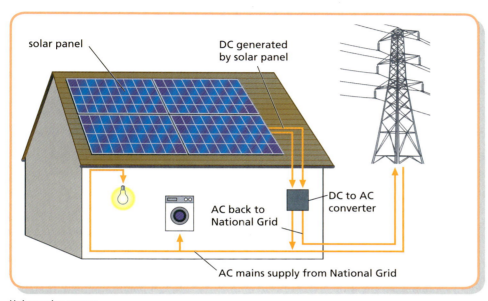

Using solar power.

ResultsPlus Watch out!

In one exam, around one-third of students lost marks because they thought that solar cells would only be widely used when their efficiency was almost 100%. There are many reasons why solar cells are not in widespread use today, but cost is likely to be the most important reason.

ResultsPlus Watch out!

Remember that solar cells only work during the day when there is light – they don't work at night.

Test yourself

1. Write down four ways in which water can be used as a renewable energy resource to generate electricity.

2. Write down three renewable energy resources that can be used to provide heating.

3. A solar cell obtains its energy from:
   - A thermal (heat) energy
   - B light energy
   - C chemical energy
   - D tidal energy

4. A homeowner buys a small wind turbine and some solar cells.
   a. Explain why these things will not provide a continuous supply of electricity.
   b. How could the homeowner obtain a continuous electricity supply?

Need more help?
For more on this topic, see pages 228–229, 244–245.

10.2: Energy and society

- P1.a.10.1 Evaluate the economic impact of different forms of renewable energy
- P1.a.10.1 Evaluate the environmental impact of different forms of renewable energy
- P1.a.10.1 Evaluate the social impact of different forms of renewable energy
- P1.a.10.2 Evaluate the possible benefits and drawbacks of implementing technology such as a new National Grid for distribution of electricity
- P1.a.10.3 Describe how scientific ideas change over time, such as the medical uses of electricity

Impacts of renewable resources

The possible impacts of different renewable resources can be considered in different ways.

All renewable resources need some kind of machinery — wind turbines, solar cells, a tidal barrage, a hydroelectric power station and dam, etc. This is why renewable energy resources are not free — we don't have to pay for the wind or the sunlight, but we do need to pay for the machinery to turn these energy resources into electricity.

Economic impacts include the cost of installing these things, how this money is to be found, and how much money might be saved by using renewable resources. All forms of renewable resources will have economic impacts.

Different renewable resources have different environmental impacts. Any resource that involves flooding an area (such as hydroelectricity or tidal power) will affect wildlife habitats. There is some evidence that wind turbines may kill birds, and they produce some noise pollution. On the other hand, renewable resources produce far less pollution than non-renewable resources.

Social impacts include wind turbines spoiling people's view of the countryside, but also include advantages such as the creation of jobs if new renewable resources are being introduced.

Wind turbines can spoil the view.

Renewable resources can have very different social and economic impacts in the developing world. In some places there is no access to mains electricity, so installing solar cells or wind turbines can provide electricity to people for the first time. This allows clinics to keep medicines safely, and provide lighting without the need for oil lamps or other sources.

New technologies

Mains electricity in the UK is distributed using the National Grid. This was set up to transfer power from a few large power stations to most of the users in the country. The National Grid is not ideal for taking small amounts of power from lots of renewable supplies and distributing it. However, it would cost so much money to start again with a new grid that this will probably never happen. The costs outweigh the benefits.

The situation is not the same in other countries, particularly in the developing world, where there may not be an existing grid. In this case, the building of a new grid for electricity distribution could transform the country, allowing faster development. But it could also have negative effects on the environment if it was not planned carefully, and there may be safety issues if people aren't educated about the potential dangers of high-voltage electricity.

Electricity and medicine

The invention of electrical generators and machines that run on electricity has allowed great advances in medicine. Electrical machines can be used for scanning the inside of the body, measuring tiny electrical currents made by our hearts, and to start failing hearts.

As computer chips and other technologies get smaller and smaller, it will become possible to implant tiny machines inside people to control or monitor their symptoms or to automatically supply drugs when they are needed.

Higher tier

Test yourself

1. Describe two ways in which renewable resources may affect the environment.
2. Why might people not want a wind farm to be built near where they live?
3. What economic and social benefits could a tidal barrage have?
4. The wind is free, so why do we need to pay for electricity generated using the wind?
5. What are some of the advantages and disadvantages of installing a new National Grid:
   a in the UK
   b in a country in the developing world?
6. Write down three medical advances made possible by electricity.

Need more help?
For more on this topic, see pages 234–235, 238–239.

10.3: Power and cost

- **P1.a.10.5** Recall that electrical power is the rate of transfer of electrical energy
- **P1.a.10.6** Use power = current × voltage to calculate electrical power
- **P1.a.10.9** Use the equation cost = power × time × cost of 1 kWh, where power is measured in kilowatts and time is measured in hours

edexcel key terms

energy Whenever something happens, energy is involved. It can exist in many different forms. It is measured in joules (J) or kilowatt-hours (kWh).
power A measure of how quickly something converts energy from one form to another. The units are watts (W) or kilowatts (kW).
voltage The difference in electrical energy between two points, which makes a current flow. The units are volts (V) or millivolts (mV).

Electrical power

Power is a way of saying *how fast* a certain amount of energy is transferred. It is a *rate* of energy transfer. The unit for power is the watt (W) or kilowatt (kW). One watt is equivalent to 1 joule of energy being transferred each second.

The power of an electrical appliance can be calculated using this formula:

power (W) = current (A) × voltage (V)

ResultsPlus Watch out!

More than half the students in one exam thought that power was the amount of energy transferred. Remember that it is the *rate* at which energy is transferred. Remembering that 1 watt = 1 joule/second should help you to recall this fact.

ResultsPlus Exam tip

You don't need to remember any formulae, as they will be given to you in the exam if you need them. But you *do* need to be able to use them, and you may be asked to rearrange them. Memorising formula triangles will help you with this. (Remember that I stands for current.)

Worked example

A 2 kW kettle uses mains electricity (230 V). What current flows in the kettle?

Convert kW to W: 2 kW = 2000 W

$$\text{current} = \frac{\text{power}}{\text{voltage}} = \frac{2000\ \text{W}}{230\ \text{V}} = 8.7\ \text{A}$$

ResultsPlus Watch out!

Be careful with the units. In the formula for power, current and voltage, the power must be in watts. If you are given a power in kilowatts (kW), you must convert it to watts first by multiplying by 1000.

Paying for electricity

Electricity companies charge the consumer for the amount of energy used. Because each household uses a huge number of joules of energy each year, electricity companies use a larger unit for energy, called a kilowatt-hour. A kilowatt-hour is the amount of energy used by a 1 kW appliance in 1 hour.

You can work out the cost of using an appliance using this formula:

cost (p) = power (kW) × time (h) × cost of 1 kWh (p/kWh)

Worked example

Joe's washing machine has an average power rating of 500 W. His electricity costs 10p for one kilowatt-hour. How long can he use the washing machine for a cost of 50p?

Remember to convert the units: 500 W = 0.5 kW

$$\text{time} = \frac{\text{cost}}{\text{power} \times \text{cost of 1 kWh}}$$

$$= \frac{50\text{p}}{0.5\text{ kW} \times 10\text{p}}$$

$$= 10 \text{ hours}$$

ResultsPlus
Exam tip

The different units used in the two formulae for electrical power can be a bit confusing. You need to remember that:
- the unit is the **watt** if you are using the formula for power, voltage and current
- the unit is the **kilowatt** if you are using the formula for cost.

ResultsPlus
Exam Question Report

The power of a heater in Alan's fish tank is 50 W (0.05 kW). Electricity costs 20p per kWh. What is the cost of using the heater continuously for 2 hours?

A 2p   **B** 5p   **C** 50p   **D** 2000p

Answer: The correct answer is A.

How students answered

Half of the students answering this question chose answer D, because they had used the power in watts in their calculation, instead of the power in kilowatts.

It helps if you think about what your answer means in questions like this. 2000p is £20, which means that Alan would be paying £10 *per hour* to keep his fish tank warm. This is very expensive!

Test yourself

1. What does 'electrical power' mean?
2. What is the unit for electrical power?
3. A small motor uses a 12 V battery. The current in the motor is 2 A. What is the power of the motor?
4. The cost of 1 kWh is 10p. An oven has a power rating of 4 kW. How much does it cost to use the oven for two hours?
   A 10p   B 20p   C 40p   D 80p
5. An electronic device uses a 3 V battery, and the current is 30 mA. What is the power of the device?
6. A 0.3 W device uses a current of 50 mA. What voltage does it need?
7. It costs Jenny 11.25p to use a 1500 W hot air paint stripper for 30 minutes. How much is her electricity company charging per kWh?

Need more help?
For more on this topic, see pages 236–237, 240–241.

10.4: Efficiency

- P1.a.10.7 Explain what 'efficiency' means
- P1.a.10.7 Use the equation efficiency = $\dfrac{\text{useful output}}{\text{total input}} \times 100\%$
- P1.a.10.10 Discuss whether an energy efficiency measure, such as insulating a home, is cost-effective
- P1.a.10.10 Use data to compare energy efficiency measures

Efficiency

Efficiency is a way of saying how good something is at transferring energy. An efficient machine transfers most of the energy put into it into *useful* forms of output energy.

You can work out the efficiency using this formula:

$$\text{efficiency} = \frac{\text{useful output}}{\text{total input}} \times 100\%$$

You can measure the energies in J or kJ, as long as you use the same units for both numbers in the formula.

Worked example

A kettle uses 500 kJ of energy, but only transfers 400 kJ to the water inside it. What is the efficiency of the kettle?

$$\text{efficiency} = \frac{\text{useful putput}}{\text{total input}} \times 100\%$$

$$= \frac{400 \text{ kJ}}{500 \text{ kJ}} \times 100\%$$

$$= 80\%$$

Cost-effective efficiency measures

We should all be trying to use less energy, both to save money and to reduce the amount of carbon dioxide being put into the atmosphere by power stations. To work out which energy-saving measures will be cost-effective, you need to know:

- how much it will cost
- how much money it will save.

You can use this information to calculate the payback time (how long it takes to save the amount of money it cost to install the energy-saving measure). Cost-effective measures have shorter payback times.

Worked example

It costs £60 to insulate the hot water tank, and this will save you £15 a year on energy bills. What is the payback time?

If it saves £15 per year, it will save £30 after 2 years, £45 after 3 years and £60 after 4 years. The payback time is therefore 4 years.

edexcel key terms

efficiency A measure of how good something is at turning energy from one form into another useful form.
insulation Use of materials to help prevent the transfer of energy in the form of heat or electricity.

ResultsPlus Watch out!

Efficiency is given as a percentage, with no unit. The formula compares two energies, so the units cancel out. In one exam, only one quarter of the students knew that efficiency is not measured in V, J or W.

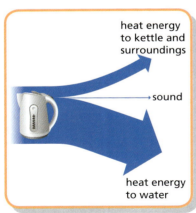

ResultsPlus Watch out!

A machine can never be more than 100% efficient. If your percentage comes out bigger than 100%, you have probably put the numbers into the formula the wrong way round.

You're in Charge 10

Exam Question Report

Selina makes four models of a house. They are the same except for the type of insulation. Selina puts a 500 ml beaker of warm water into each model house. She measures the temperature of the water in each beaker at the start and after 20 minutes.

model house	insulation used	temperature of water (°C) at start	temperature of water (°C) after 20 minutes
1	loft	84	54
2	double glazing	89	52
3	cavity wall	88	55
4	none	89	48

Which model saves the most energy?
A model 1 with loft insulation
B model 2 with double glazing
C model 3 with cavity wall insulation
D model 4 with no insulation
Answer: The correct answer is A.

How students answered
Two-thirds of students got this one wrong.

67% 0 marks

You need to work out which beaker of water has lost the least energy (had the smallest drop in temperature), so you need to work out the temperature *change* for each one. The one with the smallest temperature change is model 1, with the loft insulation.

33% 1 mark

Test yourself

1. An electric immersion heater uses 50 kJ of energy and transfers 42 kJ to the water. How efficient is it?

2. a. A light bulb uses 100 J of energy every second, but only gives out 9 J of useful light energy. What is its efficiency?
   b. An energy-saving bulb gives out the same amount of light energy, but only needs 18 J of energy per second. How efficient is this bulb?

3. Mr Jones installs draught-proofing. It costs £30 to do this, and he saves about £15 per year. What is the payback time?

4. Mrs Khan installs cavity-wall insulation, which costs her £300. Her heating bills go down from £400 to £300 per year. What is the payback time?

5. Look at your answers to questions 3 and 4. Which energy-saving measure is the most cost-effective?

Need more help?
For more on this topic, see pages 230–233.

10.5: Motors and safety

- P1.a.10.4   Label a diagram of a simple electric motor
- P1.a.10.4   Describe how a simple electric motor works
- P1.a.10.11   Explain how the earth wire, together with a fuse, provides protection for the user
- P1.a.10.12   Recall the advantages of a residual current circuit breaker (RCCB) and explain how it works

edexcel key terms

double insulation A device with a case made of an insulating material such as plastic. Double-insulated appliances do not have earth wires.

earth wire The green and yellow wire in a plug that helps to protect the user from an electrical shock.

fuse A device that melts and breaks a circuit if the current flowing is too large.

insulation Use of materials to help prevent the transfer of energy in the form of heat or electricity.

motor Something that converts other forms of energy into movement.

residual current circuit breaker (RCCB) A device to protect users of electrical equipment by shutting off the current if there is a fault.

Electric motors

An electric motor uses a magnetic field and a coil carrying direct current to produce movement. The size of the force produced by the motor can be increased by:

- increasing the current
- increasing the strength of the magnetic field
- using more turns of wire on the coil.

The direction in which the motor spins can be reversed by:

- reversing the direction of the current
- reversing the direction of the magnetic field.

(If you do *both* of these things there will be no change, as their effects will cancel each other out.)

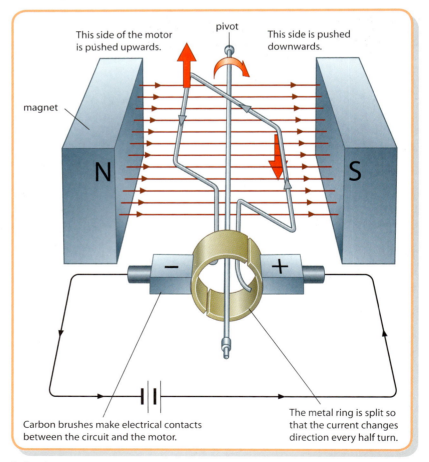

A simple motor.

Electricity and safety

Most appliances are connected to the mains with a three-pin plug. The plug includes a fuse and an earth wire to protect the user. If a fault develops in the appliance that makes the live wire touch the casing, anyone touching the appliance would get a shock. The earth wire provides a low-resistance path for the current to flow along safely. Because the earth wire has a low resistance, the current flowing in the appliance increases, and the fuse melts, cutting off the electricity.

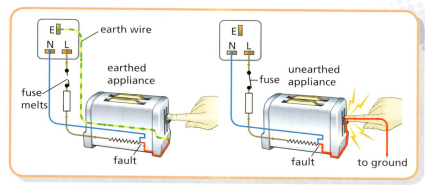

Safety measures in appliances.

Some appliances with plastic cases don't have an earth wire and fuse. They are referred to as double insulated. A fault can't make the casing live, because the casing is made from an insulating material.

ResultsPlus
Watch out!

In one exam, only about one-third of the students recalled that the earth wire and fuse are designed to protect the person, not the equipment. Remember that *both* the fuse and the earth wire are needed for protection.

Modern houses have residual current circuit breakers (RCCBs), which cut off the electricity if there is a fault. They work by comparing the current flowing into and out of the circuit (in the live and neutral wires). If these currents are different, then some of the current must be flowing where it shouldn't — in other words, a fault has occurred.

RCCBs have several advantages over fuses:

- the RCCB responds more quickly to a fault than a fuse
- the RCCB can be reset (a fuse must be replaced once it has 'blown').

ResultsPlus
Exam Question Report

Which row of the table gives the correct two advantages of an RCCB compared to a fuse?

	First advantage	Second advantage
A	an RCCB operates more quickly	an RCCB costs less to buy
B	an RCCB operates more quickly	an RCCB can be reset after the fault is corrected
C	with an RCCB, metal appliances do not need a neutral wire	an RCCB can be reset after the fault is corrected
D	with an RCCB, metal appliances do not need a neutral wire	an RCCB costs less to buy

Answer: The correct answer is B.

How students answered
Not many students got this question right. RCCBs cost more than fuses, so A and D are incorrect. There are no mains appliances that don't need a neutral wire, so C and D are incorrect. If you misread this and think about an earth wire, it is still not correct. *Double-insulated* appliances don't need an earth wire, but they don't need a fuse or RCCB either.

Test yourself

1. Look at the diagram of the motor. Which two parts are needed to create the force that makes the motor spin?
2. What will happen to the speed of the motor if you:
   a. make the magnets weaker
   b. put more turns of wire on the coil?
3. What will happen to the direction in which the motor spins if you:
   a. swap the magnets over
   b. swap the magnets *and* the connections to the DC power supply?
4. a. Why do most mains appliances have an earth wire and a fuse?
   b. Explain how they work.
5. What is a double-insulated appliance?
6. Describe how an RCCB works.
7. What are the advantages of an RCCB compared to a fuse?

11.1: Describing waves

- P1.b.11.12 Describe the similarities and differences between longitudinal and transverse waves
- P1.b.11.12 Give examples of longitudinal waves including sound waves, ultrasound and seismic waves
- P1.b.11.12 Give examples of transverse waves including seismic waves and electromagnetic waves
- P1.b.11.14 Explain the terms amplitude, frequency and wavelength
- P1.b.11.14 Describe the speed of a wave
- P1.b.11.15 Use speed = frequency × wavelength
- P1.b.11.16 Use speed = distance/time to calculate the distance to a reflecting surface

Need more help?
For more on this topic, see pages 250–251, 256–257.

edexcel key terms

amplitude The maximum distance of particles in a wave from their normal positions.
frequency The number of vibrations per second.
longitudinal A wave that vibrates parallel to the direction of travel.
seismic waves Waves produced by earthquakes.
transverse A wave that oscillates at right angles to the direction of travel.
wavelength The distance between the crest of one wave and the crest of the next.
waves A way of transferring energy by oscillations.

Transverse and longitudinal waves

All waves are oscillations that transfer energy. In transverse waves the oscillations are at right angles to the direction in which the waves are travelling. Transverse waves include waves on the surface of water, light waves and some seismic waves (S waves).

In longitudinal waves the oscillations are in the same direction as the waves travel. Longitudinal waves include sound waves, ultrasound waves and some seismic waves (P waves).

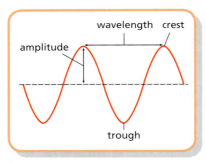

A wave.

Describing waves

A wave can be described using its:

- frequency (the number of vibrations per second)
- wavelength (the length occupied by one vibration)
- amplitude (the height of the wave from its undisturbed position)
- speed (the distance it moves in one second).

Wave speed calculations

You can calculate the speed of a wave using these equations:

$$\text{speed (m/s)} = \text{frequency (Hz)} \times \text{wavelength (m)}$$

$$\text{speed (m/s)} = \frac{\text{distance travelled (m)}}{\text{time taken (s)}}$$

Worked example

A wave has a frequency of 2 kHz and a wavelength of 0.17 m. What is its frequency?

2 kHz = 2000 Hz

speed = frequency × wavelength = 2000 Hz × 0.17 m = 340 m/s

ResultsPlus Watch out!

Sound and ultrasound waves are *always* longitudinal waves. Ultrasound waves just have a higher frequency than sound waves (they are too high for humans to hear).

Now You See it, Now You Don't

Worked example

A ship uses sonar to find out how deep the sea is. It sends sound waves into the sea and detects the echo from the sea bed 0.5 seconds later. Sound travels at about 1500 m/s in water. How deep is the water?

distance travelled by
sound wave = speed × time

= 1500 m/s × 0.5 s

= 750 m

This is the distance from the ship to the sea bed and back again, so the depth of the water is half of this.

Depth = 375 m

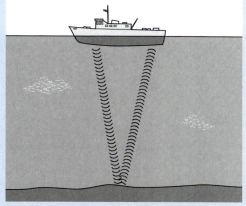

ResultsPlus — Exam tip

You don't need to remember any formulae, as they will be given to you in the exam if you need them. But you *do* need to be able to use them, and you may be asked to rearrange them. Memorising these formula triangles will help you with this. (λ is the symbol used for wavelength.)

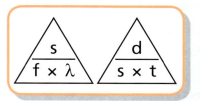

ResultsPlus — Watch out!

Be careful with the units. If you are given a frequency in kilohertz (kHz), you must convert it to Hz first by multiplying by 1000. Or you may be given a speed in km/s, which you will need to change to m/s before putting the value into the formula.

Test yourself

1. Which list shows only transverse waves?
   - A sound, light, earthquake waves
   - B light, earthquake S waves, waves on water
   - C light, earthquake P waves
   - D light, sound, ultrasound

2. Annie says 'The higher the frequency of a sound wave, the longer the wavelength.'

   Bill says 'The amplitude of a wave depends on its frequency.'

   Who is correct?
   - A Annie only
   - B Bill only
   - C both of them
   - D neither of them

3. Waves on water measure 5 cm from the top of a crest to the bottom of a trough. What is the amplitude of the waves?

4. It takes sound 0.02 seconds to travel along a steel cable 90 m long. What is the speed of sound in steel?

5. You use a datalogger to measure the time between a noise and its echo from a wall. The echo comes 0.3 seconds after the noise. The speed of sound in air is 340 m/s.
   - a How far away are you from the wall?
   - b Explain why it is a good idea to use a datalogger for this investigation.

6. A sonar in a ship uses sound waves of frequency 200 kHz, which travel through the water at 1500 m/s.
   - a Why are these waves called 'ultrasound' waves?
   - b Are they longitudinal or transverse waves?
   - c What is the wavelength of these waves?
   - d The ship is in water that is 2 km deep. How long will it take for an echo to return to the ship?

ResultsPlus — Watch out!

Don't forget that the distance travelled by a reflected wave is *twice* the distance between the object emitting the wave and the reflecting surface. So when you have used the equation to calculate the distance travelled, don't forget to divide this answer by 2.

Need more help? For more on this topic, see pages 256–259, 264–265.

11.2: The electromagnetic spectrum

- **P1.b.11.2** Describe the characteristics of ultraviolet light in terms of amplitude, frequency and wavelength
- **P1.b.11.2** Relate the characteristics of ultraviolet light in terms of frequency, wavelength and energy to the dangers of over-exposure
- **P1.b.11.3** Describe the detrimental effects of excessive exposure to microwaves (internal heating of body tissue), excessive exposure to infrared (skin burns), X-rays and gamma-rays (mutation or destruction of cells in the body)
- **P1.b.11.18** Describe the similarities and differences of the waves in the electromagnetic spectrum
- **P1.b.11.19** Recall that all electromagnetic waves travel at the same speed in a vacuum
- **P1.b.11.3** Explain the detrimental effects of excessive exposure to microwaves, infrared, X-rays and gamma-rays in terms of increasing frequency

edexcel key terms

absorption When some of the energy of a wave is transferred to the material in which it is travelling.
electromagnetic spectrum A group of transverse waves that all travel at the same speed in a vacuum.
emission The production and sending out of waves.
gamma-rays Part of the electromagnetic spectrum with the highest frequency.
infrared Part of the electromagnetic spectrum usually associated with heat.
microwave Part of the electromagnetic spectrum.
mutation When the DNA of cells is altered.
radiation Energy transferred from a point.
ultraviolet Part of the electromagnetic spectrum.
vacuum A completely empty space with no particles in it.
X-rays Part of the electromagnetic spectrum.

ResultsPlus Watch out!

Remember the similarities as well as the differences between the waves in the electromagnetic spectrum. They all travel *at the same speed* in a vacuum, and they are all transverse waves.

Higher tier

The electromagnetic spectrum is a family of waves with some things in common. All electromagnetic waves:

- are transverse waves
- can travel through a vacuum
- travel at the same speed in a vacuum.

The frequencies and wavelengths of the different electromagnetic waves vary continuously. We classify the waves into different parts of the spectrum. Each part of the spectrum has different frequencies and wavelengths, which means each part has different properties, different uses and different dangers.

The waves are often referred to as 'radiation' – but this just means that they are being emitted by something and spreading out.

The ultraviolet part of the electromagnetic spectrum is often split up further into UVA, UVB and UVC:

- UVA waves have the longest wavelength, lowest frequency and lowest energy. They are not absorbed by the ozone layer, but their low energy means they don't do much damage.
- UVB waves have shorter wavelengths than UVA, higher frequencies and more energy. They are partly absorbed by the ozone layer, but enough UVB reaches the ground to cause sunburn and skin damage, which could lead to cancer.
- UVC waves have the shortest wavelength, highest frequency and highest energy of all the UV waves. Luckily they are absorbed by the ozone layer, as their high energies mean they would cause a lot of damage if they could reach the surface of the Earth.

The higher the frequency of an electromagnetic wave, the more energy it transfers. This is why infrared waves can cause skin burns more easily than microwaves, and why gamma-rays can cause the most damage in the body.

Wave	Uses	Dangers
longest wavelength, lowest frequency		
radio waves	sending radio and some TV signals	
microwaves	sending TV and mobile phone signals, cooking food in microwave ovens	can heat the inside of the body, may interfere with equipment in aeroplanes and hospitals
infrared	heating, toasters and grills, TV remote controls	skin burns
visible light	seeing, cameras, reading CDs and DVDs	
ultraviolet	tanning, security pens, hardening dental fillings	sunburn, skin cancer
X-rays	seeing through luggage or taking pictures of bones	cells in the body may be destroyed, mutations in DNA, cancer
gamma-rays	treating cancer, sterilising food	
shortest wavelength, highest frequency		

increasing frequency
increasing energy
decreasing wavelength

The electromagnetic spectrum. You need to memorise the information in this table!

ResultsPlus
Watch out!

Don't get the uses of different waves confused. Even though microwaves and infrared can both be used for cooking, remember that toasters and grills use infrared.

Test yourself

1. Write down two properties that all electromagnetic waves share.
2. Which electromagnetic waves have the:
   a longest wavelength   b highest frequency   c highest energy?
3. Which electromagnetic waves can be used for:
   a cooking   b getting a tan
   c sending mobile phone messages   d making images of the inside of the body?
4. Which waves can:
   a cause skin cancer   b cause mutations in DNA
   c heat the inside of the body?
5. Why are you asked to turn off mobile phones before an airliner takes off?
   A So your talking does not distract the pilot.
   B So you can listen to the safety briefing.
   C In case its signals interfere with equipment on the airliner.
   D So you don't annoy other passengers.
6. UVB is the most dangerous form of UV radiation to humans on the Earth. Why is UVB radiation:
   a more dangerous than UVA   b more dangerous than UVC?
7. Explain why gamma-rays are more dangerous than X-rays.

11.3: Reflection and refraction

> **Need more help?**
> For more on this topic, see pages 252–255.

- P1.b.11.4 — Describe how reflection occurs in materials of different densities
- P1.b.11.4 — Describe how refraction occurs in materials of different densities
- P1.b.11.11 — Describe the total internal reflection of light waves
- P1.b.11.11 — Explain how total internal reflection allows optical fibres to transfer large amounts of information over long distances
- P1.b.11.17 — Use data about seismic waves passing through the Earth to draw conclusions about the types of materials that are found in the planet's interior

edexcel key terms

optical fibre A thin glass or Perspex fibre that carries light.
reflection When a wave bounces off the boundary between two materials.
refraction When a wave changes speed and direction as it enters a new material or as the density of a material changes.
seismic waves Waves produced by earthquakes.

Waves travel in straight lines while they stay in the same material (or in a vacuum). If they travel from one medium (material) to another, they may be reflected or refracted. This happens because the wave travels at different speeds in different materials. Reflection and refraction happen to all the transverse waves in the electromagnetic spectrum, and also to longitudinal waves such as sound and ultrasound.

These diagrams show what happens to light when it travels between air and glass. Light travels faster in air than it does in glass. Light also slows down when it goes into water.

If a light wave is travelling from glass (or water) to air, part of it may be reflected inside the glass. If the angle is large enough, you get total internal reflection.

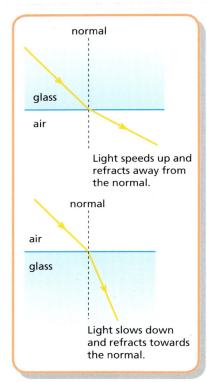

Light travelling between air and glass.

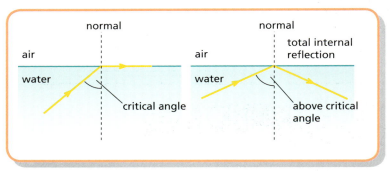

Total internal reflection.

Optical fibres are long, thin lengths of glass or Perspex. If light is shone into one end, it can travel inside the fibre. Hardly any light is absorbed by the fibre and no light escapes from the sides, so optical fibres can be used to transmit information over very long distances.

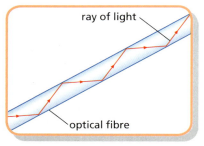

Optical fibre.

Seismic waves

Higher tier

There are many different sorts of earthquake waves. After an earthquake, detectors all around the world detect the arrival of these waves. Scientists use the arrival times of P waves and S waves to work out how the waves must have travelled inside the Earth, and so find out about the materials inside the Earth.

Scientists have used evidence from earthquake waves to deduce that:

- the density increases with depth (this is why the paths of the waves are curved – the change in density has caused the speed of the waves to change, which causes refraction)
- the outer core is liquid (as S waves are absorbed or reflected when they reach it, and don't travel through it)
- the inner core is solid (worked out from the speeds of P waves that have gone through it).

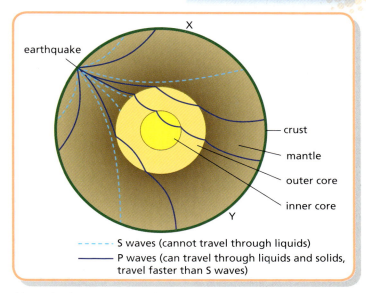

How seismic waves travel within the Earth.

ResultsPlus — Watch out!

The curving of seismic waves as they pass through the Earth is due to changes in density, *not* because they are being attracted or repelled by any part of the Earth.

ResultsPlus — Exam Question Report

Look at the diagram of the seismic waves. Which row of the table shows the kinds of waves that will be detected at points X and Y?

	X	Y
A	transverse only	longitudinal only
B	longitudinal only	transverse only
C	both types	both types
D	both types	longitudinal only

Answer: The correct answer is D.

How students answered
61% of students got this wrong.

61% 0 marks

Only 39% of students realised that, as the waves reaching X had only passed through the mantle, *both* longitudinal and transverse waves (P waves and S waves) would be received there. It is only the liquid outer core that stops S waves travelling.

39% 1 mark

Test yourself

1 Copy these diagrams and complete them to show what happens to the rays of light.

2 Look at your answers to question 1.
   a What is the name for the process happening in parts a and b?
   b What is the name for what is happening in part c?

3 You are swimming underwater in a swimming pool. Explain why you can see some reflections in the surface of the water.

4 a Which part of the Earth is liquid?
   b How do scientists know this?
   c Why are the paths of the seismic waves curved?

11.4: Using waves

Need more help?
For more on this topic, see pages 252–255, 258–261.

- P1.b.11.5 Explain how scanning by reflection can be used for ultrasound scanning of a fetus during pregnancy
- P1.b.11.5 Explain how reflection of visible light can be used in iris recognition
- P1.b.11.5 Discuss the advantages/disadvantages of scanning by reflection
- P1.b.11.6 Explain how scanning by absorption enables bone fractures to be 'seen' using X-rays
- P1.b.11.6 Explain how scanning by absorption enables rain to be monitored using microwaves
- P1.b.11.6 Explain how scanning by absorption enables forged bank notes to be detected by fluorescence using ultraviolet light
- P1.b.11.7 Explain how scanning by emission enables the use of infrared sensors to monitor temperature

 **key terms**

fluorescent Absorbs ultraviolet light and emits visible light.
scanning Building up an image of something in stages.
ultrasound Sound with frequencies too high for us to hear.

Scanning is a way of building up an image of something. Scanning is useful in security, medicine and industry. Some scanners detect waves naturally emitted by objects. Others emit a wave, and sensors detect whether the wave has been reflected or absorbed by the object being scanned.

ResultsPlus Exam Question Report

When ultrasound waves meet a boundary between two layers of the body, only some of the waves pass through into the second material.

boundary between	percentage of waves passing through
air and skin	less than 1%
gel and skin	98%

A soft jelly-like material (gel) is used instead of the air between the ultrasound source and the skin. The gel is used:

A so the probe does not feel cold
B to help the probe to move over the skin more easily
C to prevent the waves damaging the skin cells
D so that a higher percentage of waves enters the skin

Answer: D is the correct answer.

How students answered
Many students put B. The gel *does* help the probe to slide more easily over the skin, so B is a true statement. However, it is not the main reason the gel is used, so it is not the correct answer to the question. Without the gel, most of the ultrasound waves would be reflected by the skin, and so could not be used for detecting the shape of the fetus inside the body.

Scanning by reflection – ultrasound scans

Ultrasound waves can be used to produce images of the inside of the body, most often to provide an image of a developing fetus. Some of the ultrasound waves are reflected each time they enter a material of a different density (such as blood, bones, flesh, etc.). The reflected waves are detected by the scanner and built up to form an image. There may be some very small risks to the fetus from the scan, but the benefits of finding out about any possible problems are more important. Ultrasound scanning is much safer than using X-rays.

Scanning by reflection – iris recognition

Each person has a unique pattern in their irises (the coloured parts of their eyes), and these can be used to identify people. In places such as airports, special cameras take a picture using light reflected from the eye to make a picture of the iris. This picture is checked against computer records to make sure the traveller is who they say they are.

Scanning by absorption – X-rays

Broken bones and other medical problems can be investigated using X-rays, and X-rays can also be used to check luggage for dangerous items without having to open it. The scanning machine emits X-rays, and materials such as metal or bone absorb some of the X-rays. A sensor behind the objects builds up an image that shows 'shadows' of bones or metal objects.

Scanning by absorption – rain clouds and microwaves

The Earth naturally emits tiny amounts of microwave radiation. Water absorbs microwaves, so this radiation will be absorbed by rain or rain clouds. Satellites can produce images of rain clouds by detecting the amounts of microwaves that reach them.

Scanning by absorption – fluorescence

Some chemicals absorb ultraviolet light and then emit visible light. Special fluorescent chemicals are used to add marks to bank notes. These marks are not visible in ordinary light, but show up if ultraviolet light is shone onto the notes. Bank notes can be checked to make sure they are not forgeries by shining ultraviolet light on them.

Scanning by emission – infrared images

All objects emit radiation. Very hot objects, such as the filament in a light bulb, emit visible light. Objects not hot enough to glow still emit infrared radiation. This can be detected by special cameras, which show areas of different temperature. Infrared scanning can be used to 'see' at night, or to detect temperature changes in objects that may indicate faults.

Test yourself

1. What kind of scanning is used for these methods?
   Choose your answers from:

   A absorption   B emission   C reflection

   a infrared cameras that allow the police to catch criminals at night
   b iris scanners
   c X-ray images of broken bones
   d ultrasound scans of unborn babies
   e satellite images of rain clouds

2. What kind of wave is used for the following types of scan?

   a iris scanners
   b satellite images of rain clouds
   c seeing security marks on bank notes
   d checking luggage for dangerous items

3. Which two types of scan described on this page do **not** rely on the scanning machine emitting radiation?

4. The police shine a UV light on some objects they think may have been stolen. Why do they do this?

   A To see how clean the objects are.
   B To see if the objects have been marked with fluorescent security ink.
   C To see what is inside the objects.
   D To see how hot the objects are.

11.5: Digital and analogue

Need more help? For more on this topic, see pages 266–268.

- P1.b.11.9 Describe the advantages of sending information in the form of a digital signal
- P1.b.11.10 Describe how the production of digital signals has created a range of music technologies
- P1.b.11.10 Describe how digital signals have altered the way we listen to music
- P1.b.11.10 Describe how digital signals have altered the way we distribute music

edexcel key terms

analogue A signal sent in the form of a wave with a continuous range of values.
digital A signal that has two levels or states or values.

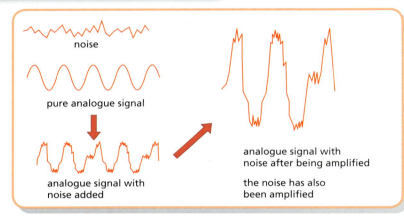

Analogue signals and noise.

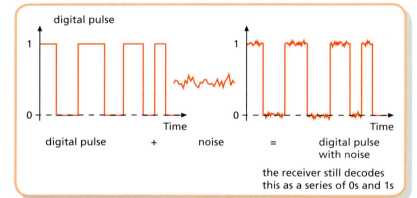

Digital signals and noise.

ResultsPlus Watch out!

One advantage of digital signals compared to analogue is that digital signals are less affected by noise than analogue signals. Both types of signal travel *at the same speed*.

Broadcasting music

When music was first broadcast by radio, analogue signals were the only type used. An analogue signal is a continuously varying wave. As an analogue signal spreads out from a radio transmitter it gets weaker. Other analogue signals may also be detected by the receiver. These other signals are called noise. When the radio signal is received and amplified (made loud enough to hear), the noise gets amplified as well and affects the quality of the music.

A computer can analyse an analogue signal and convert it into a digital code. This code is made up of just two different values, usually referred to as 0 and 1. Music being broadcast digitally is converted to a series of 0s and 1s, which are sent out using radio waves. The digital signal is converted back into analogue sound waves by the radio receiver. Even if noise gets added to the signal while it is being transmitted, the quality of the final music is not affected.

Another advantage of digital broadcasting is that the signals don't require as much 'bandwidth' – so more TV channels or radio programmes can be transmitted using the same frequencies of radio waves. Soon there will be only digital TV signals transmitted in the UK.

Music technologies

Plastic records and cassette tapes stored music as analogue signals. Modern CDs store the information as a series of 0s and 1s. CDs are read using light waves, and it is much easier to find the track you want on a CD than on a record or tape.

The information needed to record a piece of music can also be compressed, so it is easier to store on a computer or MP3 player. We can also listen to music using the Internet, and download it to transfer to MP3 players.

Once you had to buy a vinyl single or album, and play it on a large machine in your home. Today you can buy a CD or download just a single track, and listen to it on a tiny MP3 player wherever you are.

Digital technology can also be used to make music. Electronic synthesisers use digital code to recreate the effect of digital sounds. Mixing different sounds to make a music track once had to be done by trained sound engineers using expensive equipment in a recording studio. Today it is much easier for musicians to mix their own tracks using home computers. They can then allow people around the world to listen to the end result by putting it on the Internet for others to download.

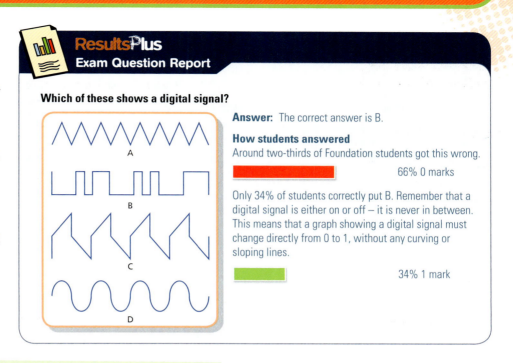

Test yourself

1. Which row of the table correctly compares digital signals with analogue signals?

	digital signals	analogue signals
A	travel faster than analogue signals	are less affected by noise
B	travel faster than analogue signals	are more affected by noise
C	travel at the same speed as analogue signals	are more affected by noise
D	travel at the same speed as analogue signals	are less affected by noise

2. Sketch a digital signal and an analogue signal.

3. Does your voice produce a digital or analogue signal? Explain your answer.

4. Fahima says 'One advantage of analogue signals is that the loss of quality from interference can be restored.'

   Explain what is wrong with Fahima's statement.

5. List the advantages of using digital technology for music.

Need more help?
For more on this topic, see pages 254–255, 262–263.

11.6: Waves and society

- P1.b.11.1 — Evaluate evidence suggesting that microwave radiation from mobile phones or masts poses health risks
- P1.b.11.1 — Discuss how evidence about possible health risks from microwave radiation has been reported in the media
- P1.b.11.8 — Discuss the benefits and drawbacks to society of a technology that is based on the properties of waves
- P1.b.11.13 — Suggest reasons why scientists find it difficult to predict earthquakes even with suitable data
- P1.b.11.13 — Suggest reasons why scientists find it difficult to predict tsunami waves even with suitable data

Are mobile phones dangerous?

Mobile phones use microwaves to send and receive information. This means that when you are using the phone, microwaves from it can travel through your head. This may heat up some of the tissue in your head. Some scientists have suggested that this may be harmful over a long period of time. Some studies show that there may be a risk from regular usage, but other studies show no significant risk, more than ten years after mobile phones were introduced. It is still possible that there may be some longer-term health effects.

Some people have also objected to mobile phone masts, particularly when these have been put on school buildings. The first suggestions that mobile phones may cause harm were reported in the press using scary headlines. Newspaper reports often simplify scientific findings to make a better story, and bad news sells more newspapers than good news.

Predicting earthquakes and tsunamis

Earthquakes can cause great loss of life and damage to property. An earthquake that happens under the sea may cause a tsunami (a huge wave) that could destroy coastal towns and villages.

Earthquakes happen because the surface of the Earth is made up of rigid 'plates' that move past each other. They do not move smoothly. Instead, forces build up until rocks break, and then the plates move with a sudden jerk. This jerk is an earthquake. Scientists know the parts of the Earth that are the most likely to suffer earthquakes. They can also measure the forces across faults in some places. However, they can't predict an earthquake accurately because they do not know how much force the rocks along the line between plates can withstand before they break.

Scientists have the same difficulties in predicting earthquakes under the sea. Predicting tsunamis is even harder, because a tsunami can be caused by the earthquake itself, or by a landslide on the coast or under the water that is triggered by an earthquake. Some earthquakes may even be caused by meteorites.

Benefits and drawbacks of wave technology

Many of the technologies that we use today depend on waves in some way. For example, you need light waves to reflect from the page into your eyes to allow you to read this book. Any time you use a radio or TV, you are using wave technology. Look at the table on page 129 for some other uses of wave technology.

Some of the drawbacks of technologies using waves come from the harm that some types of wave can cause. Even sound waves can be harmful, if they are loud enough. The table on page 129 lists some of the ways in which electromagnetic waves can be harmful.

Higher tier

Test yourself

1. How might mobile phones be harmful to your health?
2. Why don't scientists yet know if there is any harm in using mobile phones for 30 or 40 years?
3. Suggest why newspaper reports about the dangers of mobile phones may be misleading.
4. a Why is it difficult for scientists to predict when an earthquake will happen?
   b What is a tsunami?
   c Why is it difficult for scientists to predict when a tsunami will happen?
5. a Write down five things you did today that depended on technology that uses waves.
   b What are some of the possible drawbacks of these technologies?

12

12.1: Space travel

- **P1.b.12.1** Recall that there is no air in interplanetary space and that the temperature in interplanetary space can vary widely
- **P1.b.12.1** Describe why astronauts feel weightlessness in orbit or in interplanetary space
- **P1.b.12.2** Recall how lack of air, temperature variations, lack of activity and weightlessness in interplanetary space can be partly allowed for in spacecraft (by heating/cooling, using excercise machines and by artificial gravity)
- **P1.b.12.3** Explain the difference between mass and weight
- **P1.b.12.4** Use weight = mass × acceleration of free-fall $W = mg$
- **P1.b.12.9** Recall how scientists are overcoming the dangers of radiation and the deterioration of bones and heart on long space flights
- **P1.b.12.11** Use the unit of gravitational field strength, newton per kilogram (N/kg)

Need more help?
For more on this topic, see pages 274–275, 280–281.

edexcel key terms

gravitational field The area in which a mass experiences a force of gravity from another body.
gravity A force of attraction that every object exerts on every other object.
interplanetary The space within the Solar System in which the effects of planets are negligible.
mass A measure of the amount of matter in something. Measured in kilograms.
radiation Something that moves out from a point in all directions.
temperature A scale that describes whether something is hot or cold.
weight The force due to gravity.
weightlessness The feeling of having no weight.

Astronauts have visited the Moon, and many astronauts have visited and worked on the International Space Station. Spacecraft have to be carefully designed to keep the astronauts safe in the conditions in space.

There is no air in interplanetary space. The temperature in space can be very hot if a spacecraft has the Sun shining on it, but very cold if it is in the shadow of a planet or moon.

Higher tier

Spacecraft contain air, so the astronauts can breathe without having to wear spacesuits all the time. Oxygen is added to the air to replace what the astronauts use, and carbon dioxide is removed.

The temperature inside a spacecraft is kept at a comfortable level using reflective surfaces on the outside and insulating materials.

ResultsPlus Watch out!

Be careful if you are talking about 'weight' and 'weightlessness'. Astronauts in a spacecraft orbiting the Earth feel weightless, but there is still a force of gravity there from the Earth — that is what is keeping the spacecraft in orbit!

Astronauts are at risk from cosmic radiation, which can damage human tissue. This damage accumulates on long space flights. Spacecraft are built using materials that can absorb this radiation, so the astronauts inside are protected.

Astronauts feel 'weightless' when they are in space. On the ground we feel weight because the ground is pushing up on our feet as our weight pushes down on the ground. In a spacecraft in orbit, or moving between planets, astronauts feel weightless because they are moving at the same speed as the spacecraft.

Human bones and muscles (including heart muscles) get weaker when someone is in a 'weightless' environment, because they don't need to work as hard as they do on Earth. Astronauts on a long space flight must take exercise to prevent their bodies becoming too weak. They do this using special exercise machines that make use of other forces than gravity.

Higher tier

In the future, some spacecraft may have artificial gravity, so that astronauts don't need to use special exercise machines. The artificial gravity will be produced by rotating the spacecraft. To astronauts inside, 'down' will be towards the outside of the spacecraft.

Gravity on other planets

Gravity is a force of attraction between all bodies with mass. This force acting on you is your weight. On Earth, the gravitational field strength is approximately 10 N/kg. This is also referred to as the acceleration due to gravity (10 m/s^2), and you can calculate your weight using this formula:

weight (N) = mass (kg) × acceleration due to gravity (m/s^2)

The force of gravity between two objects depends on their masses and the distance between them:

- the more mass in the objects, the stronger the gravitational field strength
- the further apart the objects, the weaker the gravitational field strength.

Astronauts on the Moon would have a smaller weight, as the strength of gravity on the Moon is less, but their mass would be the same.

Exam tip

You don't need to remember any formulae, as they will be given to you in the exam. But you may be asked to rearrange this formula in an exam. Remembering this formula triangle will help you to get this right. g is the symbol used for the acceleration due to gravity.

Watch out!

Students often confuse the units for mass and weight. Remember that mass is measured in kilograms. Weight is a force, so it is measured in newtons.

Test yourself

1. What does a spacecraft need to have to keep astronauts inside it fit and healthy? Write down as many things as you can.
2. A satellite is orbiting the Earth. Explain why it could be very hot some of the time and very cold at other times.
3. a Write these objects in the order of the gravitational field strength on them, starting with the highest gravity: the Moon, an asteroid, the Earth.
   b Explain how you worked out your answer.
4. a What is the weight of a 5 kg mass on the Earth?
   b What units are used to measure weight?
5. On Mars, a 2.0 kg mass has a weight of 7.4 N. What is the gravitational field strength on Mars?
6. Which is the best explanation for your weight?
   A You ate a lot of chips yesterday.
   B There is a force of attraction on you from the Earth.
   C You and the Earth are both attracting each other.
   D Gravity on the Earth is greater than on the Moon.
7. Astronauts float around in the Space Station because:
   A there is no gravity in space
   B they have no mass in space
   C the Moon and the Earth are pulling them in opposite directions
   D they are 'falling' around the Earth at exactly the same rate as the Space Station

Need more help?
For more on this topic, see pages 282–283.

edexcel key terms
acceleration Change of velocity.
action Forces come in pairs. The force that is being applied is usually called the action.
orbit The path of a planet around the Sun, or a spacecraft or moon around a planet.
reaction The opposite force to an action.
Sun The nearest star to Earth.

ResultsPlus Watch out!
Action and reaction forces are not the same as balanced forces. Action and reaction forces are always the same size as each other, and they act on *different* objects.

ResultsPlus Exam tip
You may be asked to rearrange this formula in an exam. Remembering this formula triangle will help you to get this right.

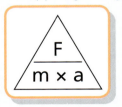

12.2: Getting into space

- **P1.b.12.5** Explain how a spacecraft might be powered in terms of action and reaction
- **P1.b.12.5** Describe the energy changes that take place when a spacecraft is launched
- **P1.b.12.6** Describe how force = mass × acceleration can be used to predict how an object behaves
- **P1.b.12.10** Describe the role of gravity on Earth
- **P1.b.12.10** Describe the role of gravity in astronomy

Gravity is the force that pulls everything on Earth towards the Earth. Rockets need to produce large forces to push spacecraft up into space against the force of gravity.

Action and reaction forces

Rockets work by pushing gases out of the back at high speed. The force pushing the gases out is the action force. The reaction force is the same size but in the opposite direction, caused by the gases pushing on the rocket. This force pushes the rocket upwards.

All forces have a reaction force. When you stand on the floor, your weight is the action force pushing down on the floor. The reaction force is the force from the floor pushing upwards on you.

Velocity and acceleration

The reaction force on a rocket makes it accelerate upwards. The acceleration depends on the size of the force and on the mass of the object being accelerated. It is calculated using this formula:

$$\text{force (N)} = \text{mass (kg)} \times \text{acceleration (m/s}^2\text{)}$$

The reaction force pushes the rocket up.

- The larger the force, the bigger the acceleration.
- The larger the mass, the smaller the acceleration.

Acceleration is a change in velocity. Velocity is a speed in a particular direction. So the acceleration of a rocket is a change in its vertical speed.

In the Solar System, moons orbit around planets and they are kept in their orbits by the pull of gravity from the planet. Planets, asteroids and comets all orbit the Sun, and they are kept in their orbits by the pull of gravity from the Sun.

Space and its Mysteries

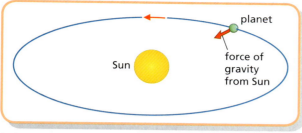

A planet orbiting the Sun.

Energy changes

A rocket needs to transfer a lot of energy to get into space. This energy is stored as chemical energy in the fuel.

Chemical energy (stored in the fuel) is transferred to heat energy when the fuel burns. ➤ Some of the heat energy is transferred to kinetic (movement) energy of the gases as they leave the rocket. The reaction force transfers kinetic energy to the rocket. ➤ As the rocket gets higher it gains gravitational potential energy (energy stored by objects in high places). ➤ Once a spacecraft is in orbit around the Earth, it is storing kinetic energy and gravitational potential energy.

Energy changes as a rocket launches.

Test yourself

1. What do each of these objects in the Solar System orbit around?
   a. a planet
   b. an asteroid
   c. a moon
   d. a comet

2. A rocket has a certain acceleration. Write down two ways in which engineers could change the rocket to give it a bigger acceleration.

3. What stops the Moon flying off into space?

4. A rocket has a mass of 750 000 kg and it accelerates at 8 m/s². What force do its engines produce?

5. A rocket with a mass of 600 000 kg produces a force of 6000 kN. What is its acceleration? (*Hint*: be careful with the units!)

6. Gases come out from the back of the rocket. The action of these gases accelerating backwards:
   A. slows the rocket down
   B. pulls on the vacuum of space
   C. pushes the rocket forwards
   D. reacts against the Earth to move the rocket

7. Which of these statements is *not* true?
   A. The Moon is travelling at a constant speed.
   B. The Moon is moving at a constant velocity.
   C. The direction in which the Moon is travelling is changing all the time.
   D. The Moon is accelerating.

12.3: The Solar System

> **Need more help?**
> For more on this topic, see pages 276–279, 286–287.

- P1.b.12.13 Discuss the chance and the possible consequences of a comet or asteroid hitting the Earth and any uncertainties in there
- P1.b.12.14 Describe how the orbit of a comet differs from that of a planet or an asteroid
- P1.b.12.15 List objects in the Solar System and Universe in order of size
- P1.b.12.15 Use data sources to compare the relative sizes of and distances between Earth, our Moon, the planets, the Sun, galaxies and the Universe
- P1.b.12.20 Describe how the existence of life on a planet is determined by the nature of the planet and its position in its solar system

edexcel key terms

asteroid A solid rock orbiting the Sun, too small to be a planet.
atmosphere The mixture of gases surrounding a planet.
comet A ball of ice and dust that orbits the Sun in an eccentric (elliptical) orbit.
galaxy A collection of millions of stars.
planet A large sphere of rock and/or gas orbiting a star.
star A large ball of hydrogen and helium gases, radiating large amounts of energy.
Universe All of space, including all of the galaxies.

The Solar System

The Earth is part of the Solar System, which consists of planets, asteroids and comets all orbiting the Sun. The Sun's gravity keeps the planets in their orbits and stops them flying off into space.

Most asteroids orbit between the orbits of Mars and Jupiter, but some are in orbits that take them close to the Earth.

Comets are in very elliptical orbits that take them close to the Sun and out to the distant parts of the Solar System.

Many of the planets have moons.

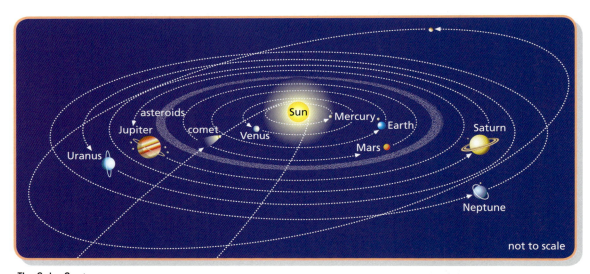

The Solar System.

Higher tier

The conditions on a planet depend on the nature of the planet and how far it is from the Sun. Planets like Jupiter and Saturn are made mainly of gas and don't have solid surfaces. Mercury, Venus, Earth and Mars are rocky bodies. The temperature of a planet depends on its distance from the Sun (except for Venus, the hottest planet, which is hotter than you might expect because its atmosphere causes a strong greenhouse effect). The Earth is the only planet whose temperature allows liquid water to exist at the surface, although other planets or moons may have ice. It is thought that liquid water is essential for life, and the Earth is the only planet in the Solar System known to have life.

Space and its Mysteries 12

The Sun is just one star in a huge collection of stars in our galaxy, which is called the Milky Way. All the billions of galaxies that exist, and the space between them, form the Universe.

[NB: Pluto was recently reclassified as a dwarf planet.]

Comet collision?

Small objects from space enter the Earth's atmosphere all the time. Most of these burn up as they fly through the atmosphere, but some are big enough to hit the Earth. Occasionally one of these objects is large enough to cause damage.

One theory to explain why the dinosaurs died out is that a large asteroid hit the Earth about 65 million years ago. Comets could also hit the Earth and cause damage.

The damage caused by an asteroid or comet depends on where it lands and how big it is. If it falls into the ocean, it could cause a tsunami (huge wave), which could destroy coastal towns and cities. If the object is big enough, it could cause changes to the climate that would kill animals and plants all around the world.

Astronomers estimate that a medium-sized asteroid will collide with Earth every 200 or 300 years. However, asteroids are quite difficult to spot in space, as they are small and often dark coloured (so they don't reflect much light). The Earth could be hit by an asteroid that astronomers have not yet discovered.

Even if an asteroid is spotted, it is not easy to work out its exact orbit to see if it will hit the Earth. Even when the orbit *has* been worked out, it can change if the asteroid passes close to other asteroids or planets.

Comets and asteroids may also hit other planets and moons. The larger the planet or moon, the more likely it is to get hit.

ResultsPlus
Watch out!

Comets and asteroids all orbit the Sun. Many students lose marks by saying that these objects orbit planets or even moons! It is also important to memorise the difference between the orbits of asteroids and comets.

ResultsPlus
Exam Tip

Exam questions often ask you to put objects in order of size. It is worth memorising this list of objects, which starts with the smallest object: Moon, Earth, Sun, Solar System, Galaxy (Milky Way), Universe.

Test yourself

1. Write these objects in order of size, starting with the largest one:
   Sun, planet, galaxy, Moon, asteroid, Universe.

2. Write down two differences between an asteroid and a comet.

3. Write down the planet that is:
   a hottest   b coldest   c furthest from the Sun   d closest to the Sun

4. Why is Jupiter more likely to be hit by a comet than Mars?

5. Why is it difficult for astronomers to spot asteroids that may hit the Earth?

6. Which statement about life in the Solar System is **not** correct?
   A The Earth is the only place known to have life.
   B The Earth is the only body in the Solar System to have water on its surface.
   C Jupiter does not have a solid surface.
   D Mercury is too hot for liquid water to exist.

7. Which statement about asteroids and comets is **not** correct?
   A A comet is more likely to hit Saturn than hit the Earth.
   B Scientists have plotted the orbits of all the asteroids in the Solar System.
   C Scientists can say for sure that an asteroid will hit the Earth in the future.
   D Scientists cannot predict the damage that will be caused by the next asteroid strike.

GCSE 360 Science

Need more help?
For more on this topic, see pages 276–277, 288–289.

edexcel key terms

black hole An object with such strong gravity that it prevents the escape even of light.
nebula A collection of gas and dust in space, usually mostly hydrogen.
stellar Associated with a star.

12.4: Star life cycles

- P1.b.12.10 Describe the role of gravity in astronomy
- P1.b.12.12 Describe stellar evolution from the nebula stage for small stars like our Sun
- P1.b.12.12 Describe stellar evolution from the nebula stage for more massive stars than the Sun
- P1.b.12.16 Describe the Solar System as part of the Milky Way galaxy
- P1.b.12.16 Describe how the Milky Way is related to other galaxies, and the Universe
- P1.b.12.10 Describe the idea of black holes
- P1.b.12.20 Describe how the position of a star in its lifecycle determines the existence of life on a planet

The Sun is just one of millions of stars in our galaxy, which is called the Milky Way. The stars are held together in the galaxy by the forces of gravity between them. There are billions more galaxies in the Universe.

Stars and solar systems form when gravity pulls clouds of gas and dust together. What happens to the star (stellar evolution) depends on how big it is.

Small stars

The Sun is a fairly small star. It was formed when gravity pulled the gases in a nebula together to form a protostar. When the gases were compressed enough, hydrogen atoms combined to form helium and release energy. The Sun is at this stage.

When the hydrogen is used up, helium atoms start to fuse to form carbon and the star swells into a red giant. When all the nuclear fuel is used up, the red giant shrinks into a white dwarf. As this star cools it will become a brown dwarf and, when it is no longer shining, a black dwarf.

ResultsPlus Watch out!

Gravity between stars is very weak, because the stars are a long way apart, but it is *not* zero. Even these weak forces are enough to make clouds of dust and gas eventually come together to form stars.

Large stars

If the star is much bigger than the Sun, it swells into a red supergiant when it has used up its hydrogen. Fusion reactions produce elements heavier than carbon. When these reactions stop there is a supernova explosion.

If what is left after the explosion is small, it forms a very dense neutron star. If there is a large amount of matter left, it may shrink to form a black hole. The matter in a black hole is so dense that its gravitational field is strong enough that not even light can escape from it.

Higher tier

ResultsPlus Watch out!

A black hole is not the same thing as a black dwarf – make sure you can remember the difference between them.

Space and its Mysteries 12

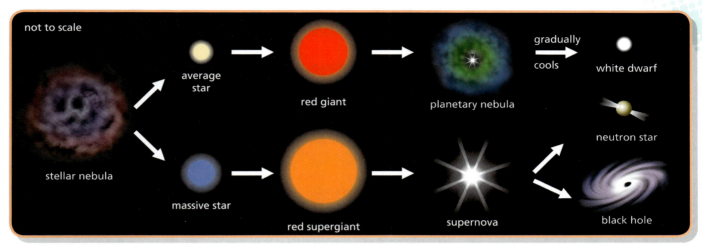

The life cycles of stars.

Stellar evolution and life

The possibility of finding life on a planet in another planetary system depends on the age of the star it is orbiting. If the star is very young, there may not have been time for life to get started. If the star has swollen to become a red giant, the expanding star may have made planets close to it too hot for life to survive.

Higher tier

Test yourself

1. Write these objects in the correct order:
   protostar, red giant, nebula, star, white dwarf.

2. What is:
   a a protostar
   b a red giant
   c a brown dwarf?

3. Suggest why there may not be life near:
   a a protostar
   b a red giant

4. A star can end its 'life' as a white dwarf, a neutron star or a black hole. What determines which of these a star will eventually turn into?

5. Which is the best description of a black hole?
   A A massive star that gives out black light.
   B An object with gravity so strong that no light can escape from it.
   C What our Sun will turn into when it has used up all its hydrogen.
   D A star that absorbs black light and reflects other colours.

Need more help?
For more on this topic, see pages 284–287, 292–293.

edexcel key terms
extraterrestrial Not from Earth.
SETI The Search for Extraterrestrial Intelligence, a project that analyses radio waves coming from space for possible signals from life forms on other planets.

ResultsPlus Watch out!
Spacecraft have visited or flown past all of the planets in the Solar System, but humans have not been further into space than orbiting the Moon.

12.5: Exploring the Universe

- P1.b.12.8 Describe ways of discovering information about the Universe that don't involve human travel, such as soil experiments on landers and the Hubble Space Telescope (HST)
- P1.b.12.8 Describe the Search for Extraterrestrial Intelligence (SETI) mission
- P1.b.12.18 Recall that there are unanswered scientific questions about the existence of extraterrestrial life
- P1.b.12.7 List and discuss the social and economic benefits of knowledge about the Universe
- P1.b.12.7 List and discuss the technological advances which might arise from exploration of the Universe
- P1.b.12.17 Use scientific evidence to develop an argument in favour of the idea that intelligent life exists elsewhere in the galaxy
- P1.b.12.17 Use scientific evidence to develop an argument against the idea that intelligent life exists elsewhere in the galaxy
- P1.b.12.17 Suggest ways of finding intelligent life elsewhere in the galaxy

The people who originally explored the Earth had to travel to different places to find out about them. Today we can investigate the other planets in the Solar System, and even planets orbiting around other stars, without having to go there ourselves.

Telescopes

We can see other objects in the Solar System because they reflect light from the Sun. We can detect this light using telescopes on Earth. We can see distant stars and galaxies because they emit (give out) light and other forms of radiation.

We can also use telescopes in space, such as the Hubble Space telescope. This can produce much better images because the light coming from distant stars and galaxies is not distorted by the atmosphere. Telescopes can also detect other radiation emitted by stars, such as X-rays or radio waves.

Space probes

Space probes have been sent to most of the planets in the Solar System. They can go into orbit around a planet and take pictures of the surface using visible light, or they can measure temperatures by detecting infrared radiation. Some probes land on planets and take samples of rocks. The information gathered by space probes is sent back to scientists on Earth using radio waves.

This rover can move around the surface of Mars and take samples.

Orbiting probes can send back data about planets and their moons.

Looking for life

Many people would like to know if there is life in other places in the Universe. This scientific question doesn't yet have an answer, but scientists are working on it! We are sending space probes to other parts of our Solar System to find out if planets like Mars may have had liquid water on them in the past. If there was once liquid water on Mars, it is possible that life may have developed there.

Space and its Mysteries 12

Planets orbiting other stars are much too far away for space probes to visit them. If intelligent life has developed on some of these planets it is possible that they may have developed radio technology. The Search for Extraterrestrial Intelligence (SETI) records radio signals coming from space and analyses them to see if there is any sign of a message in them.

ResultsPlus
Watch out!

Although people often talk about SETI 'listening' for signals from other life forms, SETI is detecting radio waves, *not* sound waves.

Higher tier

Some scientists think many of the billions of stars in the Universe will have planets similar to Earth, so it is very likely that life has developed on some of them. Some of this life may have evolved to become intelligent.

One argument against this is that if there is intelligent life elsewhere, we would have detected it by now.

Benefits of exploring the Universe

Many new inventions are made when scientists develop space probes or telescopes to explore the Universe. Some of these are new materials, which have other uses in everyday life, or medical discoveries made when investigating how to keep astronauts healthy in space.

The exploration of space also provides jobs in many industries, and helps to satisfy people's curiosity about the world and the Universe around us.

Test yourself

1. Explain what is wrong with these statements:
   a. Telescopes detect the light emitted by asteroids.
   b. The best way of finding out about planets orbiting other stars is to send space probes.

2. Which is the best way of investigating each of these things? Choose your answers from the list below, and explain your choice:
   A orbiting space probe   B a space probe that lands on a planet
   C telescope.
   a. Finding out the sizes of the mountains on a planet.
   b. Detecting planets orbiting another star.
   c. Finding out what chemicals are in the soil of a planet.

3. Which statement about life is *not* correct?
   A The Earth is the only place in the Solar System known to have life.
   B We know that the Earth is the only place in the Universe with life.
   C Scientists are looking for life on other planets.
   D The Earth is the only planet in our Solar System with plenty of liquid water on its surface.

4. What is SETI?

5. Give an argument for and against the idea that there is life elsewhere in the Universe.

6. Explain some of the benefits of exploring space.

147

Need more help?
For more on this topic, see pages 290–291.

12.6: Theories about the Universe

- P1.b.12.19 Describe the origin, current state and fate of the Universe using the main theories (Big Bang, oscillating and steady state)
- P1.b.12.18 Recall that there are unanswered scientific questions about the nature of 'dark matter' that makes up much of the Universe's mass
- P1.b.12.19 Describe the supporting evidence for the main theories including the microwave background radiation
- P1.b.12.19 Describe the supporting evidence for the main theories including red shift

There are different theories about how the Universe began and what will happen to it.

edexcel key terms

Big Bang One of the theories of how the Universe came into existence and time began.
dark matter Material in space that is very difficult to detect.
oscillating theory The theory that suggests that this Universe is just part of a repeating process.
red shift The change in frequency and wavelength of waves emitted by a moving source.
steady state theory The theory that the Universe is expanding but material is constantly being created so that the Universe always appears the same.

Steady state theory

In the early 20th century astronomers discovered that the Universe is expanding. The steady state theory suggests that new matter is created all the time so that the density of matter in the Universe stays the same.

Big Bang theory

This is the theory that most astronomers think is the best explanation for observations of the Universe. It says that the Universe started with the expansion of a tiny volume of concentrated energy and matter. As the Universe expanded, atoms formed and eventually many of these formed stars and galaxies.

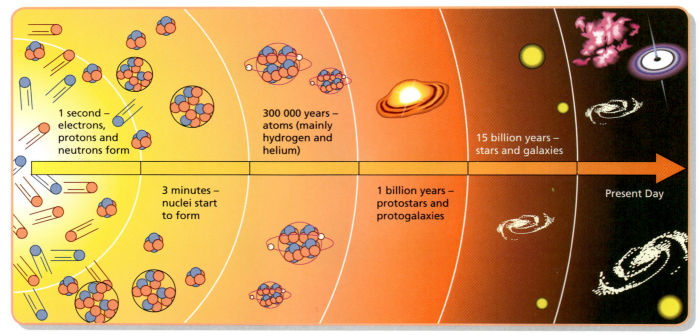

The Big Bang theory of the Universe.

Space and its Mysteries

Oscillating theory

Gravity is gradually slowing down the expansion of the Universe. Scientists do not know if the Universe will continue to expand, stop expanding, or even contract to a 'big crunch'.

If there is a big crunch, our Universe could just be one of a series of Universes, happening one after the other.

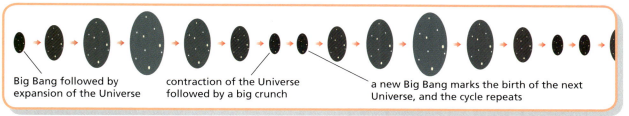

Big Bang followed by expansion of the Universe

contraction of the Universe followed by a big crunch

a new Big Bang marks the birth of the next Universe, and the cycle repeats

The oscillating theory of the Universe.

Evidence for the theories

If an object emitting light is moving away from us, the light appears to be 'shifted' towards the red end of the spectrum. Redshift is detected in light from other galaxies, and shows that almost all galaxies are moving away from us. More distant galaxies are moving away faster. This expansion of the Universe is evidence for all three theories of the origin of the Universe.

Microwave background radiation is radiation that comes from all over the sky. Scientists interpreted this as radiation emitted when the Big Bang happened, which has gradually 'cooled' with time. This is evidence for the Big Bang theory.

Current evidence is that there is not enough matter for gravity to make the Universe collapse into a big crunch. However, scientists also think that there is a lot of dark matter in the Universe, which is very difficult to detect. Until they can find out how much dark matter there is, they will not know whether the oscillating Universe is a possibility.

Higher tier

Which of these is evidence that the Universe is expanding?
A It takes millions of light years for light to reach us from some stars.
B The Universe began with the Big Bang.
C Galaxies are moving further away from each other.
D Some stars in the Milky Way are accelerating towards our Sun.

Answer: The correct answer is C.

How students answered
Some students put B, which is incorrect. The Big Bang theory does seem to fit the evidence best but we can't say definitely that the Universe began with the Big Bang.

70% 0 marks.

Statements A, C and D are all correct, but only C provides evidence that the Universe is expanding.

30% 1 mark

Test yourself

1. Write down a sentence or two describing what each of these theories says:
   a the steady state theory
   b the Big Bang theory
   c the oscillating Universe theory

2. Which one or more of the three theories says that:
   a the Universe is expanding
   b the Universe started with a Big Bang
   c the Universe will collapse and undergo a 'big crunch'?

3. What is the evidence for the expansion of the Universe?

4. What is the evidence that the Universe started with a Big Bang?

5. What is dark matter?
   A The stuff that black holes are made from.
   B Matter that we cannot see or detect in any other way.
   C Evidence that there was a Big Bang.
   D Matter that we cannot see but that has a gravitational effect.

6. Why are scientists interested in finding out how much dark matter there is in the Universe?

Answers

1.1: Chains and pyramids
1. D
2. a. A herbivore eats only plants.
   b. An omnivore eats plants and animals.
   c. A producer is a plant.
   d. A prey animal is caught and eaten by other animals.
3. a. consumer, omnivore, predator
   b. consumer, carnivore, predator
   c. consumer, herbivore, prey
4. a. There is only one oak tree supporting all the other organisms (even though it is very big), so the bottom of the 'pyramid' is very narrow.
   b. It gives a better idea of the amount of energy involved at each level.
5. a. sycamore tree → greenfly → ladybirds → bluetits
   b. Pyramid of numbers:

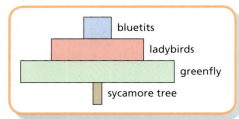

Pyramid of biomass:

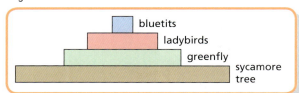

6. Energy is 'lost' through respiration and excretion at each stage in a food chain. If we ate cereal crops directly instead of feeding them to farm animals and then eating the animals, we could produce far more food from the same area of farmland.

1.2: Competition and populations
1. B
2. 'Inter-species' means between species. 'Intra-species' means between organisms within the same species.
3. a. zebra, mouse
   b. One possible answer is: impala, gazelle and zebra, because they all eat different kinds of plant.
4. a. There will be more grass for the warthogs, so they may increase.
   The extra warthogs will be extra food for the cheetahs, so they may increase.
   There will be less food for the lions and hyenas. The numbers of lions and hyenas may decrease.
   The lions and hyenas will eat more of their other prey, so the numbers of impala, wildebeest and zebra may decrease.
   b. They will hunt more impala, wildebeest, gazelle and zebra, so the numbers of those animals may go down. The numbers of hyenas and cheetahs may also go down, as there is less prey for them, and more competition for that prey.
   The plants may increase, as there are fewer herbivores eating them.
   c. The impala will starve or migrate away, so their numbers in this area will go down.
   The lions will have less food. Their numbers may go down, and they will hunt more of their other prey, so the numbers of wildebeest, gazelle and zebra may also go down.
   There will be less food for the hyenas and cheetahs, so their numbers may go down.

1.3: Modelling and human activity
1. a. Faster, and can predict a variety of different things.
   b. May be unreliable/only as good as the data fed into it.
2. They need data to set up the computer model properly.
3. a. It has increased.
   b. People produce carbon dioxide through industry and transport, so more people produce more carbon dioxide.
   c. Deforestation, increase in pollution, loss of habitats, etc.
4. People in the UK have a higher standard of living, so we burn more fossil fuels for transport (including importing food and other goods) and to manufacture goods.

1.4: Classification
1. phylum, class, order, family, genus, species
2. C
3. B
4. kingdom – Animalia (animals); phylum – Chordata (vertebrates); class – Mammalia (mammals)
5. a. birds, reptiles, amphibians, fish
   b. mammals
   c. reptiles, fish
6. Kingdom – Animalia (animals); phylum – Chordata; class – Reptilia. Their eggs are not hard-shelled or laid in water so they must be reptiles.

1.5: Natural selection
1. a. They can eat leaves on tall trees that other animals cannot reach.
   b. Some giraffes had longer necks than others because of natural variation caused by mutations. These animals could get more food so they produced more offspring. The offspring inherited the long necks. This repeated until all giraffes had very long necks.
2. Natural selection happens naturally because of competition between species and within species, without humans being involved. Selective breeding is when humans decide which animals should breed together so the offspring are more likely to have useful characteristics.
3. A

1.6: The theory of evolution
1. a. The shape of an organism preserved in rock.
   b. *Cryptolithus tesselatus*
   c. They have become extinct.
2. B
3. C
4. a. Observations of different species of animals and plants, and fossils.
   b. DNA and mutations (they also have a lot more fossils).

1.7: Organic farming and genetic modification
1. C
2. Consumers are concerned about what is in the food they are eating.
3. Organic products have a lower yield than non-organic products.

Answers

4 Natural selection occurs when competition within or between species leads to some animals that are better adapted producing more offspring.
Selective breeding is when humans choose which animals or plants should breed together to produce offspring with desirable characteristics.
Genetic modification is when humans change the genes in an organism directly.

5 enzymes

6 Any two from: to produce crops that can be kept for longer, to produce crops that are resistant to certain diseases, weedkillers or pests, to produce crops that contain more nutrients in the crop.

7 Any two from: it will only benefit big companies rather than helping to feed the world, the modified genes may get into other organisms, there may be health effects we do not know about yet.

2.1: DNA, genes and chromosomes

1 B
2 a DNA   b chromosomes   c chromosomes
3 DNA found at a crime scene can be matched to the DNA of suspects, to find out who was at the crime scene.
4 a Human Genome Project
   b A project to map all the bases in human genes.
5 If doctors know that a person's genes make them more likely to have problems like heart attacks they may be able to give them medicines to prevent them. They may be able to fix faulty genes to cure diseases.
6 Some people think it is an invasion of privacy. It may also cause people worry without helping them and affect things like getting insurance.

2.2: Reproduction and variation

1 eggs and sperm (or pollen, if you are thinking about plants)
2 a A sex cell, such as an egg, sperm or pollen cell.
   b The male sex cell.
   c The female sex cell.
   d Having half the normal number of chromosomes (i.e. only one set).
   e Having the normal number of chromosomes (i.e. two sets).
   f When a male and female sex cell join.
   g When pollen from one flower is deposited on another.
3 a sexual reproduction
   b asexual reproduction
   c sexual reproduction
4 Sexual – uses haploid gametes, requires two organisms, produces offspring with variation.
Asexual – uses diploid cells, requires only one parent organism, produces clones (with no variation).
5 Organisms need enough nutrients and water to grow (and plants also need light and enough space). They will grow well if they get enough of these things, and will not grow as well if any are in short supply.

2.3: Passing on the genes

1 Gametes always have just one copy of each allele (gametes are haploid cells).
2 a The particular combination of genes in an organism.
   b The characteristics of an organism that you can see.
3 A
4 a homozygous
   b One has red flowers and one has white flowers.
   c none   d ¼ (or 25%)
5 The plants may have RR or Rr genotypes. If two plants with Rr genotypes breed, some of the offspring may have the rr genotype, which will give white flowers.
6 a dominant
   b HH or Hh (another letter such as T is also acceptable, e.g. TT and Tt)
   c zero

2.4: Inherited diseases

1 D
2 a cc   b CC   c Cc
   d zero   e zero
3 B
4 A
5 a Putting working copies of a faulty gene into a patient.
   b It would prevent the formation of sticky mucus, so the patient would not need physiotherapy and would not have problems with breathing or get so many infections while the working genes were still present in the lungs.
   c They would not need so many tests, and would not need to worry so much about getting breast cancer.

2.5: Cloning, transgenic animals and designer babies

1 An individual with the same genotype as another.
2 There would be more organs available to transplant, and patients would not have to take drugs to stop the organ being rejected.
3 C
4 a An animal that has had genes from a different species inserted into its DNA.
   b One possibility is making 'designer milk', which contains useful chemicals.
5 a A baby selected from a set of embryos because it has certain characteristics.
   b They think it is 'playing god', or they do not think it is right to create embryos knowing that some will be discarded.

3.1: The nervous system

1 a brain, spinal cord   b the other nerves in the body
2 a axon   b insulates the axon
   c the gap between two neurones
3 A
4 A sensory neurone carries signals from receptors to the brain. A motor neurone carries signals from the brain to the muscles.
5 a The time between the stimulus arriving at the body and the muscles starting to move.
   b The faster your reaction time, the more likely you are to avoid injury.

3.2: Reflex actions

1 B
2 sensory, relay, motor
3 a The reflex that makes your pupil smaller if the light gets brighter.
   b It stops the retina from being damaged by bright light.
4 a lens
   b It gets fatter when you are looking at closer objects.
   c involuntary

    d accommodation reflex

    e It makes sure you can see clearly whatever you are looking at, so you can spot danger and avoid it.

  5 a When you move your head down in response to a moving object near your head.

    b It helps to stop things hitting your head and injuring you.

3.3: The brain

1 Any four from: cerebral cortex, cerebellum, medulla, hypothalamus, pituitary gland, midbrain

2 C

3 a cerebral cortex
  b medulla

4 a A blood clot or bleeding inside the brain.
  b The oxygen supply to part of the brain is cut off and so the brain cells in this part die. Pressure can also build up and damage the brain cells.

5 a Sudden bursts of electrical activity inside the brain.
  b People may fall down, jerk uncontrollably and lose consciousness.

6 a Problems with signals being passed between neurones, and between motor neurones and muscles.
  b Muscle tremors, stiffness, muscle rigidity and slow movement.

7 a Cells in the brain growing out of control.
  b It can interfere with the way impulses travel between cells and cause seizures, and can exert pressure on cells and damage them.

3.4: Chemical messages

1 C

2 B

3 Any three from: red blood cells, white blood cells, platelets, carbon dioxide, hormones, glucose, waste (or urea).

4 a A chemical used to carry messages around the body.
  b The organ on which a hormone has an effect.

5 a insulin, glucagon
  b in the blood plasma
  c insulin
  d Glucagon, as you would have used up all the glucose in your blood. Your liver needs to release more, and glucagon is the hormone that makes it do this.

6 a The pancreas does not make enough insulin.
  b They can be used to make insulin for diabetic patients to inject.

3.5: Hormones and reproduction

1 When the lining of the uterus breaks down and leaves the body.

2 follicle stimulating hormone (FSH) and luteinising hormone (LH)

3 oestrogen

4 they fall

5 They are used in fertility treatments, to make the woman produce more eggs.

6 D

7 B

4.1: Stimulants, sedatives and depressants

1 C

2 C

3 a Any two from: barbiturates, alcohol, solvents.
  b Any two from: paracetamol, aspirin, morphine, heroin.

4 a stimulants
  b painkillers
  c sedatives/depressants

5 a They will be slower.
  b It will be longer/increase.

6 a Ordinary painkillers are not strong enough as their pain is too severe.
  b It is addictive, and should only be used when ordinary painkillers do not work.

7 a Taking too much of a drug.
  b liver

8 It can have harmful side-effects.

4.2: Drug misuse and abuse

1 a nicotine b alcohol
  c tobacco   d tobacco
  e solvents, alcohol

2 C

3 A

4 It affects reaction times and judgement.

5 Nicotine makes blood vessels narrower and increases the heart rate, which leads to high blood pressure. This can lead to heart disease.

4.3: Transmitting disease

1 a When a disease is passed from one person to another by touching, coughing and sneezing, kissing or having sex.
  b When a disease is passed from a mother to her unborn baby.
  c When a disease is passed on via another living thing, such as a mosquito.
  d When a disease is passed on via non-living things, such as food, water, air etc.

2 a vehicle-borne
  b vector-borne
  c horizontal direct contact
  d vehicle-borne
  e vertical direct contact

3 B

4.4: More body defences

1 C

2 A

3 a A protein marker on the surface of a cell.
  b A type of white blood cell that produces antibodies.
  c Something made by lymphocytes that sticks to pathogens and marks them.

4 Chemicals released by damaged skin make the blood flow to the area increase.

5 Similarities – they engulf pathogens and destroy them.
Differences – in the second line of defence, white blood cells destroy any pathogens they find.
In the third line of defence, some white blood cells make antibodies against that specific pathogen and then other white blood cells engulf any cells with antibodies attached to them.

6 It makes the lymphocytes produce antibodies against a dead or weakened pathogen, so that if that type of pathogen gets into the body again, lymphocytes can make antibodies much faster.

4.5: Tuberculosis and new drugs

1 a a bacterium

Answers

    b Through the air in droplets when an infected person coughs or sneezes.

    c It spreads more easily in overcrowded conditions.

2 a A pill with no drug in it.

    b Because sometimes people get better if they think they are being treated, even if they are not actually being given a drug. Comparing the drug being tested with the effect of a placebo makes sure that any effects really are due to the drug.

3 a Directly Observed Treatment, Short Course. It means that patients are supervised when taking their drugs to make sure they take the whole course.

    b Many patients stop taking their drugs as soon as they feel better, even though not all the bacteria may have been killed.

    c More nurses are needed so they can supervise the patients.

4 D

5 A and B

5.1: The periodic table

1 B

2 a B   b A   c E
    d C   e D   f A, B or E
    g A

3 a Any three from: helium, neon, argon, xenon, krypton.

    b lithium, sodium, potassium

    c Any three from: iron, copper, silver, gold.

    d Any three from: fluorine, chlorine, bromine, iodine, astatine.

5.2: Atoms, elements and molecules

1 a protons, neutrons, electrons

    b Proton – positive charge, found in nucleus.
Neutron – no charge, found in nucleus.
Electron – negative charge, found outside nucleus.

2 The number of protons in the nucleus of an atom of that element.

3 atomic number

4 a H_2O b H_2
    c O_2 d SO_2

5 B

5.3: Word and symbol equations

1 a methane + oxygen → carbon dioxide + water

    b sodium + chlorine → sodium chloride

    c carbon dioxide + water → glucose + oxygen

2 C

3 potassium, sulphur and oxygen

4 $2Na(s) + Cl_2(g) \rightarrow 2NaCl(s)$

5.4: Noble gases and transition metals

1 a helium – He, neon – Ne, argon – Ar

    b the far right-hand column

    c colourless gases

2 They get more dense.

3 a Used in welding or in light bulbs.

    b Used to fill party balloons and airships.

    c Used in advertising signs.

4 a the central block

    b iron – Fe, copper – Cu, silver – Ag, gold – Au

5 C

6 a good conductor of electricity, ductile and fairly cheap

    b strong and cheap

    c stays shiny

    d very good conductor of electricity

5.5: Alkali metals

1 A

2 sodium + water → sodium hydroxide + hydrogen

3 potassium

4 a The potassium forms a molten ball that floats on the water and gives off a gas which burns with a lilac flame.

    b It is an exothermic reaction because heat is given out.

5 $2Na(s) + 2H_2O(l) \rightarrow 2NaOH(aq) + H_2(g)$

5.6: Halogens

1 fluorine – F, chlorine – Cl, bromine – Br, iodine – I, astatine – At

2 second column from the right

3 a top   b bottom

4 a sterilising water (for drinking or in swimming pools)

    b in antiseptics

5 a chlorine   b iodine   c bromine

6 D

5.7: Identifying substances

1 B

2 C

3 a Dip a clean flame test loop in a solution of the sample, then hold in the flame from a Bunsen burner.

    b If the loop is not clean, any metals in the dirt may change the colour of the flame.

4 A solid that forms when two solutions are mixed.

5 Test with sodium hydroxide, because the two metals form different coloured precipitates (and they do not give colours in a flame test).

6.1: Neutralisation reactions and salts

1 copper oxide, copper hydroxide, copper carbonate

2 a calcium oxide + hydrochloric acid → calcium chloride + water

    b copper carbonate + sulphuric acid → copper sulphate + water + carbon dioxide

3 To make sure all the acid has reacted.

4 A solid that forms when two solutions are mixed.

5 Mix solutions of barium chloride and sodium sulphate.

6 Filter the mixture, wash the precipitate that is left on the filter paper, then dry the paper (and the salt) in an oven.

7 a $CaO(s) + 2HCl(aq) \rightarrow CaCl_2(aq) + H_2O(l)$

    b $CuCO_3(s) + H_2SO_4(aq) \rightarrow CuSO_4(aq) + H_2O(l) + CO_2(g)$

6.2: Hazards and reactions

1 a toxic   b oxidising   c highly flammable

2 a sodium hydrogencarbonate and tartaric acid powder

    b The reaction only occurs when they get wet, so moisture from other ingredients in the recipe is needed.

    c neutralisation

3 D

4 B

5 B

6.3: Extracting metals

1 A compound of a metal found in the Earth.

2 a gold, platinum

    b They are very unreactive.

3 a Reduction with carbon or electrolysis.

    b The reactivity of the metal in the ore – anything more reactive than carbon must be extracted using electrolysis.

4 A compound that is more difficult to break up into its component elements.
5 a It is cheaper.
   b tin oxide + carbon → tin + carbon dioxide
   c Tin oxide is reduced and carbon is oxidised.
6 Iron(III) oxide is reduced and carbon monoxide is oxidised.
7 $SnO_2(s) + C(s) \rightarrow Sn(s) + CO_2(g)$

6.4: Collecting and testing gases
1 a It is less dense than air.
   b It does not dissolve in water.
2 Some carbon dioxide will dissolve in water, so you will not collect all of the gas produced in the reaction.
3 Less dense than air, as it can be collected using upward delivery.
4 a The gas could be carbon dioxide, as carbon dioxide will put out a lighted splint. However, other gases will also do this, so the gas may not be carbon dioxide.
   b Bubble it through limewater. If it is carbon dioxide, the limewater will turn milky.
5 For hydrogen, put a lighted splint into the gas. If it is hydrogen it will burn with a squeaky pop. For oxygen, put a glowing splint into the gas. If it is oxygen the splint will relight.
6 Dampen it and put it into the gas. If the gas is chlorine, the paper will eventually turn white.

6.5: Uses of chemicals and artificial additives
1 a A manufactured chemical added to food.
   b They are cheaper and often stronger than natural additives.
   c They think there may be health risks from artificial additives.
2 D
3 It is made from two different elements, hydrogen and nitrogen, combined together.
4 a citric, ethanoic, phosphoric
   b ethanoic, hydrochloric, phosphoric, citric
5 a carbon dioxide   b citric acid

7.1: Burning fuels
1 propane + oxygen → carbon dioxide + water
2 carbon dioxide (CO_2), carbon monoxide (CO), carbon (C), water (H_2O)
3 propane + oxygen → carbon + carbon monoxide + carbon dioxide + water
4 It stops red blood cells carrying oxygen.
5 $C_3H_8(g) + 5O_2(g) \rightarrow 3CO_2(g) + 4H_2O(l)$
6 A and C. Equation B has hydrogen as a product, which is not formed when hydrocarbons burn.

7.2: Products from oil
1 a A mixture of hydrocarbon molecules obtained from within the Earth.
   b fractional distillation
2 gas
3 a Bottled gas for caravans and campers.
   b Tar for roads, and waterproofing materials.
   c Fuel for jet engines and central heating systems.
   d Fuel for cars.
   e Fuel for cars, lorries, trains, etc.
   f Fuel for ships and power stations.
4 Neither is correct.
5 a petrol
   b Petrol – it is the vapour that burns, and petrol evaporates more easily than diesel.

7.3: Global warming
1 a carbon dioxide
   b photosynthesising organisms
   c nitrogen and oxygen
2 B
3 C
4 They are based on computer models, and the processes being modelled are very complicated.

7.4: Other fuels
1 Any three from: releases a lot of energy when it burns, does not make soot or smoke, does not leave a solid residue behind after burning, is easy to store and transport.
2 a water
   b carbon dioxide and water
   c carbon dioxide, water and ash
   d carbon dioxide and water
   e carbon dioxide and water
3 bio-fuels, hydrogen
4 When bio-fuels burn they *do* put carbon dioxide into the air. The reason they do not contribute to global warming is that they have just removed a similar amount of carbon dioxide from the air when the plants grew (as long as renewable fuels were used in the harvesting, processing, etc.).
5 D
6 All of them.

7.5: Products from air, rocks and the sea
1 a 21%   b 78%
2 C
3 D
4 sodium, chlorine, sodium chloride, hydrogen, sodium hydroxide
5 A
6 a Any two from: killing bacteria, purifying drinking water and swimming pools, used in the chemical industry to make PVC and other chemicals, making bleach (with sodium hydroxide).
   b Any two from: oven cleaner, making soaps and detergents, making bleach (with chlorine).

7.6: Sustainable living
1 A
2 D
3 C
4 D
5 a Development that does not use up resources or pollute the environment.
   b It means we get more use from resources (we do not use up resources as fast).

8.1: Modern materials
1 a Gore-tex® and Kevlar®   b Teflon® and Post-it® glue
2 B
3 a It lets water vapour out but does not let drops of liquid water in.
   b It has a membrane with tiny holes in it, which let water vapour out but are too small to let drops of liquid water in.
4 a Thinsulate®   b Gore-tex®
   c Lycra®   d Kevlar®
5 C

Answers

8.2: Nanoparticles
1. C
2. D
3. They reflect or absorb UV light without reflecting visible light, so they do not make the person look white.
4. A
5. D

8.3: Alcoholic drinks
1. a sugar, water, yeast
   b carbon dioxide, ethanol
2. a about 15%
   b The yeast are killed by the ethanol at higher concentrations.
   c distillation
3. beer
4. B only
5. Any three from: slows reactions, affects judgement, makes you become emotional or aggressive, makes you lose your balance and coordination, makes you vomit, makes you pass out.
6. The nuisance caused by drunk people, the mess they make, and the accidents they cause.

8.4: Technology and food
1. a A mixture of two different liquids.
   b vinegar and oil
   c The vinegar and oil would separate if there was no emulsifier.
2. Hydrophobic means 'water-hating' – the substance repels water.
   Hydrophilic means 'water-loving' – the substance attracts water.
3. B
4. Nitrogen is an inert gas and will not react with the food, so the food will stay fresh longer.
5. The cold slows down the growth of bacteria.
6. Bacteria need moisture to grow.

9.1: Current and voltage
1. The voltmeter can be in either of the two positions shown:

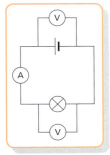

2. a amp   b volt   c ohm
3. The current is the same everywhere in the circuit, so only one ammeter is needed. The voltage can be different across each component, so it is helpful to have a voltmeter for each component.
4. a it will go up   b it will go down   c it will go up
5. D
6. $R = V/I = 230\ V/0.005\ A = 46\ 000\ \Omega$

9.2: Changing resistance
1. C
2. The filament gets hotter when more current flows through it, and this increases the resistance.
3. a increases (you are only expected to know about the kind of thermistor where the resistance gets less as it gets warmer – which means that the resistance gets bigger as it gets colder)
   b increases
4. temperature rises → the resistance of the thermistor goes down → the total resistance of the circuit goes down → a greater current flows → the lamp gets brighter (remember you only need to know about the kind of thermistor in which the resistance gets less as the temperature increases).
5. At 12 V the current is 1.60 A. $R = V/I = 12\ V/1.60\ A = 7.5\ \Omega$

9.3: Cells
1.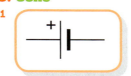
2. He can use four of the cells in series:

3. rechargeable
4. The time a battery will last at a particular current.
5. C
6. current = capacity/time = 80/25 = 3.2 A
7. Rechargeable cells cost more to buy, but they do not cost much to recharge. A rechargeable cell can be recharged many times, and overall this is cheaper than buying the same number of dry cells.

9.4: Generating current
1. Direct current always flows in the same direction. The direction in which alternating current flows changes many times each second.
2. solar cells and batteries
3. C
4. The peaks and troughs will be closer together in time, and the maximum (and minimum) voltages will be greater.
5. Using a magnet with a stronger magnetic field, moving the magnet (or the coil) faster, putting more turns of wire on the coil, adding a soft iron core.

9.5: Computers and new technologies
1. Any three things such as allowing us to use computers, electric lights, machines, etc.
2. It can be used to take readings very quickly, or over a long period of time, or in remote places.
3. It can record results more accurately and reliably than a human could. The results can also easily be plotted or averaged using a spreadsheet.
4. Any three sensible suggestions such as using TVs and digital radios, having automatic washing machines, playing computer or video games, etc.
5. Computer chips are smaller, so it does not take as long for information to be sent from one part of a chip to another.
6. Any sensible suggestion such as monitoring how much food is in the fridge, or monitoring your health.
7. A material with zero electrical resistance.
8. They are used in making very powerful electromagnets.

10.1: Renewable energy resources
1. hydroelectricity, waves, tidal barrages, tidal currents
2. solar, geothermal, biomass
3. B
4. a. The wind turbine only generates electricity when the wind is blowing. The solar cells only produce current when it is light.
   b. Buy batteries to be charged up to store energy when the wind turbines or solar cells are making more current than is needed.

10.2: Energy and society
1. Any two from: spoiling the view, damaging wildlife habitats, noise pollution, loss of homes or farmland when a reservoir is created, etc.
2. It might spoil the view or cause noise pollution.
3. It would provide jobs in the short-term and may also act as a bridge for road or rail, making journeys in the area shorter. It could lead to energy savings in the long-term.
4. The wind turbines and the wires connecting them to the National Grid must be paid for, and engineers must be paid for maintaining the turbines.
5. a. Advantages – might allow more renewable resources to be used.
      Disadvantages – it would be very expensive.
   b. Advantages – would allow more people access to electricity.
      Disadvantages – it would be very expensive, the effect on the environment, safety issues.
6. body scans, heart monitoring, restarting failing hearts

10.3: Power and cost
1. How fast electrical energy is being transferred.
2. watt (or kilowatt)
3. $P = I \times V = 2\ A \times 12\ V = 24\ W$
4. D
5. $P = I \times V = 0.03\ A \times 3\ V = 0.09\ W$
6. $V = P/I = 0.3\ W / 0.05\ A = 6\ V$
7. cost per kWh = cost/(power × time) = 11.25p/(1.5 kW × 0.5 h) = 15p/kWh

10.4: Efficiency
1. efficiency = useful energy/total energy × 100 = 42 kJ/50 kJ × 100% = 84%
2. a. 9 J/100 J × 100% = 9%
   b. 9 J/18 J × 100% = 50%
3. 2 years
4. 3 years
5. Draught-proofing, as the payback time is shorter.

10.5: Motors and safety
1. magnets and coil
2. a. decrease   b. increase
3. a. It will reverse.
   b. Nothing, as the two changes will cancel each other out.
4. a. For safety, to stop a faulty appliance giving someone an electric shock.
   b. If a fault occurs so that the casing would become live, the earth wire carries this current to earth. Because the resistance of the earth wire is low, a large current flows and the fuse melts, so no more current can flow into the appliance.
5. An appliance with an insulated case, which does not need an earth wire.

6. It detects any tiny differences in the currents in the live and neutral wires, and shuts the current off if there is a difference.
7. It responds more quickly, and it can be reset.

11.1: Describing waves
1. B
2. D
3. 2.5 cm
4. 90 m/0.02 s = 4500 m/s
5. a. $d = s \times t = 340 \times 0.3 = 102$ m; 102/2 = 51 m
   b. The time can be measured more accurately.
6. a. They are too high for humans to hear (more than 20 kHz).
   b. longitudinal
   c. $\lambda = s/f = 1500$ m/s$/200\ 000$ Hz = 0.0075 m
   d. $t = d/s = 4000$ m$/1500$ m/s = 2.7 s

11.2: The electromagnetic spectrum
1. Two from: they are all transverse waves, they can all travel through a vacuum, they all travel at the same speed in a vacuum.
2. a. radio waves   b. gamma-rays
   c. gamma-rays
3. a. microwaves, infrared   b. ultraviolet
   c. microwaves   d. X-rays
4. a. ultraviolet   b. X-rays and gamma-rays
   c. microwaves
5. C
6. a. UVA radiation has less energy.
   b. UVC cannot get through the atmosphere.
7. They have higher energies.

11.3: Reflection and refraction
1.
   a. air / water   b. air / water   c. air / water
2. A refraction
   B total internal reflection
3. Light from other objects under the water is being totally internally reflected when it reaches the surface of the water.
4. a. outer core
   b. S waves cannot go through it.
   c. The density changes with depth and this changes the speed of the waves, so the waves are refracted.

11.4: Using waves
1. a. B   b. C   c. A
   d. C   e. A
2. a. visible light   b. microwaves
   c. ultraviolet   d. X-rays
3. infrared scanners and microwaves used to detect rain clouds
4. B

Answers

11.5: Digital and analogue
1 C
2 Analogue: 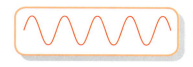 Digital:
3 Analogue – it varies continuously/is not an on-off noise.
4 She is talking about digital signals.
5 It can be used to create and mix music, you can store it in a compressed form, it allows downloading of music over the internet, etc.

11.6: Waves and society
1 They may heat up tissue inside your head.
2 Mobile phones have not been available for that long.
3 Scare stories help to sell newspapers, so newspapers do not always give a balanced view.
4 a They don't know exactly how much force is on the rocks, or how much force the rocks can stand before they break.
  b A huge wave caused by an underwater earthquake or landslide.
  c The same reasons as it is difficult to predict earthquakes.
5 a Any five things such as listening to the radio, watching TV, using a mobile phone, cooking food in a microwave, using a camera, etc.
  b Some forms of electromagnetic waves can be harmful.

12.1: Space travel
1 air, warmth, something to remove carbon dioxide, exercise machines, food, something to absorb cosmic radiation
2 It is hot when the Sun is shining on it, and cold when it goes into the shadow of the Earth.
3 a Earth, Moon, asteroid
  b The Earth is the biggest, so it has the most mass, then the Moon, and an asteroid is the smallest (with the least mass). The greater the mass, the higher the gravitational field strength.
4 a 50 N b newtons
5 7.4 N/2.0 kg = 3.7 m/s^2
6 C
7 D

12.2: Getting into space
1 a Sun b Sun
  c a planet d Sun
2 Give it more powerful engines, or make its mass less.
3 The force of gravity between the Moon and the Earth.
4 F = m × a = 750 000 kg × 8 m/s^2 = 6 000 000 N
5 a = F/m = 6 000 000 N/600 000 kg = 10 m/s^2
6 C
7 B

12.3: The Solar System
1 Universe, galaxy, Sun, planet, Moon, asteroid

2 Asteroids are mostly solid rock, comets are mostly dust and ice. Asteroids have nearly circular orbits, comets have very elliptical orbits.
3 a Venus b Neptune
  c Neptune d Mercury
4 It has a greater mass, so its gravity is stronger (it is also bigger, so it is a bigger target).
5 They are very small and do not reflect much light.
6 B
7 B

12.4: Star life cycles
1 nebula, protostar, star, red giant, white dwarf
2 a A cloud of dust and gas that is beginning to form a star.
  b A star that has swollen up.
  c A star that has run out of fuel and is cooling down.
3 a There has not been enough time for life to evolve, or there may not be any planets near it for life to get started on.
  b It may have swollen up and destroyed any planets nearby that did have life.
4 its mass
5 B

12.5: Exploring the Universe
1 a Asteroids only reflect light, they do not emit it.
  b Other stars are too far away for space probes to be sent to them.
2 a An orbiting space probe, as it can take pictures or radar measurements of the whole planet.
  b Telescope, as other stars are too far away to send space probes to them.
  c A space probe that lands, so it can take soil samples and analyse them.
3 B
4 The Search for Extraterrestrial Intelligence. Scientists analyse radio signals coming from space to see if there is a message in them.
5 For: there are so many other planets out there that life must have developed on some of them. Against: if there was intelligent life out there we would have detected it by now.
6 Development of space technology leads to new materials, medical discoveries, etc., and provides a lot of jobs.

12.6: Theories about the Universe
1 a The Universe is expanding and new matter is created all the time so that the density of matter in the Universe stays the same.
  b The Universe started with the expansion of a tiny volume of very concentrated energy and matter.
  c The Universe will eventually stop expanding, contract again into a 'big crunch' and then start all over again with another Big Bang.
2 a all of them
  b the Big Bang and oscillating Universe theories
  c the oscillating Universe theory
3 redshift
4 microwave background radiation
5 D
6 It will help them to determine whether the oscillating Universe theory is a possibility.

Index

absorption 128, 132–3
acceleration 138–41
adaptation 18
aerosols 46
alcohol 44, 46–7, 86–7, 99–101
alkali metals 54–5, 62–3
alleles 24, 28–31
ammeters 104, 106–7
ammonia 74–7
amphetamines 44
amplitude 126–8
antibiotics 31, 46, 52–3
antibodies 33, 50–1
antigens 50–1
asexual reproduction 26
asteroids 139–43, 147
astronauts 138–9, 147
astronomy 140, 143–4, 148
atmosphere, Earth's 15, 84–5, 143
axons 34

bacteria 16, 19, 22–3, 26, 40–1, 46, 48–53, 65, 90
barbiturates 44
bases 25
batteries 110, 112, 117
Big Bang 148–9
bio-butanol 87
biodegradable 92–3
biodiversity 22
bio-ethanol 87–8, 101
bio-fuels 86–7
biomass 10–11, 116
blood cells 30, 32, 40–1, 47, 49–51, 79–80
blood vessels 42–3, 46, 50, 94
boiling point 64, 81–3
brain cells 38–9
bromine 54–5, 59, 64–5

caffeine 44–5
cancer 24–5, 30–1, 39, 45–7, 128–9, 136
cannabis 44–5
carbohydrates 41, 70, 76–7
carbon monoxide 46–7, 73, 78–80, 103
carbonates 68, 70
carnivore 10
cell division 26
chemical reactions 54, 58, 62, 68, 78
chlorine 54–5, 58–9, 64–5, 74–5, 90–1
cholesterol 33
chromosomes 23, 24–6, 28
ciliary muscles 37
citric acid 77
classification 16–17
climate change 15
clones 26, 32
cloning 32–3
combustion 68, 70, 78–80, 83, 85
comets 140, 142–3

competition 12–13, 18–19
computer models 14–15, 84
condensation 80, 89
conductors 61–2
consumer 10–11, 120
contraception 42–3
copper carbonate 71
copper oxide 68–9, 71–2
crop plants 22
crude oil 81, 83
cystic fibrosis 30–1, 33

dark matter 148–9
decomposition 70–1
dehydration 70–1
density 60–1, 74–5, 130–2, 148
depressants 44–5
desalination 89, 92
desertification 15
diabetes 40–1
diatomic molecules 59, 64
diesel 81–3, 87–8
digestive system 30, 40–1
digital technology 135
diploid cell 26, 33
diseases 25, 27, 30, 33, 49, 51, 53, 78, 80, 85
distillation 81, 89, 99
DNA 18–20, 22–5, 40, 128–9
drugs 22, 25, 32, 39, 44–7, 52–3, 119

Earth's crust 72
earthquakes 126, 130, 136–7
economics 14–15, 92, 118–19, 146
ecosystem 10, 12, 14–15
electric circuits 107, 114
electrical energy 104, 113, 116, 120
electrolysis 73, 90
electromagnetic spectrum 128–9
electrons 56, 104, 108, 148
embryo 23, 33, 42–3
emissions 15, 128, 132–3
emphysema 46
emulsifier 98, 102–3
emulsion 102–3
endangered 15
endocrine glands 40
enzymes 23
epilepsy 38–9
ethanoic acid 77
ethanol 87–8, 99, 100–1
evolution 11, 13, 17, 19–21, 23, 144–5
exothermic reactions 62
extinction 15, 18, 20–1

fabrics 94
farming 15, 22
fermentation 99, 101
fertilisation 22, 26–8, 42–3, 59, 68–9, 76
fetus 48, 132
fluorine 55, 64
follicle 42–3
food chain 10–11

forensics 25, 66
fossil fuels 15, 84–5, 87, 116
fossils 20–1
fractional distillation 81, 89, 91
francium 63
fungi 16, 48
fusion 144

galaxies 142–4, 146, 148–9
gametes 26, 28–9
gamma-rays 128–9
gas syringe 74–5
gene therapy 30–1
generator 113
genetic engineering 22–3, 33
genetic modification 19, 22–3
genetics 24, 26
genotype 28–31
genus 16–17
global warming 15, 84–6, 88, 93
glucagon 41
glucose 40–1, 59
glycogen 41
Gore-tex® 94–6
gravitational field 138–9, 144
gravity 138–42, 144–5, 149

habitats 12, 15, 118
haemoglobin 40–1, 79
haemophilia 30
halogens 54–5, 64–5
haploid cell 26, 33
hazards 70–1
heart disease 27, 46–7, 99
helium 54–6, 60–1, 142, 144, 148
herbivores 10–12, 18
heroin 44–5, 47
heterozygous 28–9, 31
HIV 47–9
homozygous 28–9
hormones 22–3, 38, 40–3
Hubble Space Telescope 146
human activity 14, 19
Human Genome Project 24–5
Huntington's disease 30
hydration 70–1
hydrocarbons 78, 81, 86
hydrochloric acid 49, 68, 76–7
hydroelectricity 116, 118
hydrogencarbonates 70
hydroxides 68

immune system 50
industry 15, 77, 90, 132
infection 32, 46–50
inflammation 50–1
infrared radiation 98, 133, 146
insulation 18, 122–3, 124
insulin 40–1
interplanetary space 138
inter-species 12–13, 19
intra-species 12–13

Index

involuntary response 36–7
iodine 54–5, 64–5
iris reflex 36–7
IVF treatment 42–3

Kevlar® 94–5
kinetic energy 113, 116

light dependent resistor (LDR) 107–9
light energy 27, 116–17, 123
liposomes 31
lithium 54–5, 62–3, 65–6, 69
longitudinal waves 126, 130
Lycra® 94
lymphocytes 51
lysozyme 48–9

magnesium salts 27
magnetic field 112–13, 124
medicine 24, 45, 94, 119, 132
membranes 49
menstrual cycle 42–3
mental health 45
metal hydroxide 62, 68
metal ores 72
methane 59, 78–80, 84–5, 93
microbes 47–9, 102–3
microorganisms 40, 46, 48, 50
microwaves 128–9, 132–3, 136
mitosis 26
modelling 14–15
motor neurone 34–6
mucus 30–1, 48–9
multiple sclerosis 45
mutations 18, 20, 52, 129

nanoparticles 97–8
National Grid 117–19
natural selection 18–20, 22
nerve transmission 44
nervous system 30, 34, 44
neurone 34–7, 39, 44–46
neurotransmitters 34, 45
neutralisation 68, 70–1
neutrons 56, 148
nicotine 46–7
nitrates 27
nitrogen 22, 47, 55, 76, 84, 89, 91, 102–3
noble gases 54–5, 60–1, 64
non-biodegradable 88, 92
non-renewable energy 92, 116
nucleus 24–6, 32–4, 56, 148
nutrients 27

obesity 27
oestrogen 42–3
omnivore 10–11
opiates 44–5
opium 44–5
orbit 138–43, 146
organics 22
oscillations 126

ovulation 42–3
oxidation 70–1
oxidising agents 69
packaging 102–3
painkillers 44–5
pancreas 40–1
paracetamol 44–5
Parkinson's disease 38–9
pathogens 48–51
periodic table 54–7, 60–2, 64–5
pesticides 22
pests 22–3
petrol 81–3, 85, 87–8, 93
phenotype 28–31
phosphates 27
phosphoric acid 76–7
photosynthesis 27, 59, 84
phylum 16–17
pituitary gland 38–9, 42–3
placenta 42–3
planets 138–40, 142–7
plasma 40–1, 50
plasmids 23
pollen 26, 28
pollination 22
pollutants 78, 92, 97
pollution 80, 86, 92–3, 111, 116, 118
populations 12–14
potassium 27, 54–5, 62–3, 65–6, 69, 72, 100
precipitation 66, 68
predation 18
predator 10, 12–13, 18, 22
pregnancy 42–3, 132
progesterone 42–3
protoctista 16
protons 56–7, 91, 148
protostar 144–5

radiation 85, 128–9, 133, 136, 138, 146, 148–9
radio technology 147
RCCB (residual current curcuit breakers) 124–5
reaction force 140
reaction time 34–5, 44–7
receptor cell 34
reflection 130, 132
reflex action 36
refraction 130–1
relay neurones 38
renewable energy 86, 116–18
renewable resources 87, 116, 118–19
reproduction 18, 26–8, 32, 42–3
resistance 105
respiration 11
retina 36–7

salts 68–9
scanning 119, 132–3
scavenger 10, 13
secondary data 14, 52, 54, 56
sedative 44–6
sediments 20
seismic waves 126, 130–1

selective breeding 18–19, 22
sensory neurones 36
sex hormones 42–3
sodium chloride 59, 65–6, 68, 76–7, 89–90
sodium hydrogencarbonate 70
sodium hydroxide 66–8, 77, 90–1
solar cells 112, 116–19
Solar System 140–4, 146–7
solubility 74–5
solvents 44, 46
sound waves 126–7, 134, 137, 147
space travel 138
spacecraft 138–41
specific immune system 51
sperm 26, 33, 42–3
spinal cord 34, 36, 38
stimulus 34–7, 44
stroke 38, 99
sulphuric acid 68–70, 76
sunlight 10, 11, 52, 94, 97, 116, 118
superconductivity 114–15
supernova 144
symbol equations 58, 68
synapses 34–5, 44–5

Teflon® 94–5
telescopes 146–7
thermal decomposition 70–1
thermal insulation 96
thermistor 107, 109
Thinsulate® 94
tobacco 45–6
transgenic animals 32–3
transition metals 54–5, 60–1
transverse waves 126–7, 128, 130–1
tsunamis 137
tuberculosis 52
tumours 38–9

ultrasound 126–7, 130, 132–3
ultraviolet 97, 128–9, 132–3
units of inheritance 24
uterus 42–3

vaccination 49, 51
vacuum 114, 128, 130, 141
variation 18, 26–7, 28, 64
velocity 140–1
vertebrates 16–17
voltage 104–14, 119–21
voltmeters 104, 106

wavelength 126–9, 148
wildlife 15, 22, 118
wind turbines 116, 118–19
word equations 58–9, 62, 68, 78

X-rays 128–9, 132–3, 146

yeast 44, 99, 101

zinc 55, 66–7, 71, 97

159

Published by Pearson Education Limited, a company incorporated in England and Wales, having its registered office at Edinburgh Gate, Harlow, Essex, CM20 2JE. Registered company number: 872828
www.pearsonschoolsandfecolleges.co.uk

Edexcel is a registered trademark of Edexcel Limited

Text © Pearson Education Limited 2010

The rights of Penny Johnson have been asserted by her in accordance with the Copyright, Designs and Patents Act of 1988.

First published 2010

12 11 10

10 9 8 7 6 5 4 3 2 1

British Library Cataloguing in Publication Data
A catalogue record for this book is available from the British Library.

ISBN 978 1 846905 82 7

Copyright notice
All rights reserved. No part of this publication may be reproduced in any form or by any means (including photocopying or storing it in any medium by electronic means and whether or not transiently or incidentally to some other use of this publication) without the written permission of the copyright owner, except in accordance with the provisions of the Copyright, Designs and Patents Act 1988 or under the terms of a licence issued by the Copyright Licensing Agency, Saffron House, 6–10 Kirby Street, London EC1N 8TS (www.cla.co.uk). Applications for the copyright owner's written permission should be addressed to the publisher.

Project management by Jim Newall
Edited by Kate Redmond
Typeset by HL Studios
Original illustrations © Pearson Education 2002, 2006, 2007, 2008, 2009, 2010
Illustrated by HL Studios
Cover photo © Getty Images: Science Photo Library
Printed in Malaysia (CTP-VVP)

Acknowledgements
The author and publisher would like to thank the following individuals and organisations for permission to reproduce photographs:
Alamy Images: Dave Watts 17; **Trevor Clifford:** 66; **iStockphoto:** Bart Coenders 14; Sabrina Dei Nobili 118; **Jupiter Unlimited:** 136; **Photolibrary.com:** Steven Wooster / Garden Picture Library 26

All other images © Pearson Education

Every effort has been made to contact copyright holders of material reproduced in this book. Any omissions will be rectified in subsequent printings if notice is given to the publishers.

Disclaimer
This material has been published on behalf of Edexcel and offers high-quality support for the delivery of Edexcel qualifications.

This does not mean that the material is essential to achieve any Edexcel qualification, nor does it mean that it is the only suitable material available to support any Edexcel qualification. Edexcel material will not be used verbatim in setting any Edexcel examination or assessment. Any resource lists produced by Edexcel shall include this and other appropriate resources.

Copies of official specifications for all Edexcel qualifications may be found on the Edexcel website: www.edexcel.com